Not Quite Si

Women With Learning Difficulties Livir

British Library Cataloguing in Publication Data

A CIP record for this book is available from the Public Library

ISBN 1 902519 86 8

BILD Publications is the publishing office of:
British Institute of Learning Disabilities
Campion House
Green Street
Kidderminster
Worcestershire
United Kingdom
DY10 1JZ

Telephone: 01562 723010
Fax: 01562 723029
E-mail: *enquiries@bild.org.uk*
Website: *www.bild.org.uk*

Please contact BILD for a free publications catalogue listing BILD books, reports and training materials.

BILD Publications are distributed worldwide by
Plymbridge Distributors
Plymbridge House
Estover Road
Plymouth
United Kingdom
PLS 7PZ
Telephone: 01752 202301
Fax: 01752 202333

Contents

A Note on Terminology

People with learning difficulties have been given many names over the years. During the period covered in this book, 1913-1996, legal definitions have included idiot, imbecile, moral defective and feeble-minded in the 1913 and 1927 Mental Deficiency Acts. Later the 1959 Mental Health Act definitions were redefined to include subnormality, severe subnormality and mental disorder. In 1971 Mental Handicap was used and in 1990 'learning disability' was first used by the Department of Health.

Most of the labels have negative connotations and despite their legal and medical status they have, over the years, been used imprecisely, often providing a pretext to segregate people whom, for one reason or another, wider society did not accept. I have only used these terms to point out historical attitudes and definitions, not to indicate my own position on labels. In most of the book I use the term learning difficulties influenced by the self advocacy movement who see this term as less offensive and in line with Bogdan and Taylor's (1982) assertion that any definition is socially constructed. In other words we label people, not necessarily as an accurate reflection of their abilities, but rather as a reflection of our current social attitudes.

The book details the history of women who lived in two catholic convents. It is therefore necessary, at times, to use terminology that is employed by Catholics. For example, on page 27 I refer to 'the Religious'. This is a term used by 'men and women of religion', or nuns and priests, as a way of distinguishing themselves from lay members of the church. I have attempted throughout the book to provide footnotes to highlight this distinctive language to help the reader understand the context.

Introduction

> *I do not know why I wasn't allowed to fulfil my potential then. Perhaps it was thought then that people who were seen as slow learners should not show what they could do with their lives. We, like children, should be seen and not heard. We were labelled as people with a mental handicap, and were not to be seen to be mixing with normal people . . . I wished that my parents . . . had shown more affection towards . . . myself . . . I wished that my parents had not treated me like a person who could not look after myself (Adams, 1995: 40).*

Mary Adams, who wrote these words, lived nearly fifty years of her life in a convent home for women 'in need of care'[1] in the south of England. Her words reveal a thread of welfare history that consigned many thousands of men and women to a life removed from wider society in institutions.[2] She talks of 'slow learners' who were called 'mentally handicapped' and thought to be ineducable. What defined someone as ineducable in the earlier part of the twentieth century was often dependent on a number of factors, which were sometimes unrelated to their intellectual ability.[3] Mary was herself an extremely able woman, who could read and write effectively and in the time that I knew her, researched her family history, wrote her autobiography, *Those Lost Years* (1995) (see Figure 1), and worked as a co-tutor with me on a reminiscence project until she became ill and died of cancer in 1995.

Her story is not unusual for people who have been labelled 'mentally handicapped', 'slow learners' or as someone with a learning difficulty. After attending a variety of schools, she was given two IQ tests which suggested that her '*intelligence was quite low*'[4] (Mary, 1992). This experience dogged

---

[1] A term commonly used to refer to people who were institutionalised in the 19th and 20th centuries.
[2] 'Institution' is used here as a broad term to cover a range of residential segregated provision including, from the nineteenth century, asylums, colonies, established after the 1913 Mental Deficiency Act, hospitals that replaced them in 1959, and voluntary sector religious homes, a thread of residential provision that ran throughout the period.
[3] See my note on terminology at the beginning of this book.
[4] I use italics for spoken speech taken from interviews throughout the text. This distinguishes the words of interviewees from written original material gathered for the book.

Figure 1

Mary for most of her life, creating deep insecurity that she only overcame in her sixties. At the age of eighteen in 1947, her parents took her to a convent which accommodated women who were considered to be in need of care. There she remained until she finally moved out in 1993, only to be diagnosed with terminal cancer a year and a half later.

Mary and the rest of the women who lived in her convent were like many other people with learning difficulties who lived in institutions during the twentieth century. Their stories have been largely absent from our social history. This hole in our understanding of our past is particularly grave especially as some 'new' philosophical thinking is arguing for parents to have the choice to kill their disabled infants (Singer, 1986). The definition of 'disability' itself has changed over time and one of the greatest challenges to thinking such as Singer's is the fact that 'disability', of whatever form, is constructed within a social context, not just determined by impairment. The stories in *Not Quite Sisters* reveal the extent of this construction. Many of the women who lived in the convent homes described in the book would not necessarily today be thought to have a 'learning difficulty' and in many other cases they certainly would not be thought to need institutional care.

The women in *Not Quite Sisters* shared their lives with the nuns or Sisters[5] who cared for them within a strict hierarchy of authority. The women residents were in some senses the *Not Quite Sisters* in the convents; not quite as privileged, not quite enabled to made decisions about their lives and not quite as valued. Yet the women and the Sisters did share similar experiences. They both lived a life removed from wider society. They shared daily activities and they lived under the authority of a Mother General, the director of the convent movement, who, in turn, was responsible to the Holy Father, leader of the Catholic Church. Both Sisters and residents were subjected to a male-dominated religion and culture even though they lived in a women-only environment. The story of convent life goes back to the beginnings of the development of institutional care for people with learning difficulties in the nineteenth century and continues

[5] I use the term 'Sisters' specifically to describe the 'nuns' of the convents. Catholic Sisters have several names. 'Nuns' is the most commonly used by lay people but the term 'Sister' denotes a working nun rather than a nun who is contemplative. Sisters and nuns themselves often use the term 'Women of Religion' or 'Religious' to denote their distinctiveness from lay members of the church. When a woman enters a convent, she goes through training of between four and seven years to become a nun. During the training period she is called a postulant or a novice. Where I use terms other than 'Sister', in talking about nuns in the book, I am referring to nuns in other religious orders than the one studied.

into the 1990s when the NHS and Care in the Community Act (1990) enforced the closure of larger long-stay institutions.

As we move into the twenty-first century, it is important to reflect on our history, a history which includes stories from people who were excluded from the mainstream. This inclusive history can help us to challenge our current assumptions about rights and provision of care. These stories sound a note of caution for developing an ethics that highlights a belief in our ability to make judgements on the contribution of disabled people. The histories of people with learning difficulties over the twentieth century indicates that our science, although certain of its knowledge at the time, has always been shot through with inconsistencies and social and cultural meanings. It is, therefore, vital that we listen to our past before making decisions about our future.

Historical Roots

The convent movement that cared for the women discussed here began in 1872, a time when concern for the safety and morals of young women was a major preoccupation in British society. This concern about young women fed into debates about young people who were ineducable. These debates led to the passing of the Mental Deficiency Act in 1913. The Act provided for the certification and segregation of people who were deemed to be either feebleminded, morally defective, idiots or imbeciles.[6] Certification was the process used to remove people from wider society into institutions. Two medical doctors were expected to examine individuals suspected of being 'mentally deficient' and advise on their mental state. If the person was certified, they would be institutionalised. By 1959 when certification ended, nearly 100,000 people had been placed in institutions.

As well as certification, other processes were used to institutionalise people. An 'order of care' could be evoked and many people, especially young women, were placed in institutions using this process (Cox, 1997). Orders of care were seen to be a less permanent form of certification but, in practice, once people had been placed in an institution many simply

[6] I use this terminology here as they are the historical terms that were wielded but in the rest of this book I use the current terminology that People First encourage: people with learning difficulties. For further clarification on terms, see my note on terminology at the beginning of this book.

remained there. Many of these people were not placed in large-scale public institutions which flourished during the first half of the twentieth century, but lived in smaller private or voluntary sector provision. While both men and women were institutionalised through this legislation, it is clear that the reasons for institutionalisation were different for each sex. Women were considered particularly at risk of certification if they were sexually active (Thomson, 1992). Evidence (Cox, 1997; Thomson, 1997) has also suggested that problematic young family members were placed in institutions by their families by evoking an order of care or by convincing doctors that they required certifying. This argument is developed further in the next chapter which details the history of institutionalisation of women labelled as having learning difficulties.

Mary Adams' story and experiences find echoes in this research and in many other stories from people who describe themselves as having 'learning difficulties'. Cooper, who was also institutionalised for over twenty years, says in her autobiography:

> *In them days if you had learning difficulties or anything that's where they used to put you . . . They would just say, 'You, you've gotta go into a big hospital' and that's it (1997: 29).*

The experience of living in an institution with a label has only recently begun to be documented and this book seeks to add to those accounts from people with learning difficulties who lived in institutions for many years. The text focuses on one particular form of segregated living provided by the Catholic community in Britain for women. Unfortunately, there are few accounts that represent the stories of women with learning difficulties (Williams, 1992; Walmsley, 1995). The majority of published autobiographies by people with learning difficulties are men's stories. This book focuses on women's accounts and the history of institutionalisation for women. This is not to suggest that men did not experience painful and unnecessary separation through the certification process but rather to point to the specific history of women who were labelled as having a learning difficulty.

In *Not Quite Sisters,* I discuss life in two convent homes which cared for women with learning difficulties between 1872 and 1996. Each chapter details how life was organised in these homes, focusing on the residents' experience of their care, the routines in their lives, and the changes which led to the closure of the convents in the 1990s.

From the Residents' Perspective

The majority of our accounts of institutions for people with learning difficulties has focused on public provision, usually from the perspective of professionals, such as doctors, care staff and managers (Morris, 1969; Jones, 1975; Alaszweski, 1986). Although a few early studies, such as Edgerton (1967), worked with people with learning difficulties as informants, it was not until the late 1980s that in Britain interviewing people with learning difficulties about their lives became a more commonly used research approach (Atkinson and Williams 1990; Booth, Simons, Booth, 1990; Potts and Fido, 1991; Booth and Booth, 1994 and Walmsley, 1995). A few autobiographies by people with learning difficulties have been produced, including Deacon (1977), Hunt (1982), Barron (1989) and most recently Cooper (1997) and Lewis (1997).

This book builds on that tradition of highlighting the perceptions and accounts of people with learning difficulties themselves. The material was gathered from the stories of the women who lived in the convents through interviews with convent residents and written materials and pictures given to me by the women. In addition to the interviews, I spent time in the convents participating in activities such as celebrations, attending Mass, as an adult education tutor and helping with daily activities such as washing up and sharing meals. This enabled me to gain some sense of the day-to-day experience of the women and to gather information from women whose use of speech was limited. The emphasis on the women's interpretations of daily life over the twentieth century throws light on how services and activities were perceived by residents.

A few accounts examine the role of spiritual communities (Vanier, 1982; Segal, 1990) but no other research has been found that focuses on life in a women-only institution such as a convent. This is despite the extent of religious communities' involvement in providing care homes (Morris, 1969; Emerson, Cullen, Hatton and Cross, 1996). In some ways, the focus of the material, women and convents, makes the book unusual. Convents are regarded by many as secretive and unknowable institutions and the Sisters within them as ethereal spiritual beings (Loudon, 1992). While in some senses this does make the book unique, the stories also provide an interesting perspective on caring and the experience of care provision through the last century. This special nature of convent life made the encounter with the convent women even more fascinating for me.

A Chance Meeting

I came across the convent movement almost by chance. I was teaching drama at a local adult education centre in London during the 1980s. I was asked if I would take on a new class for women with learning difficulties. The women came from one of these convents. I did not know anything about the convent's mission and was only beginning to learn about people with learning difficulties. The women fascinated me.[7] They were polite and well spoken, having a sort of 'old-fashioned air' about them, indicating a different world view to others around them. I was aware I had some affinity with the experience of convent life; I am from an Irish Catholic background and had been schooled in a convent. I was labelled at school as 'remedial' and sent to special classes because of my spelling, with the traditional stigma that goes with such actions. My mother had also left me at a convent when I was four. This common ground, the language of Catholicism and having some understanding of the shame and hurt that the women felt about their lives enabled me to interact more immediately with them. The idea for the book grew out of these early encounters and I determined to examine in more detail how these women experienced and interpreted their world.

The Content of the Book

The women's stories of their lives in the convents cover a period of extensive change in social policies in Britain, from the introduction of the Mental Deficiency Act in 1913, through to the introduction of the NHS and Care in the Community Act, 1990. Their life stories also span the 'modernisation' of Catholicism from a close-knit closed community in the earlier part of the century to the more open community of post Vatican II (1962 – 1966). The book consists of eight chapters that explore different aspects of daily life, creating a social history of the convents from the residents' experience.

Chapter one provides the historical context for the convents. It details the development of segregated care provision for women with learning

[7] I use the terms 'women' or 'resident' to denote the women who lived in the convents who are now labelled as having learning difficulties. As in many long stay institutions, these women's abilities varied; some seemed, by my estimation, to be extremely capable of living in society unaided while others were less so.

difficulties, Catholic welfare provision and the background to the convent movement itself. At the end of the chapter, there is an annotated time-line for easy reference.

Chapter two discusses how the book came about, providing some examples of the process of information gathering and how I communicated with different women, some of whom had limited use of speech. It includes background information on the women who feature in this book, including their age, class, ethnicity and brief biographical details.

In *chapter three,* the accounts detail how the women came to live in the convents and their relationship to the Sisters who cared for them. *Chapters four* and *five* detail daily life in the convent, their work and leisure activities. Both these chapters highlight how power relations between the Sisters and the women residents, and between the women themselves, were organised and how they permeated daily life.

The right to sexuality has been hard fought for people with learning difficulties and is still precarious (Craft, 1987; McCarthy and Thompson, 1994). The women in the convents had feelings and emotions and their stories and experiences of sexuality in the convents form the basis of *Chapter six. Chapter seven* focuses on those women who moved into the wider community and the closure of one of the convents. This chapter analyses why the convents were unsuccessful in transforming themselves into providers in the new era of community care. In a book that focuses on the life stories of a group of largely ignored people, the final chapter reflects on how people tell their stories and how particular stories come to have prominence in our social histories. It examines the different approaches taken by two convent residents to their life histories.

There are two *appendices.* The first provides biographical details of all the women interviewed for the book, while the second provides the reader with some of the personal material given to me by residents when I began working on this project. This includes poetry, an early version of Mary Adams' autobiography and some of the residents' drawings.

The book has been a fascinating journey for me. I have learned about life in the convent homes but, more importantly, I have learned a great deal from the women who were kind enough to help me. I would like to thank them for all their enthusiasm and commitment to the project. I dedicate this book to them.

Chapter 1

The History of Institutionalisation, Women with Learning Difficulties and the Development of Convent Care

This chapter provides background detail on how women such as Mary Adams came to be seen as being 'in need of care', providing a context for the stories recounted in the rest of the book. It discusses the history of institutionalisation and the development of Catholic care provision from the later nineteenth century until the end of the twentieth century. This account focuses on the experience of women during this period, showing how women's experience of certification and institutionalisation was different to men's experience. The chapter also argues that definitions and categories such as 'learning difficulties' have had a chequered history and were not always precise or truly scientific.

The Historical Roots of Institutional Care for Women with Learning Difficulties

From the mid-nineteenth century, the number of specialist 'idiot' asylums grew to provide education to 'improve' the behaviour of 'idiots' (Wright, 1997). These developments were based on the explosion of medical research that created 'scientific' classification systems of 'types' of people (Foucault, 1978; Digby, 1997; Gladstone, 1997). Before this period, definitions of particular diseases, ailments and disabilities were often unclear and at times unnamed. This catagorisation affected both men and women but often specific diseases and deficiencies were deemed to be particular to one or other sex. Towards the end of the nineteenth century, British society was concerned about the shifting role of women, creating a climate in which women were increasingly blamed for social ills, such as venereal diseases and under-nourished children (Walkowitz, 1982; Cox, 1997). In the late 1880s, British society became fearful of what was called the 'residuum' (Stedman Jones, 1981), a sub-group within the working class who, it was alleged, had no desire to work and lived criminal lives. The growing concern about women's behaviour was connected with this debate in the media of the time. The 1913 Mental Deficiency Act, which implemented large scale institutionalisation for people who are now labelled as having learning difficulties, grew out of these debates along with eugenicist ideas which suggested that there was a 'scientific' category of degenerate people (Jones, 1986; Alaszewski and Nio Ong, 1991; Williams, 1996). The Eugenics Society was an influential organisation of largely middle and upper class people who used the ideas of social Darwinism (Jones, 1986). It was in this period, leading up to the 1913 Act, that definitions of mental deficiency and feeble-mindedness began to emerge. The process of placing a person in an institution required a certificate signed by medical practitioners but as Wright (1997) argues:

> The importance of family indicators of mental ability need not be inferred, for contrary to the design and purpose of the certificates, with one section for practitioners' comments and one for those of the family, many practitioners simply repeated the anecdotal evidence of the family (Wright, 1997: 126).

This suggests that families, at least in the early stages of mental deficiency asylums, were influential in drawing up the criteria for defining admission to asylum. Thomson also confirms that in the early part of the twentieth century 'mental testing (was) imprecise' (Thomson, 1997: 210). Wright goes on to argue that seeking asylum care had less to do with 'an acceptance of a medical approach to idiocy . . .' (Wright, 1997: 131) than a range of social factors, including family poverty and the attitude of family members. In other words, the new 'science' which focused on experiment and examination, while important, was only one part of the emerging category of 'mental deficiency'. Once labelled ineducable and morally depraved, people could be put away in institutions.

At the same time, definitions of women's position in society shifted. Women, potentially, occupied two opposing moral positions. They could be seen as either 'good' mothers – angels in the home – or wicked, fallen women. A kind of moral retribution was heaped upon so-called wayward girls, limiting their rights and their freedom (Cox, 1997). Medical science developed a fascination with women's behaviour and bodily functions, often voyeuristically so, although it defined it as scientific investigation (Jacobus, et al, 1990). New diseases, and with them, categories of women, were named, including the now discredited 'Hysterical Woman'. This so-called science was as much rooted in popular Christian moral perceptions and conceptions of women as in any rigorous clinical investigation.

Walkowitz notes that, as the nineteenth century progressed towards the twentieth, the dividing lines between scientific and religious reformers became blurred:

> Increasingly, medical reformers joined with purity advocates in a concerted effort to educate the population to the values of chastity as the best prophylaxis against V.D. Out of this medico-moral coalition the social hygiene movement of the early twentieth century was born (1985: 254).

As well as this blurring in campaigns over venereal disease and moral purity, attitudes towards the classification of 'idiots' were also blurred. The growth of eugenicist ideas during the later part of the nineteenth century underpinned the development of hereditary theories to show that women who were morally degenerate produced feebleminded children (Jones, 1986). D'Arcy, a leading Protestant Bishop in Ireland and a member of the Belfast Eugenics Society, argued that the 1913 Mental Deficiency Act provided a way of relieving the burden of tax for the undeserving poor:

> What we really wanted above all things, was to prevent the marriage of the unfit and almost anything would be worth doing to that end (D'Arcy, 1914).

Thomson argues that 'girls were often seen as in need of tighter moral control than could be provided by supervision at home so a place of refuge or voluntary religious home, away from the allures of London was preferred' (1997: 211). Separating women out was seen as a necessary social control. The Mental Deficiency Acts of 1913 and 1927 were explicit about women's role in degeneracy. Girls, who were rescued by philanthropic care organisations, were put away and described as 'morally contaminated' (Cox, 1997: 194). This term suggests a particular way of viewing women's behaviour and highlights the fear of women's ability to spread disease and corrupt men.

The process of certification was used to limit young women's fertility. Many certificates were issued for women who did not behave in what was considered an appropriate manner. Hence the history of institutionalisation for women who were labelled in this way was not always about their mental ability, but rather about their perceived morality or their need for protection from 'contamination' (Thomson, 1997, Cox, 1997).

During the early part of the twentieth century, Thomson (1992) argues, women were particularly targeted as 'mental defectives' and institutionalised. Thomson also suggests that in this climate it was not uncommon for girls to be segregated without certification to ensure their 'moral safety'. In other words, while many men were caught within the labels of the time, it is clear that part of the classification and certification of the so-called 'mentally deficient' was influenced by perceptions of women's appropriate role in society.

During the nineteenth century, Christian morals bolstered and legitimatised developing social policies. Most of the major social reformers and politicians of the nineteenth century were professing Christians. Many of the philanthropic voluntary societies and feminists' involvement in campaigns against practices such as child prostitution and the Contagious Diseases Acts of the 1860s were not secular but explicitly religious (Yeo, 1992). Gladstone argues that much of the care provision in Victorian England was undertaken by philanthropy:

> . . . the response to those with the condition of mental deficiency was part of a broader social fabric of Victorian society. Notwithstanding the growth of government in social affairs and the development of mutual aid and self-help organisations, philanthropy played a major role in the supply of welfare in Victorian Britain (Gladstone, 1997: 140).

Religious belief at the time argued that men and women should live their lives in different spheres of influence. Men should focus on the world of work, while women were encouraged to provide a supportive role centred on the home. A 'good' woman's demeanour would show restraint and control.

Not only were women expected to behave in certain ways in wider society, but women who found themselves institutionalised would be expected to live according to the principles of correct behaviour for women at the time. This affected the organisation of daily life in institutions. Cale (1993) and Mahood (1988) argue that this thinking created particular structures within female penitentiaries. Cale highlights the case of Mary Carpenter, a Unitarian who established several girls' reformatories in the 1850s. She notes that in the reformatories relationships with superintendents were based on familial structures. There was explicit encouragement for the girls to see superintendents as father or mother figures. Equally important were the moral principles that highlighted the girl inmates' sins. In other words, the Victorian Christian values which provided the background for much of the philanthropic work in establishing the idiot asylums in the nineteenth century (Wright, 1997), were founded on ideas of what it was to be a 'good' woman. This suggests that the role of religion in definitions of welfare, morality and the provision of care, is perhaps as significant as the development of medical science.

The development of institutional care grew out of a mix of social ideals which drew together emerging science and Victorian religious morality, providing a particular role for women both in and outside of institutions. The next section describes the history of institutionalisation through the twentieth century.

Institutional Care for Women 1927–1990

After the introduction of the second Mental Deficiency Act in 1927, care provision for women was given priority in institutions during the 1930s (Potts and Fido, 1991), because of these fears of hereditary transmission of degeneracy and feeble-mindedness. Care provision in asylums or institutions in this sense were used as a method of control, restricting women's right to sexuality. With the loss of their civil rights through being institutionalised, these women also lost their right to adult status (Walmsley, 1993a).

During the review of mental deficiency, in the early 1950s it was recommended that categories changed and certification was ended. While many people 'escaped' confinement in the first half of the twentieth century (Walmsley, 1995), many others did not. In 1971, as Jones notes, as many as 59,000 people who were now called 'sub normal' or 'severely sub normal' were still in institutions (1975: 5). During the 1950s and 1960s, there were several scandals about the quality of provision in long-stay hospitals, in particular Ely and Farleigh Hospitals. The National Council for Civil Liberties also campaigned (1951) on behalf of people 'locked away' in institutions.

In 1971, the idea of community rather than segregated care was introduced through the *Better Services for the Mentally Handicapped* policy document (Alaszewski and Nio Ong, 1991) partly in response to an enquiry into institutional provision resulting from the scandals (Morris, 1969). While the moral tone taken in the earlier legislation was removed and women were no longer cited as the cause of social ills, sterilisation of women with learning difficulties continued in Britain into the 1980s indicating that, legally, women with learning difficulties were still considered 'unfit' mothers and in need of care themselves (Brown, H, 1994).

During the 1980s, the demand for community care grew due to the criticisms of segregated service provision by theoreticians espousing the principle of Normalisation in services (Wolfensberger, 1972) and to the self advocacy movement arguing for a greater sense of rights to citizenship and adult status (Simons, 1995; Barton, 1996). The theory of Normalisation suggests that people who use services are socially devalued because of the abnormal organisation of provision. Wolfensberger emphasised that 'physical integration . . . is only a potential facilitator of actual individual valued social participation' (Wolfensberger and Tullman, 1982: 217). Inclusion required the devalued person to be able to live valued social roles to 'pass' as a 'normal' person.

At the same time, neo-liberal ideas of care became popular with demands from government for economies. The resulting NHS and Community Care Act (1990)[1] provided new parameters for debates and practice surrounding questions such as adult status. More recently, the principle of Normalisation has been challenged by a number of writers who have pointed out that 'difficult questions arise when trying to identify what exactly such norms or valued social roles are, or should be' (Ramcharan, Roberts, Grant and Borland, 1997b: 245). Walmsley and Downer have pointed out that 'Normalisation implies that disabled people are not normal' (1997: 39) even if this is not what Wolfensberger meant. Other critiques of Normalisation highlight that as a theory it accepts traditional social roles and does not recognise difference within the wider society. Walmsley notes:

> It (Normalisation) fails to identify those barriers to full participation in society such as poverty and exclusion from the labour market. . . . (and) particularly in terms of gender, critics have shown that adherence to the prevailing norms of society reproduce inequality based on gender stereotyping (1995: 26).

In a study of mentally handicapped (sic) women in Ireland in the 1980s, it was found that:

---

[1] This legislation established new divisions in health and social services creating a series of quasi-markets developing a divide between providers and purchasers of care in both sectors. It acknowledged the work of the voluntary sector and, some have suggested (Reading, 1994, Atkin, 1996), offered potential for expansion in this sector. It also sped up the closure programme of long-stay institutions for groups such as people with learning difficulties. In January 1998, the Secretary of State for Health announced a revision of Care in the Community, which may affect people with learning difficulties but is more likely to be focused on people with mental health difficulties.

> Women were . . . more likely to attend day care services than vocational training workshops. In addition, their patterns of ability differed in two key areas – women were more adept at traditional domestic tasks with lower personal independence (Noonan Walsh, 1988: 71).

Women were also encouraged to 'resist adventure', and to assist with 'domestic duties'(Noonan Walsh, 1988: 72). In other words, women with learning difficulties continued to be constrained within the traditional gender roles of wider society (Mitchell, 1971; Wilson, 1977) which indicates a need to examine how women with learning difficulties are socialised and provides a challenge to aspects of the ideas of Normalisation. One of the threads woven throughout the history of welfare from the nineteenth century to the present day is the different experience of women who today are labelled as having learning difficulties. The connection between the role of women in society and welfare is not limited to women who were institutionalised but can also be drawn in examining women as providers of welfare. Since the nineteenth century, we have seen both the expansion and contraction of publicly funded welfare provision – provision that was rooted in institutional care. However, this provision, although dominant during the middle of the twentieth century, was not the only form of welfare provision in Britain during this period. The next section details the development of Catholic welfare provision and the role of Catholic women in providing care.

Difference in Welfare – Catholic Culture and Community

For nearly two centuries, Catholics were banned from organising publicly in Britain. They gained full civil rights only after the removal of the Test Acts in the 1820s and during the nineteenth century developed a subculture as a minority religious group in Britain. Brothers emphasises this point:

> (Catholicism) is not a set of beliefs and ideas that exist in the spiritual sphere alone, but a way of life involving the commitment of the whole person (1964: 158).

When Catholics gained the right to organise openly in society, they established a separate way of life for their community, including their own schools, hospitals and care homes. In 1880, Catholics in Britain codified their doctrine. They emphasised their 'denominational exclusiveness' from other Christians, separating themselves from the activities and values of Protestants (Heimann, 1995: 116). Catholics took on charity work as a mark of their religion. Unlike Protestants, who saw poverty as a sign of degradation, Catholics believed poverty to be a mark of 'unfortunateness' (Heimann, 1995: 158). Williams (1996) notes that Irish Catholic immigrants experienced racism and discrimination when applying for welfare. A flood of Religious Orders began to work in Britain, increasing from fourteen convent Orders in 1850 to over 140 Orders by 1950 (Buchanan, 1996). These Orders 'played a disproportionately large role in all areas of Catholic life . . . (and their role) was paramount in the development of Catholic education, conversion and of course charity' (Buchanan, 1996: 254).

In February 1872, the Daughters of the Mother of God,[2] the convent movement that ran the convents discussed in this book, was founded. It was the first British Catholic Order of nuns to be established since the repeal of the Test Acts in the late 1820s. The Order was founded by an Englishwoman, daughter of an Anglican rector, who converted to Catholicism while working as a 'lady-helper' during the Crimean War. The mission of the Order was to take on charity work.

The life of a nun was different to the life of a lay woman, no matter how devout. Campbell-Jones, a social anthropologist who studied nuns in Britain, illustrates this point:

> The beliefs of the laity have always been recognised as belonging to a different order from those of the clergy in the Catholic Church. But that was more an expression of hierarchy than of an understanding for the beliefs of ordinary people (1979: 149).

In other words, the separate world of the 'Religious' placed them on a different level to other believers. These ideas are echoed in the biography of the Foundress of the convent movement studied. The author identifies her message to her Sisters:

[2] The actual name of the convent movement has been disguised. In order to gain permission to carry out the research for the book, I agreed to the Sisters' request not to use the full name of the Order.

> To her daughters, Mother . . . would say that, as real nuns, the Kingdom of God was within them. To some Sisters who might have said to her or who would say today, 'But all Christians have the Kingdom of God within them, not just us', she might reply, 'Yes but all Christians are not nuns; only a few are called. You are of that few and of that few, you have a special mark' (Gilpin Wells, 1988: 211).

This process of separation was written into convent life and was highly structured and symbolic. These structures were what enabled the Sisters to be special, to be set aside for God, to be pure. It was essential that these rules of purity should permeate their work with the poor. It is this interface between good and bad, chastity and sexual freedom, which dominated the morality of the Movement in the nineteenth century. Although distinct as Catholics, with a particular set of beliefs, there were parallels between their behaviour and the rest of British society. In other words convent life could be seen as an extreme version of many of the values and practices of Victorian England.

Throwing light on perceptions of care and women's role in caring, Yeo (1992, 1996) shows how 'motherhood' became an ideal in the new social science of care in the late nineteenth century. She suggests that middle-class women took on the ideal of 'social motherhood' to give themselves a justification for their voluntary work outside their homes:

> Beside the icon of the married mother, . . . (another) . . . image of a virgin mother engaged in self-sacrificing work with the poor and needy in the public world and introducing a home influence into it (was created) (Yeo, 1992: 75).

Yeo suggests that these mothers could come in different guises. They could provide 'care' in different ways, as punishing and cruel mothers, as protecting and suffocating mothers or as empowering mothers who enabled their 'children' to develop independence (1992: 78). A clear example of 'social motherhood' activity is found in Mary Dendy who established the Lancashire and Cheshire Society for the Permanent Care of the Feeble-minded in 1898. As Jackson states, she:

> was carving out a niche for herself in a public arena from which women were often excluded. Her success in this endeavour is evidenced not only by her notoriety as the

> matriarch of a family of feeble-minded children at Sandlebridge but also by her appointment as a paid commissioner to the newly created Board of Control in 1913 (Jackson, 1997: 178).

Dendy used her role as a woman, as a 'matriarch' to enter the public arena, exactly as Yeo describes. Dendy established Sandlebridge as a home for the 'mentally deficient'. She was an active member of the Eugenics movement. A Unitarian by belief, her commitment to a 'scientific' eugenicist method was firmly rooted in a distinctive 'morality', providing a clear example of how the values of motherhood and morality were used to find space in the public arena of science.

As well as lay women's involvement in the establishment of 'welfare', spiritual Sisterhoods developed welfare concerns in the same period. Convent philosophy, whether Protestant or Catholic, centred on women who separated themselves from the world and its corruption. 'Women of Religion' were deeply influenced by the charitable attitudes of nineteenth-century philanthropy and set up convents that took 'good works' very seriously and exemplified the ideals of the virtuous woman (Campbell-Jones, 1979; Gilpin Wells, 1988).

In other words, the Daughters of the Mother of God were not unique in their practice but rather shared the social values of the time. The perpetuation of these values in their extreme form of separation, into twentieth-century Britain however, created a particular culture within the convents, which can be traced to the teaching of the Foundress of the movement.

To be recognised as a convent movement of the Catholic Church, it was necessary for the Sisters to prepare a constitution to be accepted by the Pope, the 'Holy Father'. With spiritual mothers, of necessity, within Catholicism, came spiritual fathers. However, the picture cannot be seen as simply oppressive or the women as totally passive. The movement needed a father confessor as part of Catholic doctrine because women could not absolve their own sins. However, it was possible for each Order to choose its own 'father'. Mother Foundress was careful not to allow this 'father's' authority to take away the Sisters' autonomy. She wrote in a letter to her Sisters:

> It must not, however, be understood that the priest governed the Institute. He always told them (the Sisters) that God gave

> them light. . . . All that he was to do was teach and counsel (Gilpin Wells, 1988: 156)

The priest also acted as teacher and led their spiritual retreats, explaining to the Sisters the doctrines of the movement that they themselves had founded (Gilpin Wells, 1988). Despite her insistence that their priest was not in control of the movement, he did often write to Mother Foundress chiding her for her mistakes as in this letter:

> Don't act impulsively. It may only be a ruse of the devil . . . One result, at least, is coming out of this trial – it is making you a better nun (Gilpin Wells, 1988: 171)

The religious family of Mother, Father and the poor they cared for as their children mirrors much of the development of modern British social policy. The role of care was established. Yeo makes this point lucidly:

> Women would also help to moralise the professions, especially medicine. . . . The presence of women auxiliaries would soften and sweeten medical inspection . . . Finally women's social work could help to transform class separation and antagonism into the loving relations of family . . . (which) persisted well into the twentieth century (1992: 71)

The family principle worked in a number of professions: the medical profession, 'father' doctor, 'mother' nurse; the social sciences, 'father' scientist or academic, 'mother' social worker or religious guardian of moral values and with the parental figures, the 'children', the sick, the poor, the prostitutes, the feeble-minded and the disabled.

The Daughters of the Mother of God took on a range of 'good works' including setting up and supporting hospitals for the poor, work with 'wayward girls' and women who were considered in need of care. In 1888, Mother Foundress signed a lease for a house in south London, which became one of the two convents examined in this book, Angel convent.[3] It was already equipped with a laundry and Mother Foundress wanted to use the house as a resting-place for 'girls' from their house in Soho, who proved to be worthy (Gilpin Wells: 1988). Angel convent was, therefore, tied

[3] This is a pseudonym.

directly into work with wayward girls. As the biography of Mother Foundress states, 'the girls could live . . . and leave behind the dangers and evils of Soho' (Gilpin Wells, 1988: 191). The so-called girls were at least fourteen years old.

The other convent discussed in the book, Mother convent, was founded in 1904 after Mother Foundress died, but the aims and structure of the convent were the same. These were: a laundry to remind the women of their sins as in many female institutions (Mahood, 1988; Cale, 1993), and a home to provide a haven from the wicked world with 'Sisters' and a 'Mother' who would provide care. Families could be assured that their female children were protected from 'the allures of London' (Thomson, 1997: 211). In other words, from its earliest beginnings, this convent movement was establishing a familial relationship between the women they cared for and the Sisters who cared for them. This theme of motherhood and family, mature and immature women, provides a central motif in the structuring of life within the convents and is used in examining relationships between the women and the Sisters in the following chapters.

From Vocation and Self-sufficiency to Subsidy and Professionalism 1904–1960

Apart from work with women, the movement established hospitals, hospices and schools and expanded its influence to America, Ireland and Africa in the early twentieth century. From the beginnings of the movement, finances came largely from wealthy supporters (Gilpin Wells, 1988) and, as each convent was established, some sort of livelihood for its sustainability was developed. The regime within the convents continued to be based on the principles of Mother Foundress.

As indicated in the time chart at the end of the chapter, during the first half of the century the convents relied on the support of parishioners' subsidies, families' payments for their children and income from the laundry businesses. While eugenicist ideas were dominant in state provision, Catholics spoke out against this form of social policy. Jones notes that the Catholic Church was the only religious group in Britain that was opposed to eugenics (Jones, 1986: 49) and during the 1920s and 1930s a Papal Bull (1929) denounced the philosophy and practice of Eugenics. Jones (1986) argues that Catholic MPs were instrumental in the failure of the Sterilisation Bill (1931). Both the eugenicist position and the religious belief advocated regulation of sexuality. While Catholics were opposed to eugenics (Jones, 1986: 49), one Catholic doctor who was bitterly opposed to sterilisation suggested in 1906 that 'marriage of the mentally unfit should be prohibited' (Jones, 1986: 49) indicating that there was support for some form of segregation and regulation. Catholics believed in the rights of family to act as the main component of welfare. If the family was unable to manage their own care, small charitable organistations, such as convents, would be brought in to support the family. This principle of 'subsidiarity' lay at the heart of Catholic welfare (Coman, 1977) and was at odds with eugenicist philosophy that believed in state control of fertility. Subsidiarity was also at odds with the development of the welfare state, and Catholics continued to organise much of their own welfare separate to state welfare until the 1960s.

Women who lived in the convents were there because of the breakdown of families, when they were placed there through Catholic orphanages or because families themselves were looking for voluntary institutions that would care for their 'problematic' young women. These women were outside of state control. They were not certified but were often placed in the convents under 'orders of care' and were financially supported by their own families creating a separate trajectory for Catholic segregated care in Britain during this century.

Kelly (1988) argues from Christian scripture to identify the 'place' of people with learning difficulties in society. He says, 'unless you change, and become as little children, you will not enter the Kingdom of Heaven', a reference to Matthew chapter eighteen, verse three. Kelly goes on to argue that the behaviour and identity of people with learning difficulties is childlike, saying 'People who have a mental handicap often maintain a childlikeness throughout their lives' (1988: 164). This is a complex view, a moral and religious perspective that centres on a Catholic doctrine of purity and childlikeness, not simply childishness. Catholic doctrine states we all should become trusting, childlike, and dependent on God. Kelly argues that people with learning difficulties maintain this childlikeness. This is particularly significant for women with learning difficulties who, it has already been noted, are seen to be more dependent than their male counterparts. How this philosophy is expressed in the day-to-day structures of the convents is an important theme in this book.

For the Sisters who cared for the residents, the shift from this ideal of childlikeness to support for an ordinary life (Sperlinger, 1992) and adult status expressed in more modern policies has raised many difficult and problematic issues regarding their beliefs and their practice.

The particular culture of the convents, described in detail in the following chapters, followed the teachings laid down in the nineteenth century by the Mother Foundress. In other words, the environment provided in these homes was developed in line with the Foundress's notions of the Sisters caring as spiritual mothers for those in need. For example, the older convent residents commented that until the second world war, they worked in silence (a favourite penance of Mother Foundress), that retreats included specific rituals and prayers that had been used since the beginning of the movement and that the Sisters said that some routine activities in the convents dated back to the time of the Foundress (Mary, 1992; Maria, 1992, 1993; Elvera, 1992; Laura, 1992).

A Life Apart

Daily life in the convents in the early part of the century was routinised. Work was the major activity common to many female establishments such as penitentiaries and other long-stay institutions where laundries and workshops occupied the women for the majority of their time (Mahood, 1988; Walmsley, 1995; Cox, 1997 and Gladstone, 1997). Mother and Angel convents took in washing to make ends meet, from their establishment in 1888 (Angel) and 1904 (Mother). Both convents had large laundries that, until 1939, provided a service for wealthy parishioners and the local priest's house. Initially, the women lived in the back of the main house, but by the 1930s there were too many residents (approximately forty women) and additional dormitories were built, at the same time as hospitals and colonies prioritised the building of 'female villas'.[4] Hence, even though the women coming to live in the convents were not subjected to a medical certification process as those who went to colonies were, there was a growth in segregated care in the convents indicating that the wider social discourse identifying women as 'dangerous' impacted on Catholic welfare as well.

Apart from the laundry, both convents had a farm, making the cost of feeding the women cheaper. Mary describes the farm at Mother convent in

[4] See the time line at the end of this chapter

the 1940s. She tells us there were 'Cows for milk, 200 chickens for eggs and the table, 12 geese, potatoes, cabbages, cauliflowers, swedes, parsnips, brussels sprouts and corn for hens and cows . . . fruit from the orchard' (Adams, 1995: 29). The diet was described as 'good' by most of the women (Adams, 1994). As well as the farm and the laundry, women worked as domestics in the convents. Again Morris (1969), Jones, (1975) and Potts and Fido (1991) note this practice in their studies, indicating that while Catholic provision was particular, it was also similar to other institutions.[5]

During the 1940s, state provision of welfare increased. Mental Deficiency colonies were incorporated into the new National Health Service between 1946 and 1948. As Ayer and Alaszweski note, 'The colonies renamed hospitals were left with a confusing role' (1984: 20). In the Catholic community, however, attitudes to new social policies remained the same. Coman identifies that 'in 1951 it [the Catholic population in England and Wales] was estimated to be 4.67 million' (1977: 9). Catholics clustered in specific areas in Britain, particularly Liverpool, Manchester and London, and conducted their daily life in Catholic groups. Membership of the community consisted of three distinct groups:

> The masses of Irish immigrants thus joined the two smaller indigenous English Catholic groups – the old Catholic families and the converts. Frequently the two latter groups shared high social class and were often linked with the land-owning gentry . . . A key factor in . . . binding together very diverse social and national groups, was allegiance to the Papacy (Coman, 1977: 11).

Apart from allegiance to the Pope, the particular language of Catholicism directly affected the way Catholics saw the world and organised their community. Catholics worked within the community, centred on the local parish church under the direction of men and women of religion, priests and nuns (Mathew, 1955). They were in effect a community within a community.

Coman (1977) and Buchanan (1996) argue that during the development of the welfare state there was much opposition from Catholics to state welfare. Catholics saw state education as a threat to their community,

[5] Further details on work arrangements can be found in Chapter Four.

because schooling was an important part of maintaining a Catholic culture. Catholic Religious communities had cared for 'their own' and saw state intervention in the field of welfare as competition and weakening the responsibility and control of the core unit of society, the family (Coman, 1977; Norman, 1985; Buchanan, 1996). While the state accepted the teaching of the Catholic faith in Catholic schools to enable the inclusion of Catholic schools in the new state funded education system, the story of Catholic hospitals was different. Catholic opposition to birth control was fundamental to their beliefs. Catholic hospitals were withdrawn from the plans for the NHS and they continued to function as private hospitals (Norman, 1985). The Daughters of the Mother of God ran a number of hospitals as well as their provision for women in Mother and Angel convents. They continued to organise their welfare work outside of state control and contact with the expanded welfare state was minimal. This lack of contact was not unusual and even by the 1960s most independent sector homes were not visited by professionals (Morris, 1969). By 1969, both convents had increased in size to accommodate just under 100 residents. Overall, life in the convents did not change until the 1960s (Adams, 1995: 42). It was at this point that life for Catholics all over the world was significantly altered. The unchanging pattern of Catholic ritual was called into question by a sea change in doctrine instigated by the Second Vatican Council, which deliberated between 1962 and 1966.

Catholicism and Change – The Holy Father and the New Nuns 1960–1990

Allegiance to the papacy had always been a central feature of the Catholic community in Britain and still, in the 1950s, it was vital to the maintenance of the community of the convents. The Pope is the father of all Catholics and Catholic doctrine taught that the Pope was able to interpret God's words to his people. The decrees of the Second Vatican Council were an important watershed in Catholic thinking. The time line at the end of the chapter highlights the changes described in the following sections.

The Second Vatican Council reconstituted what it was to be a Catholic in the modern era. It discussed all aspects of Catholic life, both the lay community and the communities of nuns and priests. It challenged the basis of religious organisations such as convents and re-defined their role in 'the community'. The lives of the Sisters working in the convents were re-ordered. As a result, they also re-ordered the possibilities for the women who lived under their care. The roots of change in the convent homes came from the new values espoused by Pope Paul who outlined the new role for 'Religious':[6]

> This sacred synod highly esteems such a life, since it serves the pastoral work of the Church so usefully by educating the young, caring for the sick, and discharging other services. The council supports such Religious in their vocation, and entreats them to adapt their life to modern times (Paul Bishop of Rome, 1966: 473).

It was these values that forced the Order to adapt to the wider society. An English nun from another Catholic Order describes the enormous sense of upheaval that followed:

> You have to remember that at this time the Second Vatican council was beginning to make radical demands on religious Sisters. Our entire way of life was crumbling and changing. The religious community I had joined was undergoing immense transition, and to be part of that cauldron of bubbling ideas, and to see them changing the very way we lived, was immensely exciting (Byrne, 1992: 151).

American nuns and Sisters writing about the changes were equally excited about the potential and at times fearful of what change might mean (Borromeo, 1968). They wrote:

> Vatican II has also made clear that much of what we thought in the past was natural is cultural. Once we realise that something is cultural, we enter the realm of free choice (Sister Loyala Parsons and Sister Thomas Dunleavy CSC, 1968: 140).

The decrees of the Second Vatican Council were to drag the Catholic Church and its members into the twentieth century:

> Communities should faithfully maintain and fulfill their proper activities. Yet, they should make adjustments in them according to the needs of time and place and in favour of what

[6] This is a particular term used by nuns and priests to distinguish themselves from lay Catholics. See the note on terminology at the beginning of the book.

> will benefit the universal Church and individual dioceses. To this end they should resort to suitable techniques, including modern ones, and abandon whatever activities are today less in keeping with the spirit of the community and its authentic character (Paul, Bishop of Rome, 1966: 480).

The modern techniques which Paul is referring to became understood as offering mass in the vernacular rather than in Latin, dissolving the Friday abstinence from meat and for 'Religious', a modernisation of their dress, and community organisation. As Douglas points out, the meanings of Catholicism were bound up in the practice of Catholicism. In *Natural Symbols* (1973), she discusses the abandonment of Friday abstinence and suggests that the threads between the different classes that bound English Catholicism together would be unraveled by this change. She goes on to argue that the ritual of Friday abstinence is a vital part of the meaning of Irish Catholicism:

> Loyalty to my Bog Irish ancestors would not in itself lead me to defend ritualism. Without being Irish, any anthropologist knows that public forms of symbolic expression are not to be despised . . . (Douglas, 1973: 26).

The effect of abandoning rituals such as Friday abstinence and the Latin mass was to abandon a universal Catholic community. It created a space for uncertainty and flexibility. One American nun noted this uncertainty when she wrote about her religious community, 'By now it is clear that . . . forming a community . . . is an ongoing project . . . full of perils, . . . menaced by all sorts of perversions' (Sister Mary Aloysius Schaldenbrand, 1968: 115). This climate had a major impact on the day-to-day lives of the Daughters of the Mother of God. Sister Bartholomew, a woman in her late fifties at Mother convent, told me: '*it* (the changes from the Second Vatican Council) *was like a revolution. We are all different now. There is no coherence.*' (1992). Sister Bartholomew, unlike many of the other Sisters in the movement, had not modernised her dress.

Coman (1977) suggests that Vatican II was a major factor for British Catholics endorsing the developments in the welfare state. He suggests that 'in the early 1960s it (the Catholic identity) was . . . weakened by internal divisions within the . . . Catholic community itself' (Coman, 1977: 109). Their loss of a single identity meant that there was no longer a need for such a tight-knit community and different opinions on the provision of welfare within Catholicism developed, finally leading to the ending of opposition to the welfare state in Britain.

The role of Religious men and women was re-defined within Vatican II. Their role was now more focused on partnership with other providers of care than with separateness. Hence from believing that Catholics needed to provide services separately for all their community, a gradual acceptance of partnership with the state developed as the nature of Catholicism was redefined in Vatican II (Coman, 1977).

From the late 1960s, the convents began to interact more directly with the outside world. The Sisters started to claim Department of Health and Social Security (DHSS) money for the women who lived in the convents. Joanna, the first lay care manager of Mother convent, told me:

> *It wasn't until the sixties that they started actually claiming – I suppose it was supplementary benefit in those days – they didn't claim proper income, I think they were actually getting quite low money until the early 80s, a lot of people were on about fifty quid a week whereas in fact they could have got about 150, so I think there was quite a perceived loss over the years . . . (1996).*

At the same time as changes in Catholicism were being introduced, changes in policy for state institutions developed. Both the Mental Health Act 1959 and *Better Services for the Mentally Handicapped* (1971) changed the direction of state care. Partnerships 'with' secular authorities became more possible as state providers also looked to their wider community. Once the convents took DHSS payments for the women residents, state legislation and policy had a more direct impact on the convents.

The impact of Vatican II on the Sisters also affected the way the convents were organised. There was greater interaction with parish events, including special bazaars held in the convent grounds to raise funds. During the 1970s, many of the women became known in their local villages and some developed friendships with 'outsiders'. People who worked in the village near Mother convent continued to call the women '*the girls from the convent*' into the 1990s (social worker, 1996).

The women residents of the convents identify the period of the late 1960s and early 1970s as a time when life began to change, creating more freedom. This growing freedom is reflected in the attitudes of nuns around the world. One nun writing about the new era said:

> (The inference that) because people profess evangelical poverty, they must all look exactly alike and use exactly the same things in exactly the same way seems less evangelical than totalitarian . . . Differentiated members, not faceless members, compose the true community (Sister Mary Aloysius Schaldenbrand, SSJ, 1968: 125).

Sisters were able to train as professional care and social workers and lay staff were employed to work in the convents (Mary, 1994) as the boundaries between the outside world and the convents began to break down.

The Sisters had always seen their work as 'care in the community', but their community was the closed community of 'Religious' with a powerful Mother overseeing their daily lives. Through the permeation of state funding, the convents, like other long-stay institutions, were being faced with a new definition of 'care in the community' born out of the end of segregated 'care' in the state sector and with a growth of professionalism within the convent movement. The convent communities were drawn into the direct frame of state social policy and were making links with a variety of different state institutions, including adult education institutions, and social services and health authorities. In addition, increasing inspection powers during the 1980s gave the convents an outside authority beyond the rule of the Pope to contend with.

By the late 1970s, the laundries had gone into decline and by 1984, when the first adult education tutor started at Angel convent, twenty hens were all that was left of the farm. Both convents had sold off large parts of their land during the early 1970s to raise funds. Lay domestic workers were also introduced, although the women continued to engage in cleaning and cooking activities in both convents until the 1980s. By the early 1980s, the laundries were running at a loss. In 1988, the laundry at Angel convent burnt down, not to be replaced, and Joanna, the lay care manager at Mother convent, closed the laundry at Mother convent in 1993. For most of the women who worked in the laundry, the closure at Mother and the fire at Angel were described as traumatic events. The laundry was an important symbol of the value of their existence and many of the stories that the women told me in both convents indicated a pride in their work.[7]

---

[7] see Chapter Four

Changes in convent life mirrored many of the changes in state institutions.[8] However, the changes had special significance for the women and the Sisters who lived in a Catholic environment where the decree of the 'Holy Father' through the Second Vatican Council was the impetus to re-shape their lives. As the convents altered, further changes in social policy were implemented and the convents sought to maintain an identity as providers of care.

Care in the Community: The 1990s

In the 1990s, the Mother General was in control of the Order's affairs. She had a team of religious advisers, the Generalate, and a Social Care Board. The convent movement hoped to benefit from the 1990 NHS and Community Care Act and developed plans to expand its day service provision (SMG, 1992). It established working parties to examine the potential of the new legislation in different areas including learning difficulties. This one, the 'Social Care Advisory Board – Learning Difficulties' – was established as part of the revision of care in the convent movement.

The Advisory Board reported positively on the possibilities of adapting provision in line with the 1990 Act:

> After several meetings the board recommended: That there be a comprehensive ASSESSMENT of every resident both in community houses and institutions within the next 14 months. These assessments, at which it will be essential to include representation from the resident's Authority of origin, social worker and family member must be so designed and managed to ascertain individual need in terms of accommodation, day care provision, health care, etc. (SMG, 1992) (upper case in original).

In examining the role of the voluntary sector in community care, Reading suggests that there were possibilities for increasing voluntary sector power within the new legislation:

---

[8] see the time line at the end of the chapter

> Community care legislation and money offers new ways of providing services and encourages local authorities to look for voluntary, not-for-profit, and private agencies to bring these about (1994: 26).

The social care board was attempting to find ways of benefiting from the changes in state policy in the 1990s. The quasi-markets of the new era (Brigden and Todd, 1993) could offer possibilities for more service provision for the movement and financial rewards. The Social Care Advisory Board document states:

> The Board would recommend that the Government's broad approach to achieving better care as contained in its White Paper 'CARING FOR PEOPLE' be accepted as the Congregation's own approach to its services . . . (SMG, 1992) (upper case in original).

The Board recommended that respite care be developed and day care expanded. Training of staff using NVQs was to be implemented and Sisters with formal training were to become accredited practice teachers to 'generate a small income from placements'. They also advised that a lay coordinator should be appointed and better links with other care agencies were developed.

In 1993, the Generalate appointed a lay manager, a man, to advise the Order on all aspects of their care provision. He established a separate charity foundation for the care work, accountable to the Generalate, but separate from, the day-to-day lives of the Sisters. The new foundation took on its own name. Continuing the link with Mother Foundress, the foundation took on her birth name, removing the religious connection to the Daughters of the Mother of God and emphasising the professional secular side of the work. The mothering role of the Sisters was being altered and re-shaped just as their religious lives had been re-shaped. The implications of this ideological shift for the provision of care in the convents are taken up in more detail in Chapter Seven. Decisions on development or closure, 'client groups' or work areas were taken by the Generalate. Despite the professionalisation of the work, all meetings continued to begin and end with a prayer (Joanna, 1996). Part of the finances from each convent were also still returned to the headquarters in London, for '*administrative costs*' (Joanna, 1996). In 1993, at Mother convent this amounted to over £30,000 a year.

Even in the 1990s, all the Sisters' salaries were returned to headquarters in London as is traditional in convent movements. In other words, Sisters did not keep their pay. Sisters were allocated to convents, and were usually moved between convents fairly regularly, about every four years, '*unless they are very useful*'(Joanna, 1996).

In the late 1980s, both the convents I have studied moved some women into cottages in the grounds. From dormitories sleeping about twenty women, the convents began building works to create smaller units within the convents themselves. In the early 1990s at Mother convent, Joanna '*saw opportunities to give the women who lived there a life where they had choice and safety*' (Joanna, 1996). She produced glossy publicity leaflets advertising their services. The residential services were described as 'on-site flats and community based housing' (Francis Taylor Foundation, 1993).

The 'community based housing' grew out of parishioner networks taking in residents for a fee. The convent had developed a complex symbiotic relationship with the Catholic parish, establishing through their work with local parishioners a community outside of the convents that offered the women a window into the wider society, but still located within the Catholic faith. The changes to the care service implemented by the convent movement in the 1990s were building on the changes that had been taking place in the convents since the late 1960s, where 'Religious men and women' were told through Vatican II to work in the wider community. The link between the religion and the care work had not been entirely severed but had been severely fractured. The final story of the two convents from 1993 – 1996 is taken up in Chapter Seven.

No organisation functions outside social values and historical developments, but individual institutions and movements will have their own particular interpretation of social life. The story of the convents shows how the relationship between wider society and small communities with deeply held beliefs is often contradictory. There are clear indications of the impact of wider social forces on the development of convent life but there are also unique and specific practices which only convent residents and the Sisters experienced. The day-to-day experiences of the residents, the Not Quite Sisters, are taken up in the rest of the book.

Time-line of events

Date	Convents	Social/Policy	Catholicism	Wider Social/ Theory Influences
			Catholic Emancipation Act 1829	
1840s	Foundress working in poor relief	Development of specific asylums for idiots including the establishment of Charity for Asylum of Idiots 1847	Catholics grow in numbers	Improvement of 'Idiots' e.g. Senguin's School 1831
1850s	Foundress in Crimea converts to Catholicism	Further asylums established	Nuns in Crimea	
1872	Convent movement established		Catholics active in their own welfare provision. Racism Growth of 'working orders'	Philanthropy and Social Motherhood[1] against Irish Immigrants
1888	Angel convent established	Moral panics Social fear of residuum		

[1] See page 17 in chapter one.

EARLY MODERNISM

Date	Convents	Social /Policy	Catholicism	Wider Social Influences
1890		Lunacy Act		
1900	Foundress dies			
1904	Mother convent established	Royal commission on feeble-mindedness reporting in 1908	Self Sufficiency Opposition to eugenics	Women blamed for 'degeneracy' in the nation[3] Eugenics movement grows – segregation
1913	Mary enters convent	Mental Deficiency Act		
1920–30	Laundries and Farms Financial contributions from families.	Expansion of public provision Growing number of female villas a priority	Papal Bull (1929) against eugenics	Sterilisation proposed as a solution to 'problem' of mental deficiency
1926		2nd Mental Deficiency Act (1927)		General Strike
1920/30s	Self sufficiency/charity			

HIGH MODERNITY

Date	Convents	Social /Policy	Catholicism	Wider Social Influences
1930s	Building campaign	Expansion of colony building	Catholic MPs vote against Sterilisation Bill	
1935	Elvera enters convent	1931 Sterilisation Bill fails	Subsidiarity principle	

3 See page 11 in chapter one for a fuller discussion.

Date	Convents	Social /Policy	Catholicism	Wider Social Influences
1940–45	Laundries benefited from war – took in washing from soldiers	1944 Education Act	Expansion of state welfare	
1945–72	Sr. Margaret Mary at Mother convent Martha enters 1947	 Beveridge Report 1945	 Catholic opposition to Welfare State continues	
		1946 Association of Parents of Backward Children founded (later MENCAP)		
1954		Royal Commission on Mental Deficiency and Health (1953-1959)		1951 NCCLs '50,000 Outside the Law' raised awareness of detention of 'mental defectives'
1959	100 residents in convents	Mental Health Act (1959)		
1960	Sr. Ruth at Angel convent	Scandals at Ely, Farleigh	Vatican II	Goffman's work on institutions
1963/7	First TV contact with outside world Relationship with local authority established	Morris Commission	Welfare State accepted	

Date	Convents	Social /Policy	Catholicism	Wider Social Influences
1971	Farm closed at Mother Dormitories go at Mother convent. Sr. Ursula arrives at Mother convent	Better Services for the Mentally Handicapped Disability Alliance Founded (1974) National Development Team to advise on policy (1975)	Religious to work in wider community	Normalisation theory espoused Community care ideas growing in influence
1979		Jay Report	New conservative Pope	
1984	Adult Education at Angel convent	First People First group in England		
1986		Audit commission (1984)	Declining numbers of Sisters/ Priests/ Brothers in West	Neo-Liberal Government begins restructuring of Welfare State
1988	Laundry burns down at Angel	Griffiths Report (1988)		
LATE / POST MODERNITY				
1989	1st lay manager at Mother (Joanna)			
1990		NHS and Community Care Act (1990)		

Date	Convents	Social /Policy	Catholicism	Wider Social Influences
1992	Social Care Board Report Lay chair of care established Foundation separate to convent movement set up		Larger number of Catholics in Latin America and Africa than in Europe	Belief in integration of people with learning difficulties into community life
1993	Day care and respite established	Community Care Act implemented		
1994	Laundry closed at Mother			
1994	Closure of Mother announced Joanna, lay care manager resigns			Re-appraisal of Normalisation Inclusion and difference
1995	Sr. Ruth replaced at Angel	Disability Discrimination Act 1995		Recognised as issues to shape practice
1996	Mother Convent closes Angel Convent all services in house 30 residents left			

Chapter 2

The Curiosity of a Cat: Finding Out About the Residents

This chapter introduces the thirty women who contributed to the accounts of life in the convents detailed in the book. Their personal stories enabled me to gain a sense of daily life in these homes, which I hope to convey in the rest of this book. The women came to live in the convents in different periods during the twentieth century. My oldest interviewee, Martha, began her adult life in Mother Convent in 1913 when she was sixteen, and the most recent arrival that I interviewed, Diana, moved into Angel convent in 1988.

My first visit to Angel convent was in 1985. Set in a leafy suburb of south London, the convent was housed in an impressive listed building with well tended gardens, a gatehouse and a long winding driveway up to the front door. I taught my drama class in a prefabricated 'hut' at the back of the main building. Over the weeks that I visited the convent, I became friendly with several of the women and Sisters. They often referred to their history but it was clear that little of this history was recorded to help me conduct my research. Having decided to find out more, I asked the Sister-in-charge and some of the women at the convent if they would agree to be interviewed. The Sister-in-charge, Sister Ruth, explicitly asked that I did not name the convents or convent movement in my research. I agreed to this request and have given this convent the name *Angel convent.* I also discussed and agreed pseudonyms for most of the women, the Sisters and other professionals who I interviewed.

After spending some years working with the residents at Angel convent, I made contact with another of the movement's convents in the south of England, which I have named *Mother convent.* The stories recounted in the book are based on events in these two different convents. I visited both institutions regularly for a period of seven years and shared many of the daily activities with the women, including eating meals, washing dishes and attending celebrations. Working in two convents provided me with further detail on convent life and access to more residents' stories and experiences. It also enabled me to draw comparisons between the two convents and highlight similarities. Overall, I was struck by the similarities between them, suggesting that convent life was more dictated by a set of guiding principles and beliefs than by its immediate surroundings.

The Women Residents

When I first visited the convents, each had about eighty women residents. Some would not, by modern definitions, be thought to have learning difficulties but had been placed in the convents and left there for other social reasons.[1] By 1996, Mother convent was closed and Angel convent had only thirty women living in the convent itself, with several women boarding in homes 'in the community'. The women's ages ranged between twenty and ninety-five. They were of mixed religious background, although most were Catholic, either English or Irish. Twenty-seven of my interviewees were white and three were black. The black women all lived in Angel convent. I interviewed women who had entered the convent in each of the decades since 1913 up until the 1990s. Working with women of different ages provided continuity and helped chart changes and developments in convent life. From 1913 to the 1920s, six of my interviewees came to live in the convents: Martha, Amanda, Myra, Laura, Beth and Maria. By the time I interviewed these women, they were in their eighties and nineties, but several of them claimed to remember clearly the early days of convent life. During the 1930s and 40s, another six of my interviewees arrived: Elvera, Gloria, Mary, Joan, Moira and Alice.

Mary and Elvera played a very important role in gathering the material for the book. They provided a range of material and were very supportive of the project. Elvera wrote poetry which was often performed during celebrations at Mother convent. She recorded these poems on tape and gave them to me. Hearing the tapes gave me a sense of her performance as well as providing historical details of events. During the time I worked in the convents Mary wrote her autobiography, researched her family history and made a video interview for trainee social workers. All their material provided me with useful information for the book.[2]

The next two decades, the 1950s and 60s, saw most of my interviewees, nine in all, arrive at the convents: Athena, Louise, Roberta, Tess, Jane, Anne, Jessica, Lucy and Sara. It was in this period that the convents had the largest number of residents and contact with social services became more common.[3] The final five interviewees, Zarina, Susan, Diana, Tembe and Claire, began convent life during the 1980s. For many of these younger

[1] For further discussion on why these women came to live in the convent see Chapter Three.
[2] For a more detailed discussion on Mary and Elvera see Chapter Eight.
[3] More detail on the reasons for entry into the convents can be found in the next chapter.

women, life in the convents was a temporary home before they moved into the wider community.[4]

Gathering Information Using Different Communication Skills

Communication with most of the women flowed easily. Most used speech as their main form of communication, but two women, Lucy and Roberta, were less verbal. As Walmsley (1995) points out, research with people who have major communication problems is a complicated and difficult field. I, like Walmsley, do not feel I have resolved all these difficulties but I describe below how I tried to include Lucy and Roberta's perceptions of convent life in the book.

Communication is about a two-way engagement and meaning should be checked by referring back and ensuring that the understanding gathered is what the interviewee meant. This can be done with speech and a number of other clues can also be used, such as facial expression and listening to tone of voice which can indicate certainty or a lack of clarity about a point being discussed. I also used drawings as another tool with both Roberta and Lucy which gave me some insights into their world. Sharing with them the development of their pictures helped me find out some of the things that were important to them. Drawings can be valuable but they often present difficulties in gaining an accurate understanding of the artist's meaning. This was particularly problematic when working with people like Lucy who had virtually no speech. It was more successful when people, like Roberta, were able to use their pictures to flesh out limited speech. Roberta drew a picture of her convent building, placing the Sister-in-charge's room in the centre of the building (Figure 2). Working with her, I found out that the room was not actually in the centre of the convent but that, for her, the Sister was metaphorically at the 'centre' of the building and she knew what was happening all the time. She also points out in her drawing that the front door had a path leading up to it but that the workroom had a separate entrance where the women spent most of their day. This story indicates the positive uses of drawings but also highlights their limitations. The image of the Sister-in-charge at the centre of the convent could mean that Roberta felt she was all powerful, or possibly it indicates that she felt a form of safety through being watched over, or perhaps it suggests a bit of

[4] Further biographical details of the women can be found in Appendix One.

Figure 2: Roberta's drawing of the convent

both. The image is powerful but it is difficult to be certain of its meaning and required working with Roberta over several sessions to gain her own understanding of the picture. Finally, Roberta told me that Sister was like '*God*' and '*our mother watching us*' (1995) indicating that she did feel the Sister-in-charge had a powerful role in surveillance in the convent.

Another example of the use of drawing is the story of Lucy,[5] who had very little speech and almost no Makaton. Lucy carried with her a bag of dismembered dolls, legs, arms, heads, and bodies. If she was given a whole doll she would pull the limbs apart. Through a series of sessions with her, drawing complete dolls then letting her add to the drawing, I became aware that she always crossed out the arms and legs (see Figure 3). Crossing out the limbs reminded me of her dismembering the dolls in her doll bag. It seemed that she was attempting to communicate as she always looked up at me as she passed the drawing back and waited for a response. The breakthrough in understanding her meaning came when one day after making her drink she returned to the table where we had been working. On the table were her doll parts. I had arranged them as a doll, with the arms, legs, heads and bodies in correct relation to each other but still

[5] Lucy was one of two women who did not choose their pseudonyms, as they did not generally use speech to communicate. The other woman who did not choose her 'name' was Roberta. The other twenty eight women all chose their 'names'.

Figure 3: Lucy's Doll

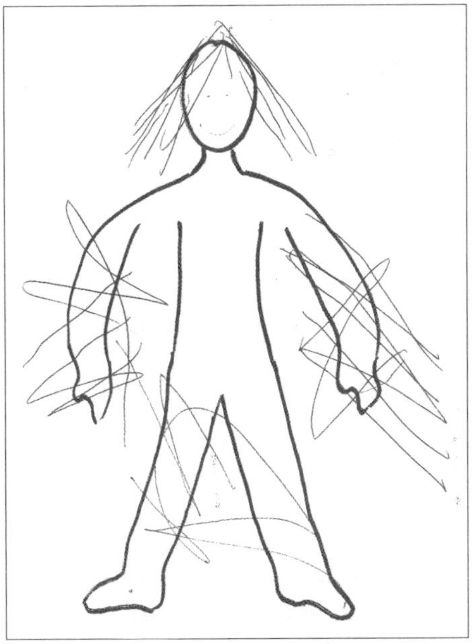

disconnected. Lucy dropped her cup on the floor, looked at me and shouted one word, '*mama*' (Lucy, 1991). On discussing this incident with one of the Sisters, I was told that Lucy had found her mother lying dead at the bottom of the stairs before a social worker had brought her to the convent. I felt that Lucy was attempting to tell all who met her about this incident and make sense of it for herself. It was not possible ever to confirm this feeling as Lucy was not able to explain her actions but it did seem there was some connection between her experience and her dolls.

My work with Lucy was conducted using drawings, observing her communication patterns through her behaviour and, most important of all, giving her the time to build mutual trust with me and develop her confidence in being able to communicate. Lucy is an extreme example. The majority of the women I interviewed were effective speech communicators, but the convents were home to very different women, and as in many institutions for people with learning difficulties (Morris, 1969; Alaszewski, 1986; Potts and Fido, 1991), the range of their communication, physical and conceptual abilities varied considerably. It was important to attempt to include that range. Inevitably, the stories and voices reproduced in the book focus on the women who were most able to communicate,[6] but I have been keen to include some work with people whose verbal communication skills are limited.

Despite the difficulties, drawings by people with learning difficulties add a richness to data, by including people who are usually excluded from research because of the emphasis of either written or oral sources. It also provides a different perspective on experience to that gained from words.

[6] For more discussion on this point, see Chapter Eight.

As Atkinson and Williams say in their editorial to the anthology of people with learning difficulties experiences, *Know me as I am*:

> There are accounts and drawings that appear, at first glance, to be slight and rather inconsequential but which, in fact, represent for the author or creator a major step in a communication with the outside world (Atkinson and Williams, 1990:234).

As well as drawings produced by the women for the book, I also examined, with the women's consent, some of their possessions and photograph albums.

Possessions and Photographs

Many people with learning difficulties who have lived in institutions have few personal possessions (Atkinson, 1993; Stuart, 1997). Morris, who conducted her research in the 1960s, found that few people had their own clothing and most shared dormitory space. These circumstances did not provide an environment to collect and maintain their possessions (Morris, 1969). Several of the women in the convents I worked with did not have personal possessions or photographs of their family or prior lives whilst others had family albums, record collections and books, ornaments and memorabilia. Simply asking who had possessions and who did not revealed a wealth of knowledge about the women's experiences of life.

The types of possessions that the women held also revealed aspects of their personality. On one occasion I had a fruitless yet polite interview with one woman, Maria, but when she showed me her Catholic icons, I gained an understanding of the depth of her religious belief and commitment to life in the convent that I had previously not fully grasped. Possessions and photographs can be useful prompts for conversations and can help people who find speech difficult to use a number of other symbols to help understand their past. Jackson has pointed out that photographs can provide us with a fertile source of data. He also points out that any photographs of institutions can increase our understanding of the institution:

> Photographs of workers can therefore be used to enhance our understanding both of the day to day management of an

> institution and of the strategies adopted to legitimate that management (Jackson, 1997: 70).

Photographs of convent life are rare, especially ones of events before the 1970s. I could find no photographs of the women working in either the laundry or on the farm. Joanna, the first lay care manager at Mother convent, told me that she had wanted to photograph the laundry as some record of working conditions but she did not manage to organise this before it closed in 1994. The photographs that do exist are in the possession of individual women, not held formally by the convent. It was the women themselves who were keeping the past of the convents alive.

Telling outsiders about their lives was important to the women who helped me to gather the data for this project. In one of the reminiscence books I helped the women to produce, the contributors wanted the cover design to include their statements about the value of the book. Each woman wrote her thoughts; one put down, 'people don't often listen to me'; another said, 'not many people know about the kind of life I've lived' (The Remembering Project, 1988).

I also interviewed five Sisters and three lay care staff, including the care manager of Angel convent, several Sisters who were care workers, both lay care managers of Mother convent and a lay care worker. In these interviews I was not concerned to gather material about the Sisters' or the care managers' lives, but rather, firstly, to flesh out details from the interviews with the residents and later to gain more information on the convent movement. These interviews provided me with information about the Order of nuns and how wider social changes affected the two convents studied. The residents gave me a sense of changes within the convents, the religious meanings of the convents, the structuring of daily life and their personal experience of convent living.

I also interviewed two 'outsiders', a social worker who had close links with Mother convent, from 1992 until its closure, and the first adult education tutor to teach in Angel convent whose experience dated from 1984 until she retired in 1994. These professional perceptions gave me an idea of the attitudes and views of people who came across the convents from the 'outside', and provided me with a reference point for my own perceptions.

Both convents were located within suburbs and I initially thought that neighbours might have been able to provide additional data, but people who lived near the convents knew little about them. The adult education tutor of Angel convent told me that few locals seemed to be aware of the purpose of the convents. She said:

> *People who lived locally had no idea who lived at Angel. When I told them they were surprised – most said they had thought it was just a regular convent* (Adult Education Tutor, 1996).

Equally, residents' families, who were still in contact with the convents, could have proved useful informants. However, during casual conversations with them they seemed to have a limited knowledge of convent life. Joanna said that relatives '*never went beyond the parlour or the dining room if it was a disco night*' (1996). For many of the families, and in the local communities, there was a kind of silence connected with the convents, perhaps a lack of interest, or a religious reverence that did not question or pry, meaning that 'outsiders', whether relatives or neighbours, seemed to have little to offer an exploration of the experience of life within the convents.

Working from the women's accounts of life in the convents was the most appropriate method to gain a detailed description of convent life. As Atkinson suggests, the history of 'learning disability' is still 'a partial account, based on documentary evidence . . .The history (or histories) of people with learning disabilities, from their point of view, remains largely unwritten' (1997:3). The women's stories themselves are a valuable and unusual source of information and, as Walmsley states:

> Studies in which people with learning difficulties have been asked for their views, and have been able to speak for themselves are rare and relatively recent (1995:53).

The choice to use the women's stories rather than the more traditional documentary evidence was also made because documentary material in the convents was scarce. Writing in the introduction of Mary's autobiography, the care manager, Andrew, explained why:

> Formal documentation held at (Mother) . . . omitted the rich detail of people's personal lives. Scanning the files for 'significant life events' you could be forgiven for thinking that women living at. . . had done little in fifty years. For many individuals it seemed that their only recorded achievements

> were the date on which they arrived and the day they started work in the laundry. An entire lifetime of feelings, loves, losses, personal joys and triumphs as well as heartache was left to memory (Saunders, 1995:5) (My brackets).

This is in sharp contrast to hospitals, which produced extensive records. However, even here, Jones notes that in some hospitals' records were 'deficient' (Jones, 1975:56) which suggests that documentary sources did not adequately account for people's lives and certainly did not contain information on personal achievements. Joanna, the first lay care manager of Mother convent, told me '*files had little more than 'arrived at* (Mother) *on 25 June 1935. Father unhappy as she has no job and walks the streets*' (1992). In addition, the convents were not hospitals, they were 'homes', and kept no other formal records, such as medical records. Perhaps most significant of all, the women who lived in the convents, despite being part of a 'learning difficulties' service today, had never been certified,[7] as this excerpt from an interview with Joanna illustrates:

> (MS:) . . . and so I mean I would have thought the vast majority of your older population didn't have learning difficulties at all
> (Joanna:) *No*
> (MS:) . . . that was to do with the history? . . . they still went through, . . . did they go through the process with the doctors and certification? . . .
> (Joanna:) *No, there was no reason (why they came to live in the convents), I only found one person who was detained by any section, umm, all of the rest of the people were not . . . and in fact she was under the 1890 Lunacy Act . . .*
> (MS:) Oh right so they really weren't certified?
> (Joanna:) *No*
> (MS:) But then why . . .?
> (Joanna:) *The majority of the people were actually placed by families directly and they paid* (1996).

Joanna saw my research as '*the first account of life in the convents*' (1992).

[7] Certification was a process used from the later part of the nineteenth century until the 1959 Mental Health Act that assigned people to a life in an institution. For further discussion on this process, see Chapter One, and for more detail on the women in the convents and their reasons for living in these homes, see Chapter Three.

The experience of convent life was held in the residents' memories, not in official records. Personal detail and personal meaning provide more useful indicators of how daily life was organised than the limited information on record and it is appropriate that the majority of the material used in this book is taken from interviews with residents and from written or performed materials owned by these women. Where women found speech difficult, I worked with them to generate drawings. I fleshed out this information through interviews with staff and professionals and by reading some of the limited documentary evidence available. That the women, in their memories and in their possessions, kept the only detailed record of convent life, has created a particular flavour and poignancy in constructing the history of these institutions. The story of the convents that emerges in this account, therefore, focuses on the residents' perceptions of their own lives, revealing a history that is filled with humour and affection as well as pain and oppression.

Chapter 3

Removal from the World – Coming to the Convent

In the few life history accounts from people with learning difficulties that we have such as Barron (1989), Atkinson and Williams (1990) and Potts and Fido (1991), the stories of entry into institutions are painful. In these accounts, people describe how they were forcibly taken from home, often without any knowledge of why they had to leave. Most of the stories of entry into the convents echo those feelings of pain and shame. However, four of the women I spoke to said they had chosen to live in the convents, suggesting, perhaps surprisingly, some autonomy in their decision to enter a convent. On the other hand, of the thirty women I interviewed, seventeen were placed in the convents by family members and of these, nine women went to live in the convents on the advice of their fathers. This perception of being abandoned by their families came across very strongly in many of their stories. For some of the women, the convents became the only 'family' they had. Additionally, many of the accounts of the process of entry suggest links between the Sisters' first experiences as postulants and the women residents. This contrasts with stories from publicly funded long stay hospitals where staff and inmates' experiences were considerably different (Potts and Fido, 1997). This chapter therefore compares stories of entry from women who came to live in the convents at different times. It indicates that there is not one account of segregation, but rather there are many different experiences in different institutions and between different individuals.

The Family of the Convents

Institutions for people with learning difficulties are often characterised by unequal dependency between staff and residents but there are many types of unequal dependency relationships (Alaszewski, 1986: 4). In British society, we have often catagorised people with learning difficulties as dependent, but they are not only seen as dependent but also infantilised. In other words, they are seen to be dependent because they are thought to be like children. Walmsley refers to Hockney and James (1993) who studied dependency in older people: 'In western cultures, the child is the dominant model of dependency, hence the infantilisation of older people and disabled people . . . ' (Walmsley, 1995: 31). Many other accounts of life in hospitals for people with learning difficulties point to infantilisation (Morris, 1969; Jones, 1975; Alaszewski, 1986; Ryan and Thomas, 1980). If people with learning difficulties are treated as children, it may be the case that staff, rather than relating to them as 'patients', may see themselves playing a parental role.

Many of the convent residents suggested that relationships in the convents were like a family. Some developed special relationships with particular Sisters, saying they had been like 'mothers' to them.

One of the residents, Elvera, uses the image of family in one of her poems to describe the relationships between convent residents and the Sister in charge:

> *For God's little chosen ones*
> *A spot was in your heart*
> *They often went for a cuddle*
> *And this to them you would impart*
> *We were a very big family –*
> *Over eighty or even more*
> *But you coped with all quite happily*
> *And never closed the door* (Elvera, 1988).

Hearing the women use this image, and uncovering the emphasis placed by Mother Foundress on her role as 'Mother' to her 'Sisters', the theme of family seemed to emerge as a common thread that shaped life in the convents.

In describing daily life in the convents as familial, I am not suggesting a romantic ideal of family life. The 'convent family' was constructed within quite specific power relations. Another resident, Mary Adams, wrote in her own autobiography: 'The Sisters loved us so much that they punished us for our own good, but if you had any problems they were kindness itself' (Adams, 1995: 35). The right to punish was conferred through 'love', hence this family could be extremely harsh and some of the stories the women told me echo stories of mistreatment found in other accounts of convent life or other institutions[1] (Humphries, 1998). A process of infantilisation

[1] See Chapters Four and Six.

where all the women were called 'girls' and those that were less able were called the 'little ones' also sustained 'The family'. This process of infantilisation not only cemented the familial roles of the Sisters as mothers and the women residents as children but it made the women dependent on the care provided for them. Dependency created vulnerability and women were, at times, left exposed to mistreatment. Equally the Sisters lived within a hierarchy.

The 'Sisters' were both sisters to each other and 'mothers' to the women. They too had 'mothers' who watched over them. Through her teachings that continued to inform convent policy into the 1990s, the Mother Foundress 'watched over' the Sisters. The role of 'Superiors' who managed individual convents and a 'Mother General' at headquarters who was in charge of the movements' affairs across the world were each a mirror for the ultimate 'Mother', the Mother of God. As well as using mothering to maintain the process of infantilisation, it was also used to maintain the authority of the Superiors over their Sisters. Thus the Sisters were also subjected to harsh treatment which limited their freedom and created, in the name of the religion and in the name of care, a strict regime of authority with controls on behaviour if members of the community acted inappropriately. This was the discipline of the Religious Order that dominated all the women's, Sisters, and residents' lives. The notion of family in the convents was therefore a continuation of the ideas of spiritual motherhood used by the Mother Foundress, which was discussed in Chapter One. Her writing and teachings were considered special and her story, in a variety of forms, was often repeated to me. For example, Maria, who had pictures of the Foundress, as well as statues of the Virgin Mary, in her room, would say each time we met, '*That's Mother Foundress, she started everything*' (Maria, 1993). The Foundress was often compared to favoured Sisters, suggesting that her teachings were embodied in the work of a 'nice' Sister. Mary wrote her own autobiography:

> I wonder what Mother Foundress would have said if she had seen all her big buildings being shut down, but I am sure she would have agreed that everyone should be respected, and gain their independence to a certain degree (Adams, 1995: 49).

In Mary's mind, the Mother Foundress was present even at the time of closure of the convent. Mary, Elvera and Maria all described convent life in familial terms; sometimes their perception of this family was caring and sometimes controlling. Life in the convents was constructed through a sort of symbolic language of care. It was care by mothers and sisters for daughters, but the language, either real or symbolic, could be used differently. It could be used as a method of controlling and silencing (punitive), of protecting and limiting choice (protective) or as a way of supporting and enabling (empowering). For example, a punitive mother would be strict, believing that punishment was for the good of her children, a protective mother would not give sufficient space for her children to develop independence and an empowering mother would create safe environments to enable her children to develop new abilities.[2] Hence the language of care and caring needs to be understood as a language of power, power over the women and powerful in maintaining the hierarchical relationships between the women. Describing certain women as 'the little ones' suggests that they required care but it is also a powerful way of affirming their place within the hierarchy of convent life. 'Eat up your dinner' is also a common phrase that I heard in the convents while I visited the convents in the 1980s. It suggests caring but, at times, I noticed that the women were made to finish what was on their plates before they were allowed to leave the table. The language of familial care was made more effective in structuring life in the convents as it was interwoven with religious belief and values. A series of familial figures such as Mothers and Sisters maintained authority through the religion but 'Fathers' were also evident. Local priests, who heard confession of sins performed by both Sisters and women, were the representatives of the 'Holy Father' in Rome, who led the church and symbolically represented God the 'Father' on earth. Fathers could be called upon to adjudicate between the Sisters and at times between the women and the Sisters.[3] Priests were given particular authority in the convent, not unlike the authority of a Victorian father who was often not seen but when he was he was always heard. For some of the women with Mothers, Sisters and Fathers, the 'family of God' was being created before their eyes.

On entry, the women took on the role of child, a symbolic daughter. While I was gathering the women's stories about their entry into the convent, I found similarities between the women, especially when they had come to

---

[2] Elvera and Mary talk about punishments from Sisters (see Chapter Four). Sister Ruth provides several examples of protective behaviour (see Chapter Six) and Mary talks about Sr. Ursula who gave her the chance to develop her skills in organising and planning events (see Chapter Five). All these examples illustrate how the role of carer can suggest different forms of caring.

[3] For examples of the role of priests as fathers see Chapter Five and the account of Christmas in the convents and the story of the apples in Chapter Eight.

live in the convent in a similar time. There were clear connections between the women's experiences and developments in social policies and social attitudes in Britain. The stories of entry are categorised in this account using this theme of daughters. Each set of 'daughters' is discussed chronologically, from 1913 to the 1980s, to explore changes and continuities in the entry process and in the reasons for entry. The daughters are catagorised as: daughters of moral retribution; daughters of the colonies; daughters of the state; daughters of prejudice; daughters of mixed economy care and the Sisters themselves – the Daughters of the Mother of God. Exploring continuities and discontinuities in this way reveals similarities between the process of entry for the Sisters and the women and draws a number of comparative points with other state institutions. The next section explores the process of entering a convent for women who came to live there as residents in the 1920s and 1930s, at a time when moral panics about appropriate behaviour for women led to a kind of moral retribution against young women.

The Daughters of Moral Retribution – Notions of 'Good' and 'Bad'

As the Mental Deficiency Act was going through Parliament to intern people in colonies or hospitals in 1913, Martha started her life in Mother convent. Rather than her experience being one of force, she told me that coming to live in the convent was '*my choice*' (Martha, 1992). At ninety-five she was the oldest resident alive in the convent. She was frail but lucid:

> (Martha:) *No one forced me to come here, not like some. I wasn't bad, not like the others. My mother died and I talked it over with my father and he thought it was a good idea so I agreed.*
>
> (MS:) Why did you agree?
>
> (Martha:) *There are worse places you could spend your life. My father told me of all the wickedness in the world and said I should stay pure and I wanted to. I wasn't like the others.*
>
> (MS:) Who do you mean?
>
> (Martha:) *Those who did the bad thing, you know the types; you never can tell what they'll get up to with men* (1992).

For Martha it was important that she came to the convent through her own choice. She, like the majority of the women in the convents, was not certified by any doctor and was not held in the convents by legislative power. She was keen to emphasise that she had not had any relationship with a man and that she had agreed to move to the convent because her father had suggested it. Thus, although Martha emphasised her own choice, the role of her father was important.

Martha was not the only woman who was 'encouraged' by her father to go the convent because her mother had died. Of the residents in their eighties and nineties, ten who survived in Mother convent in 1993, four went to the convent on the advice of their father when a mother had died. It is difficult to be certain of the reasons for this advice but ideas about appropriate morality for the women seem to have been important, which confirms evidence presented by Gladstone (1997) and Cox (1997) as discussed in Chapter One. These women were 'daughters' who lives were severely affected by the morality of the time. Fathers perhaps felt unable to raise a teenage daughter without a wife, especially as young women's moral behaviour was a serious social concern at the time. The Sisters could provide substitute female care. If, as with Martha, men were left to look after their young daughters because of the death of their wife, it seems that the convents were seen as an appropriate alternative.

Loss of family through abandonment or inability to care can also be seen in the biographical accounts of Elvera who entered in 1935, Maria (1925), and Joan (1933). All these women came from Catholic orphanages run by another convent Order, the Nazarene, who cared for abandoned children. As the women turned fourteen, they were sent to convents such as Mother or Angel where they could work and learn a trade.

Equally important for the women, who entered in the early part of the last century, were notions of purity. Myra, another woman who believed in staying pure, was born in Newhaven and lived in Angel convent:

> (Myra:) *My mother was French and my father English. She was lovely. I was very happy as a child. We had an orchard. My mother was a good cook. She made wonderful apple tarts. She died when I was sixteen. Then I had to come here.* (the convent)
>
> (MS:) Why did you come to the convent?

(Myra:) *My father said I should, said it was for the best ...he didn't, well, he was a man. He didn't know what to do with me. He said my mother would have wanted it, I would stay good* (1990).

All the women I spoke to who had come to the convent before 1930 had clear perceptions of 'good girls' being women who had nothing to do with men and 'bad girls' having some sort of involvement with men. The panic around morality and control of women's sexuality and fertility, traditionally seen to be determined by coercion and scientific control (Jones, 1986), is only part of the story. Ideology operates in different ways and withdrawing from the world through a desire for purity, as Martha and Myra did, could be seen as a manifestation of the morality of the time. During the years of institutionalisation, many people were put away unnecessarily (Potts and Fido, 1991). Jones (1986) argues that working class people were segregated in the main because of middle class moral panics about working class fertility. The extent of confinement through family decision or by personal choice uncovered by these accounts of convent residents challenges the notion that segregation was only about the social control of working class fertility. The panic around morality and feeble-mindedness created a social environment where Catholics, often middle class family members, created their own solutions and withdrawal to a convent on a permanent basis, without becoming a nun, was acceptable. The role of the state or local authority did not affect this particular community.

Alongside the 'good girls', like Mary and Myra, were 'bad girls' like Margaret who came to Angel convent in 1919. She told me:

I was a bit of a lass, if you know what I mean, a bit bad. I had a baby you know. I grew up in the East End of London. My dad was a sailor. He went all over. I got letters from India and South Africa. He went all over, but when he came back and found out, he sent me to this home. They took the baby away and when I was better the courts sent me here.

(MS:) How did you feel about leaving your baby and coming to the convent?

(Margaret:) *Well it was the way they did things and I suppose I was a bit wicked you know. I've been here ever since* (1990).

What seemed to me to be particularly interesting is the way these ideas of good and bad have remained. The women have no other explanation for why they came to the convents. Both Margaret and Martha accept the moral reasoning given to them. This notion of 'good' and 'bad' is also prevalent in the accounts of the other women who came to the convent in this early period. Several of the women – Laura who arrived in 1922, Elvera who came in 1935, Joan who came in 1939 and Maria who came in 1925 – came as a result of having been abandoned. Most state the traditional definition of 'bad morals':

> *'The Sisters said I was wayward'* (Elvera, 1992).
> *'They said I was too brash to live in the world'* (Joan, 1992).

In Maria's case, it was a question of needing protection from the bad. She told me: *'I was too delicate, too much could happen to me, they said'* (Maria, 1993). In other words, confinement in the convents represented moral retribution for the bad girls and moral purity for the good ones, although both resulted in a life removed from the world. The labels that the women adopted were religious, labels such as 'pure', 'good' and 'bad' that grew out of Catholic belief rather than scientific definitions such as 'defective' or 'feeble-minded'. Hence, there are contrasts with public welfare provision in the process of labelling. Welfare provision in Catholic convents did provide labels for their residents, but the labelling process was focused on a religious familial discourse (good/bad girls) rather than a scientific one as was the case with public sector hospitals. These daughters were institutionalised, not because of scientific definition, but because of moral values and ideals of care, both powerful notions in shaping people's lives.

The process of entering created a sense of new identity for both the women residents and also for the Sisters. It was an identity that was shared although each Sister or resident was placed in a different part of the hierarchy, with the Sisters as the carers and the women as dependents. Both groups were labelled by a religious language suggesting a different approach to that prevailing in public institutions.

Connections between Postulants and Residents

Rituals of entry for both postulants and the women residents were similar and rich in the metaphor of birth. Having arrived in the front parlor of the convent, usually a large circular room, you were led through long winding passageways, doors to each side, darkly painted walls, and dim lighting, through to your new quarters in the convent. The women who were left at the convent often have clear visual memories of the spatial aspect of entering the convent. Jane told me:

> *I remember being led through the corridors; it seemed to take a long time. I looked back and my mother was getting smaller and smaller at the other end, if you know what I mean. Then the door opened and I was in the hall (1990).*

Entrants moved out from the dark silent passageways akin to a birth passage, leaving behind their 'mother' 'getting smaller and smaller' in the circular womb-like front parlour.[4] They moved through a set of doors into the 'girls' quarters which were bright and noisy, a kitchen, dormitories, dining hall and recreation area. They had entered their new 'world'. They had been 'born'.

The symbolism of birth was important for the women in the convent. Most saw their entry, either positive or negative, as a 'new' beginning. For many it was a complete break with their old lives. Many of the women never had contact with family or friends from 'outside', after entering. The connection between this 'birth' and the arrival of a new Sister is highlighted in this poem of Elvera's about the arrival of Sister Ursula in 1974:

When you arrived at our front door
Not knowing what was in store
You rang the front door bell, the rest only fate can tell.
. . .
First impressions are lasting
There's a saying that's very true –
Maybe your heart was lonely but the smile came shining through (Elvera, 1988)

Elvera connects the Sister's feelings with her own feelings of entry, talking of 'fate' and 'not knowing what was in store' as well as suggesting that her 'heart' would have been 'lonely'. In other words, Elvera saw the

[4] See Figures 4a and b, which illustrate the convents' layout.

Figure 4a

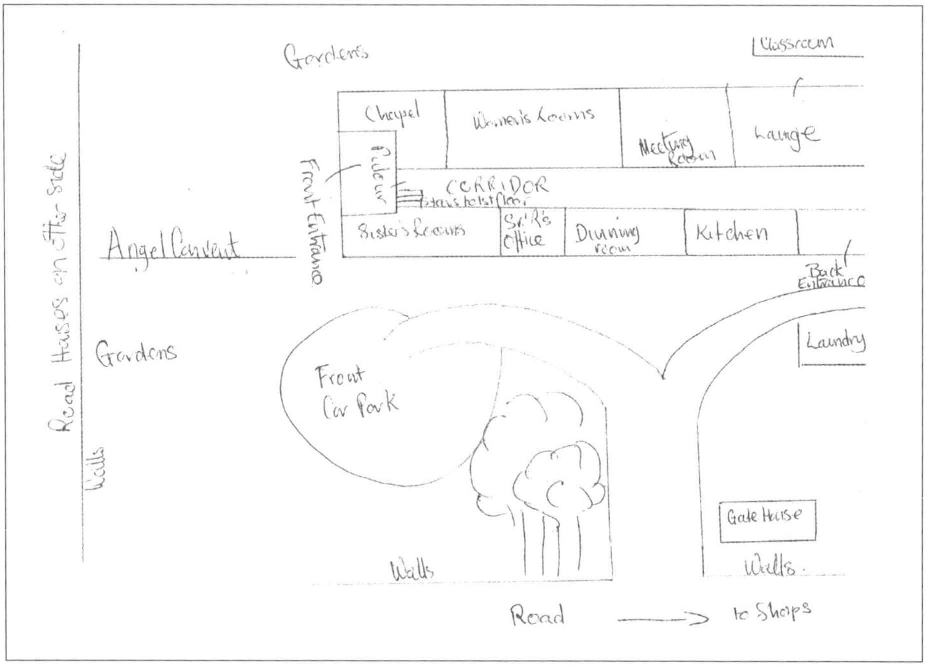

Figure 4b

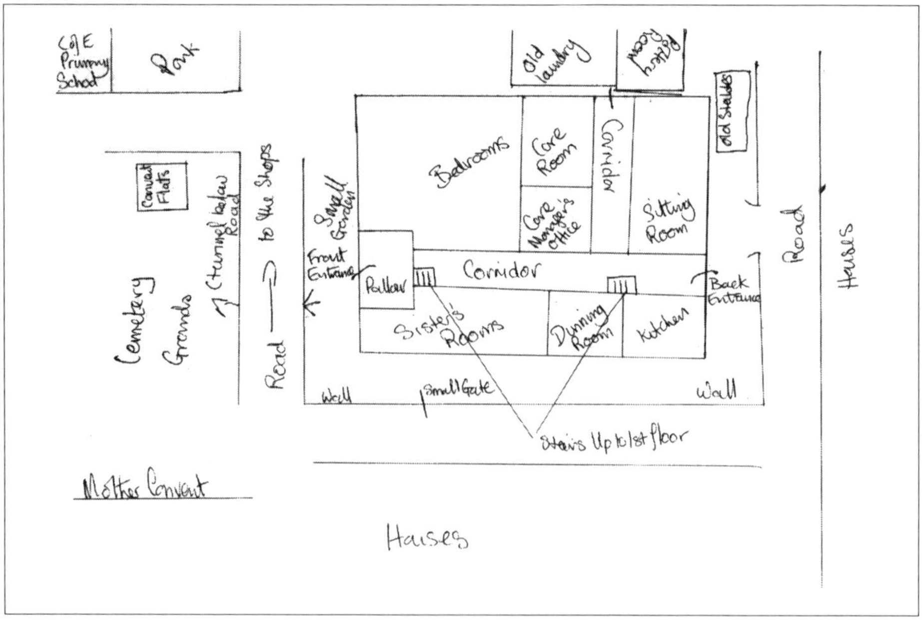

connections between the Sisters and residents coming to live in the convents. For both, the experience was immediate, physical and psychological and for most it was also permanent. The process of birth and re-birth are common themes within Christianity and are powerful symbols about a change in lifestyle. They are used to indicate turning away from the world and entering into the 'family of God'. Christians have a range of symbolic metaphors for this process, with baptism being the most potent symbol. For the women coming to the convent, the architectural structure produces a similar physical metaphor for birth. The structure of a large circular parlour with long winding corridors that lead maze-like from the hall, to the 'real' convent, where the life of the Sister or resident is conducted, is common across many Orders of nuns (Loudon, 1992). The movement from dark to light, from quiet to noise, from the old world to the new all focused the women's minds on change and new life.

The front entrances to the convents were beautiful and peaceful. Both had carved wooden doors with brass knockers, a porch area with a lantern to light the door and gardens with flowers surrounding the entrance creating an atmosphere of sanctity and composure. For parents, the convents must have seemed a haven for their daughters. The back entrance, on the other hand, housed the laundry on one side, the kitchens and their dustbins on the other. The architecture and geography of the convents emphasise the duality of experience for those who lived there and in some respect is not unlike most houses where front rooms and entrances are kept for visitors. The work areas were situated away from the sight of visitors and parents and, as Coward (1984) suggests, this hid the labour of the women.

Potential nuns were often encouraged to take up religious life by devout parents and, when entering a convent, had their clothes taken from them and, until the early 1970s, had their hair cut close to their head. This ritual was also imposed on the women who came to the convent. Elvera told me:

> *When I arrived (at Mother convent), I remember Jenny looking down on me as I stood in the hallway and she said, "Oh no, they've cut her beautiful hair" – I had lovely long black hair and they cut it. They said it was for the machinery in the laundry, but I didn't go near the machinery to begin with. I was ironing* (1992).

Elvera's experiences are typical. Many of the women who arrived in this early period told me of having their hair cut on their first day.

Anthropologists and psychologists cite hair-cutting ceremonies as a means of controlling sexuality. Campbell-Jones in her book on nuns states:

> The nun's cutting their hair close to their heads therefore symbolised the repressive nature of the chastity vow and the hiding of all sexuality (1979: 176).

This ritual act was part of a broader set of social practices, which served to control the women and the Sisters. The Daughters of the Mother of God lived within similar constraints as the other 'daughters'. Many women told me of name changes on entry. As with the Sisters who leave their old world name behind, and take a name of religion, several of the women were made to change their names. In many Catholic families, women were called Mary. Once there was one Mary in the convent, new 'Marys' had to take new names to '*avoid confusion*' (Mary, 1992). This again has echoes of name changes for Sisters, although it is not clear if the new names taken had particular meaning for the women as they did with the Sisters.

As the Sisters were expected to wear a habit, so the women wore a uniform. After entering the front parlour, the women's personal possessions were removed: '*They took all your things, everything like hair slides and all*' (Gloria, 1993). The clothes were removed and replaced, after a bath, by '*. . . a blue dress and an apron made out of coarse material, a beret and wooden clogs. No hair slides or anything like that*' (Margaret, 1990). These accounts are similar to stories from state institutions (Morris, 1969; Potts and Fido, 1991) and have clear echoes of Eving Goffman's description of a total institution (1961), where staff in mental hospitals removed identity-forming possessions and clothing. They also, of course, have connections with the experience of becoming a Sister described above.

From the inception of the convent movement until the 1970s, the Sisters wore a long blue habit, their dress, a wimple, a kind of starched covering around the face and neck, and a long veil to hide their shaven head (Gilpin Wells, 1988). The clothing of the Sisters – the covering of the head and the loss of personal and sexual expression – was mirrored by the clothing allocated to the women who came to live there. While entrants to state institutions early in the last century also had their personal clothing taken away (Morris, 1969), within the convent movement new clothes were worn by both the Sisters and the residents, and neither had their own possessions. The meaning of the loss of possessions is rooted in a religious commitment to withdrawal from the world and a denial of self and sexual expression. Any attempt at sexual expression was stamped out. As Margaret told me:

> *Anyone who tried to wear their beret in a sort of fetching way, you know sort of sideways, like that, well they were told to take it off and had to put it on straight. They were very strict about that* (1990).

While I would agree in broad terms that 'the working class' were particularly affected by the development of institutionalisation, especially through the pervading influence of eugenics which gained prominence during the 1920s and '30s, this is not the whole story. Of the thirty women interviewed, fourteen women came from the professional classes. Joanna told me that, '*There's a Lady tucked away in most of the convents. Parents paid. These were not homes for the poor*' (1992). Hence, rather than Catholic welfare providing only a form of control of working class fertility, it seems that these convents provided a 'safe' environment for young women from the middle classes who had in some way been seen as 'out of place' from the rest of society (Douglas, 1970). Being out of place has, historically, been enough to label people as deviant, as evident in some of the accounts of inmates in voluntary asylums during the nineteenth century (Gladstone, 1997). This theme of being out of place can also be found in stories from the next category of daughters, the daughters of the colonies.

The Daughters of the Colonies

'*I came to England to get a good education, but I couldn't*', so Beth, who has lived in Mother convent since 1927, told me. She went on to describe her background:

> *I come from Grahamstown in South Africa. My mother and father wanted me to get an English education. They took me to Cape Town and we went to Stuttefords and they bought me a lovely fur coat, just right my mother said, for the English winter* (Beth, 1993).

Beth spoke to me after remaining silent for many years. Some of the care staff and other residents had even thought she was suffering from dementia. In fact, it seems she felt she did not want or need to speak. This conversation came out as a result of my disclosure that I had grown up in

South Africa. Perhaps she saw a connection between us. She went on to say:

> *They said an English education was the best in the world, but I couldn't get it.*
>
> (MS:) Why? What happened?
>
> (Beth:) *I didn't get on with the mistress, she said I couldn't learn anything.*
>
> She had tried to make contact with her mother and father in Grahamstown but:
>
> *My aunt was looking after me, she lived in Cornwall, then she died. I wanted to go back to Grahamstown, but I couldn't. There was no money so I had to come here. I never heard from my parents since I came here* (Beth, 1993).

After this conversation, Beth did not wish to talk again. I was unable to find out any further details as convent records had only the name of her aunt who had died (Joanna, 1992), but Beth's story is not unusual. Another woman, Alice, came from India. She told me:

> *I lived in India when I was young. I remember it was very hot. My sister and I never wore much clothes; it was too hot. I went to boarding school when I was four.*
>
> (MS:) Why did you leave India?
>
> (Alice:) *They* (her guardians) *put us on a boat back to England. I was very seasick. Then they told me my mother and father had died. They didn't tell me while I was still in India. I couldn't go to the funeral. I didn't know* (1990).

When she came to England she went to stay with her aunt. When Alice was thirteen:

> *She sent us to boarding school. The headmistress said I was too stupid to learn so I had to wait on her, bring her supper and that in her room. I taught myself to read and write, so I'm not stupid. But when I was 18 my sister said I should go to the*

> *convent because I needed looking after and she couldn't do it. I went to lots of different places, nursing homes and convents. I wanted to get a job but she said no* (Alice, 1990).

Alice came to Angel convent in 1943 and lived there until she died in 1992 in a car accident.

Moira, a resident of Mother convent, grew up in China and during the difficult evacuation of English officials in the Second World War, was traumatically separated from her parents. She was thought to be mute and spent her childhood in 'deaf and dumb' schools, before coming to the convent as an adult.

Jane was born in Egypt, and after spending most of her childhood in boarding schools, was placed in Angel convent after a distressing divorce between her parents. Mary came to the convent in 1947. Having spent several years in Ghana where her father was a schoolteacher, she returned to England because she became ill. She then spent several years in various institutions including convent boarding school until 1945 and then a farm school. On one occasion, when I was interviewing Mary, I asked her if she would elaborate on the reasons for entering the convent:

> (MS:) When we talked before, Mary, you said your parents had told you you should come here (the convent) because you cried a lot. Was that the only reason?
>
> (Mary:) *Well, I had lots of tests at school, I had to see the psychologist twice and he said my I.Q. wasn't up to scratch and you see when I was four my mother had a nervous breakdown and the social worker found us and we were both just screaming and the social workers said I should go to boarding school. Boarding school from four, then Tattingstone, then on here* (1993).
>
> I asked her how she had felt coming to the convent. She replied: *Awful, I always wanted to get out, but my mother you see, she wouldn't let me, so I thought I had a life sentence* (Mary, 1993).

Mary told me of the process of entry. Because she had found her separations from her parents difficult over the years and had cried, the Sisters attempted to make the separation easier. Mary was:

> . . . told by one of the Sisters to go and join them (the other women) while she talked to mother. In reality she wanted me not to notice mother leaving as she had been told it was always a wrench for me to part with her . . . (Adams, 1995: 24).

Later, when she discovered her mother had left, she 'cried then and thought how horrible of her not to say good-bye to me. I felt so hurt . . .' (Adams, 1995: 24). Morris argued in her work in 1969 that the process of entry into institutions may have been more distressing for families than for those entering institutions. Many of the women I interviewed expressed enormous distress, feeling unwanted and unloved by their families. This, perhaps, suggests a contrast with the Sisters I interviewed who definitely viewed their lives as a vocation. Only a few residents, Martha, Maria, Elvera and Myra, saw their lives in the convent as devotional and, even then, recognised that families had left them in the hands of the Sisters.

Despite their middle-class backgrounds, the experiences of Beth, Alice and Moira show that these women were put away. Most were placed by family members who did not want to be burdened with their relatives' children. These women had little choice about their lifestyle because they were 'misfits', unable to find their place in society. Their parents were unable to care for these women, as a result of either death, dislocation or distance. England was their 'home' in that they were British citizens but their experience was that of the colonies. Relatives may have felt disconnected from these children or perhaps the women were caught up in family battles that had caused the move to the colonies in the first place. Only the Sisters of the convent would accept them. Families paid fees to keep the women in the convents and although these women were never certified, they were left to live a life removed from the world.

Legal definitions altered with the 1959 Mental Health Act, but when certification was removed, institutions continued to keep people in hospitals:

> From the mid 1950s the image of people as a eugenic danger vanishes from sources such as the Minutes of the Mental Health sub Committee. However, this did not end the confinement of people . . . People continued to be regarded as the subjects of care . . . (Walmsley, 1995: 144).

The next wave of residents who came to the convents marks the beginning of direct links with the welfare state.

Daughters of the State

While listening to younger women's stories, I began to hear the figure of the social worker replacing the parent as the person who actually brought women to the convent. Parents continued to make the decisions about the care of their daughters but, during the 1960s, they were assisted by the local authority.

Yvonne came to the convent after her mother died in 1968. She told me:

> *The social worker came to our flat. My mum was lying on the floor. I couldn't get her up, the social worker said she was dead. She sent me here. I never saw her again* (Yvonne, 1990).

While the social worker in this story surfaces as the instigator of Yvonne's entry, later she told me:

> *My aunt didn't want me. She said I should go to the convent. She never comes to see me* (Yvonne, 1990).

Social workers followed the career of particular families, especially working class families and picked up children whose abilities seemed 'slow'. Parents who found care difficult did not receive adequate support (Ayer and Alaszewski, 1984). Sara, who moved into Angel convent in the sixties, at eighteen, was one such woman. She told me:

> *I found it hard at school but my mum said I didn't really need to go. I could stay at home. So I did. I hated the teacher anyway. I stayed at home 'til my mum had her op and my sister got pregnant and had to move in. Then the social worker said it was too much for my mum and she looked for a place for me to go and I came here* (Sara, 1990).

I asked her how the social worker became involved and she told me:

> *She came all the time, well not the same one, sometimes a different one, but my dad didn't work and my brother was trouble, real trouble, so she came all the time* (Sara, 1990).

I asked her how she felt about coming to the convent. She told me she found it 'all right'. She went on to say: '*I go home at weekends when my mum can manage it*' (Sara, 1990).

By the 1960s the convents were beginning to change. The women increasingly identified their life there as a sort of boarding school, from which they could go home. Life within the convent changed as well. Many of the women who had entered in earlier phases, including Mary, Myra and Moira, found the changes difficult and see the sixties as the turning point in the convent life. Moira told me, *'I am used to the Victorian ways. If I have to change, I have to change, I accept my lot'* (1993).

The process of entry changed too. No longer were women expected to wear uniforms or to change their given name. Hair cutting, although still prevalent, could now be avoided, if you promised to keep it tied back. *'I said I always plait it, so Sister said all right it could stay, but the minute it got untidy, it would be off* (Sara, 1990). Later the same year, however, I noticed that Sara had had her hair cut.

The role of the 'professionals' in internment of people in Britain in the twentieth century has been emphasised in the learning difficulties literature discussed in Chapter One. The significance of educational psychologists' IQ tests, the legal framework, social workers, doctors and health workers is highlighted in a number of important texts (Barron, 1989; Atkinson and Williams, 1990; Potts and Fido, 1991; Cooper, 1997). However, this study consistently reveals the equally important role of families in placing people in institutions and as Walmsley (1995) notes, the role of families in care provision. Not just in the early part of the century but through to the 1990s, parents, usually Catholic middle class parents, used the convents as an alternative form of care for their female children because they thought they were at risk. Joanna told me that one referral document from 1967 gave the reason for sending a woman to the convent as *'she walks the streets daily and her father is worried that she would "get into trouble"'*(Joanna, 1992). There was no easy relationship between the public services and the convents:

> *The majority of the people were actually placed by families directly and of course that led to quite a conflict later on post '93 to establish points of origin and, umm, me getting data on originating authorities and they were coming back saying, no we could have accommodated this person, they could have had a day service in the sixties or seventies or whatever but the families chose to place them there and they did that against social services' wishes* (Joanna, 1996).

In other words, families continued to have responsibility for their members who were seen to be in need of care and their involvement in placing the women in the convents continued in the latter half of the century. As Walmsley points out:

> Family care has always been in practice the mainstay of services. Even in the pre-war era when families were officially stigmatised, they provided the bulk of care for people. The requirement for families to continue to pay maintenance for those in institutions is formal evidence of this (1995: 143).

Several of the women told me of abuse by family members. In particular, the story of Anne who came to Angel convent in 1951 highlights how families used the convents when abuse was present. She told me she had been raped by her cousin and she said, '*The worst thing was he didn't even want me, he wanted me dead. After that they sent me here*' (Anne, 1990).

Her mother was dead but she spoke to her father about the incident:

> *He said I should come here, to protect me. The social worker came, she told daddy it was for the best. I had all my bottom drawer ready and he said I wouldn't need it any more* (Anne, 1990).

Again, like the women in the earlier part of the century, Anne was sent to the convent by her father. Her cousin continued to live in the wider community. He did not visit Anne, whose story highlights the complexity of family involvement in these women's lives. Her father, wishing to protect her, sent her to a convent, effectively punishing her for the wrong doing of another male family member.

Most of the women who lived in the convents were white. However, the convents also took black women during the 1970s when a small number of black women came to live in Angel convent in south London. Again a notion of being seen to be 'out of place' figures in these stories of entry.

Daughters of Prejudice

Much of the literature on people with learning difficulties identifies that working class people (Jones, 1986) were particularly affected by definitions of feeble-mindedness and learning difficulty (Thomson, 1992; Cox, 1997). Equally, some of the literature has pointed out that these concepts been defined in racist terms in educational and welfare settings (Leicester, 1989; Ferns, 1992; Ahmad and Atkin, 1996). This has partly been because of the scientific definition of race, fueled by eugenics, but has also sprung from cultural prejudice about what is considered to be appropriate behaviour, a kind of in-built belief in the superiority of white culture (Bhabha, 1986). Williams (1996) notes that welfare provision was racist long before the establishment of the welfare state. In nineteenth-century Britain, Irish Catholics and Jews experienced discrimination in gaining access to welfare. The convents are an example of Catholic welfare that developed partly because of racist attitudes towards Catholics in Britain. During the 1950s, racism within welfare took on a new slant focusing on black immigrants to Britain. Ahmad and Atkin (1996) argue that black people in Britain experienced different kinds of discrimination, including access to welfare resources and in terms of perceptions of black people's abilities. Leicester (1989) highlights how black children were seen to be less intelligent when in fact they were simply coping with bilingualism. Service provision has more recently taken on the notion of anti-discriminatory practice but, during the 1960s and 1970s, discrimination and mislabelling were common.

The convent movement had, since the 1960s, taken women from other cultures who were sent there because of social pressures in their families, often using residential care as a solution because of the cultural prejudice by social workers (Ahmad, 1990). Tembe, a young Nigerian woman, was moved to Angel convent by a social worker at the age of seventeen. Her mother, having escaped from a violent husband in Nigeria, was being forced to return. Tembe had no learning difficulty and later proved her abilities by gaining five GCSEs. After two years at Angel, on her mother's return to England, she moved into her own flat and began studying fashion at a college in London. She told me on one occasion when we spoke after she left the convent:

> *I often feel that if I'd stayed there, I would have gone as stupid as the others. I had to get out. I was only eighteen, just think, your whole life like a nun. I couldn't have stood it* (Tembe, 1991).

Similar stories can be told of Zarina from Somalia, a refugee from the war who still lived in the south London convent in 1996 and hoped to return to Somalia when the war was over. She told me: '*I don't have a job and my family were told by the social worker, it's best I stay here*'(Zarina, 1990). Later she told me:

> *I'm Muslim and they make me eat bacon. Why can't they find me somewhere I can practice my faith?* (Zarina, 1990).

The lack of recognition of Zarina's religious and cultural needs highlights the inability of the social worker or the convents to acknowledge difference. Not only was Zarina placed in an English home for women with learning difficulties, she was placed in a convent home that observed Catholic religious practices.

Jessica, who was from Jamaica, had been abandoned by her parents. She lived in the convent from 1980 until 1992 when she moved into a bedsit. Jessica often complained of racism from the other women in the convent. She told me her social worker had suggested she speak to the Sisters but that she should, '*remember that the other women don't understand when they call you Blackie*'(Jessica, 1990).

Whether the decision was being made from family pressure or identified family need, the convents were used to place women who had nowhere else to go, even if it was inappropriate. These black women's experiences highlight another theme that runs through many of the stories. It seems quite common for any woman to be placed in the convents for their protection, even when they have no learning difficulty. I was told by one of the social workers who worked with the women at Mother convent during the 1990s that at least nine women of the thirty I interviewed would not be defined as having a learning difficulty '*under present conditions*' (Social Worker, 1996). In other words, the convents were prepared to take in any woman who was defined as being in 'need of care', even if the service offered was not entirely appropriate. Connected to this point is the fact that the convents were fee-paying institutions and as well as being in need of care, the women would need someone to contribute to their living costs. This has been a feature of young women entering the convents even when moving people out of institutions became policy. The last category of 'daughters' exemplifies this process.

The Daughters of Mixed Economy Care

The process of entering the convent in the 1980s is a markedly different experience to those I have already described. The cohesion of convent life has been altered by changes from Vatican II, by changes in social policies evident in the reports that encouraged community care such as *Better Services for the Mentally Handicapped* (1971) and the *Jay Report* (1979) and by theories of Normalisation. Certainties were replaced with insecurities (Lyotard, 1992). As Atkinson argues:

> Normalisation heralded the demise of modernity . . . it challenged the old certainties about institutional care . . . (1997: 140).

In the convents, lay staff used different approaches to care provision. In the earlier part of the last century the Sisters and the residents knew their place, even if convent life was oppressive. During the 1990s clear boundaries between the internal community of the convents and the outside community dissolved and were reformulated in contradictory ways. Lay professionals worked alongside the Sisters to accommodate the changes which community care had brought. The Sisters found their initial reason for working with the women, that of 'nurturing', was no longer required. As Joanna argued:

> *(The Sisters) are ever so good at terminal care for people who want to be in that kind of situation, wouldn't suit me, but yes, if you're a very strong Catholic it's quite nurturing there . . . (there is now) the recognition that people with learning difficulties don't need nurturing* (1996).

In 1995, many of the women I interviewed were living in group homes or with foster families outside the walls of the convents. In the 1990s, women who came to live in the convents, did so on the understanding that it was a temporary home. However, despite this multi-agency approach of community homes and convent homes, with lay and religious staff working side by side, the changes that took place were framed within a context of continuity. I will illustrate this by another woman's story of her reasons for entering the convent.

When I interviewed her, Diana was a young woman in her early twenties. She was articulate, could read and was interested in drama. She participated in a number of community theatre events and was always a hard working, enthusiastic performer. She told me she had come to Angel convent in 1988 after finishing at a special boarding school in Sussex:

> *My parents said it would be good for me, help me to become more independent, but really I think it's because I have a boyfriend, my mother's frightened I'll run off with him. Parents just don't understand teenagers, it's like 'Neighbours', you know Charleen*[5] *and that* (Diana, 1990).

Diana did not remain in the convent but moved to a hostel in 1994. Despite the emphasis on care in the community in the late 1980s, in studying the overall pattern of referrals to the convents, I was struck by the similarities between Diana's story and those of the women who have come to live in the convent since the beginning of the twentieth century. There are similar reasons why these women ended up living in the convents and these centre on conceptions of women's sexuality, safety and family 'need'. Consistently, the convent is being used as a safe haven, by families, by social workers and by women themselves. Equally, as the convents took fees from families there were more middle class women living in the homes, even in the 1980s. The convents seemed to have been used by middle class Catholic families as an alternative to public care, perhaps because public care would not have been available or acceptable.

Continuities through the Changes – Unequal Sisters

In the 1990s, the Daughters of the Mother of God looked and behaved differently to their earlier 'Sisters' as the movement was in transition. Many Sisters dressed without a veil and saw themselves as professional career women. However, even the Sisters who were the most radical felt the need for separation and the protection of the convent. Sister Ruth told me she felt '*safe*' and saw her work as '*different and special*' (Sister Ruth, 1992). She liked the security of living inside the convent walls. She added that it had become much easier for Sisters to break their vows or to live in ordinary houses. Similarly, residents were more able to leave the convents, creating a continuity in experience between the Daughters of the Mother of

[5] 'Neighbours' is an Australian soap opera, which was very popular in Britain in the 1990s. Charleen was one of the characters from the series.

God and the daughters they cared for. The comment that most emphasises this link, from the past to the present, came from Maria:

> *When I came here, we lived in dormitories, now we have our own bedrooms and the Sisters used to have cells; now they have bedrooms too* (Maria, 1993).

In other words, the women who shared convent life, both the Sisters and those cared for, had changed lifestyles. Unlike many state institutions where workers lived very different lives to the people they cared for, the Sisters in the convents shared many similarities to the women. Like the women, they were expected to be celibate, were subject to a strict regime, living with few possessions, and their 'cells' were bare with only a small locker and a bed, not unlike the description of mental handicap hospital wards (Morris, 1969; Jones, 1975; Potts and Fido, 1991). Hence the Sisters in these convents had lived like many people with learning difficulties who had been institutionalised and these connections create particular values that make the daily life different to that of the large long-stay hospital where staff lived somewhat differently. The changing social structures which led to the closure of long-stay institutions also affected the way the convents operated but the changes in the convents were also mediated through Catholic belief, especially through the shift that took place in Catholic doctrine through Vatican II. As changes in Catholicism developed during the 1970s and 1980s, the controls over the Sisters' lives lessened, giving them greater comforts and more freedom and the residents also gained more freedom and some comforts.

Nevertheless, although similar, the experience of life for the two groups of women could not be directly comparable. Convent relationships were constructed and maintained through unequal power relations with the Sisters in authority over the women, yet the lifestyles of both the Sisters and the residents were connected from their moment of entry, which symbolised their removal from the outside world, either as residents or as postulants. Removed from the wider society, they had been expected to make their lives within a specific community which had clear rules and which shared a common language. They were truly *Unequal Sisters*. How this tension between similarity of experience and clear hierarchies was organised is detailed in the stories in the rest of the book. The Sisters were, for many of the women, the only family they had and despite their limited experience of life, many women were able to find spaces to live their lives with fervour as is revealed in the following chapters.

The women entered the convents for a variety of reasons, but not through a medical or legal process of certification, and often on the advice of family. The convents took in women from across class and cultural barriers, although many of the convent residents came from Catholic middle class families. The convents were seen as a safe haven from the rest of society, by families, by the Sisters and even, surprisingly, by some (but not all) of the residents. Unlike long-stay hospitals that, during the twentieth century, were developed as part of a process of containment of the working class and a fear of working class fertility (Jones, 1986), the convents were an alternative form of care provision that had a philosophy of protection, providing segregated provision for women whose families could not or did not want to 'manage'. The reasons for entry even in the 1980s have echoes of decisions made by earlier generations and their families and show a distinct continuity, reasons that remain related to protecting women and focused on family choice. The next chapter discusses how work activities and power relations between the women, both Sisters and the women they care for, were organised throughout the twentieth century.

Chapter 4

Clean and Dirty – Work Arrangements in the Convents

Work and working is a major feature of most people's lives and this was equally the case for the women who lived in the convents. However, in a convent institutional environment, working for a salary was not an option. This chapter explores how work in the convents developed and changed over time. It examines how a women-only work environment could reproduce accepted social patterns of work activity and values. Work structures in the convents were also infused with religious symbols that helped shape the work environment.

Working long hours is a central feature of the life stories of the older women in their seventies and eighties. By the end of the twentieth century, most of the women spent their days in 'leisure pursuits'. This shift from a predominantly work-orientated environment to a leisure-based environment parallels policy and ideological shifts in other services for people with learning difficulties over the last hundred years. The experiences of the women in the convents raises questions about the employment of people with learning difficulties and highlights, from the convent women's experiences, some of the difficulties of a normalisation theory of citizenship. I begin with a description of the work activities in the convents.

The Family Business – Working for Income

While work tasks were exploitative, paying in some cases as little as 6d per week in the early part of the twentieth century, Morris (1969), in her study of institutions for people with learning difficulties, argues that working in voluntary sector and religious institutions was undertaken for a purpose and in some respects fulfilled a similar function to work found in some family businesses. In other words, the labour of inmates in voluntary sector homes was more directly needed to maintain the financial viability of the institution than was the case in institutions that received public funds. Work was therefore a necessity for economic self-sufficiency for such institutions, as well as potentially offering some sense of purpose to the inmates. Walmsley notes in her study on caring that her interviewees who had lived in institutions during the twentieth century 'valued contract work, low paid and repetitive though it may be, over the activities currently offered' (Walmsley, 1995: 262), indicating that work in most institutions provided a sense of self worth for some people. This sense of purpose was echoed in the accounts of work from some of the older residents in the convents.

From their beginnings, both of the convents were organised to be self-sufficient. To provide income, both convents established laundries. To provide food, they both developed farms. Until the 1960s, work began early and finished late, six days a week. Weekdays were organised as follows:

> *6am mass and breakfast*
> *8am work*
> *lunch at noon*
> *1pm work*
> *6pm supper*
> *7–9pm recreation time, where we would be able to talk to friends in the day room.*
> *Silence from 9pm* (Martha, 1992).

On Saturdays and Sundays in Mother convent, Mary said, they had to go to the '*blessed beach every* (emphasised) *weekend*' (Mary, 1992). Each member of the community had a specific work task, and work was quite separate from the leisure time.

In her biography of Mother Foundress, Gilpin Wells (1988) indicates the importance of laundries for the convent movement and notes their development in each of the convents as they were established:

> Sister . . . had spent weeks in training for laundry work in the convent in Antwerp, was at Beaumont training novices in the work (Gilpin Wells, 1988: 130).

and

> By December 1882, the Sisters assigned to St. Helens were operating a laundry, giving an instruction class, having a night school for miners and visiting the poor (Gilpin Wells, 1988: 174).

The laundries took in washing wherever it was lucrative. During the early part of the century, washing came from individual wealthy parishioners, and during the Second World War, from soldiers billeted nearby. From the 1950s, the laundries took on contracts with private boarding schools and more recently from the 1980s, the laundries had large social service or health authority contracts. Laundries were common in many institutions and were used to provide additional income for colonies, hospitals and asylums in the nineteenth and twentieth centuries (Potts and Fido, 1991; Walmsley, 1995; Gladstone, 1997). The lay care manager who closed the laundry at Mother convent commented that the local social services department had a vested interest in maintaining the convent's laundry even in the 1990s:

> There seemed to be much investment in the continuation of the status quo. It also needs to be acknowledged that the local authority had a considerable conflict of interest since several of its Part III homes had contracts at a very advantageous rate! On discussing this aspect with an East Sussex Team Manager responsible for resources, he referred to the yearly dilemma of whether or not to 'pull the plug' on the use of (Mother's) laundry, and the fear of the implications for the residential provision (that used the service) (Brown, Y, 1994: 5)

Throughout the years of the laundries, Sisters worked alongside the women although activities were clearly divided between Sisters and residents. Neither Sister nor resident was paid. The work was done to enable the home to continue. Even in the 1980s, the conditions were poor. 'There was no proper ventilation. A hot and humid atmosphere predominated' (Brown, Y, 1994: 1). Many of the women and the Sisters worked beyond retirement age. Sister Ida worked until she was seventy-seven and Maria worked until she was seventy-nine.

Many of the older women speak with pride about their contribution to the running of the convent. A typical comment on laundry work came from Martha:

> *We worked hard but they needed the laundry, don't think there's much happening now down there, they can't be bringing in much money now (1992).*

The laundries grew in importance at a time in British social life when servants were becoming scarcer and washing machines were yet to become a feature of the average home. Lewenhak (1988) notes that laundry work was seen as women's work:

> Throughout the nineteenth and early twentieth centuries in west Europe and America, the poor but enterprising woman with a water supply, a backyard in which to boil the wash, a mangle, an iron and a kitchen table, to use it on, could earn a living (Lewenhak, 1988: 73).

The convent movement took on 'washing' with enthusiasm. As well as being quite lucrative in the early years, the laundries were also used to train those women who would be moving out to work in a variety of positions. Tasks were divided. Some worked in the wash house, some the drying room, others ironing and some in the packing room. The day started early as Martha, who worked in the laundry from 1915, explained:

> *Do you know what time we used to get up?*
>
> *Five o'clock, five o'clock every day and we only had Sundays off. Yes, Monday to Friday we'd be in the laundry then Saturday we'd have to clean the machinery out. We didn't start in the laundry at five. There'd be prayers and breakfast and mass. We used to go to mass every day in the old days. We started in the laundry at eight o'clock then we'd stay there till twelve then lunch then back at one o'clock then stay there 'til five in the evening, six days a week that was, six days.(Martha, 1992).*

The work arrangements were harsh, long hours in damp and humid conditions. However, despite the oppression, some of the women told me they were able to get to positions in the laundry that they could enjoy:

> *I started in the ironing room, I really hated it, I burnt all the hankies so they moved me. I won't exactly say I did it deliberately, no, well yes, that was the intention and I was glad to move on. They sent me to the drying room but the machine hurt my arms so I played up a bit and I ended up in packing and sorting. I liked packing; it was warm in there but the sorting was cold. I always had bronchitis in the winter (Maria, 1992).*

These stories show the harshness of the women's lives in the convents. However, in the later nineteenth and early twentieth century's accounts of factory work for women has echoes of this harshness noted by Maria above. At the time of the development of Angel convent, Chew wrote to the *Crewe Chronicle* in 1894 explaining the position of working women:

> To take what may be considered a good week's wage the work has to be so close and unremitting that we cannot be said to 'live' – we merely exist. We eat, we sleep, we work, endlessly, ceaselessly work, from Monday morning until Saturday night, without remission (Chew, 1982: 76).

Chew was a campaigner for working women's rights and her account indicates that some working women worked similar hours to the women in the convents. Examples of hard working conditions can also be found in accounts of women's factory work in the early part of the twentieth century:

> A standard working day was from 8am – 6pm with an hour for lunch and from 8am till 12 on Saturdays. During overtime, they worked to seven or eight at night. These hours were little changed from Victorian times (Phillips, 1994: 60).

While there are some similarities between work in factories and convents, there were also significant differences. Sisters' salaries were returned to the headquarters of the movement,[1] and while the women who worked in the laundry in the convents called the small amount of money they did receive[2] '*a wage*'(Jane, 1990; Elvera, 1992), many also told me that their labour was for the convent itself (Martha, 1992; Maria, 1993). In other words, both the Sisters who organised the work and the women who undertook the work shared a sense of common purpose where they laboured daily for almost no money to maintain the convents themselves.

---

[1] See Chapter One.

[2] £1.90 in the convents in 1960, as opposed to £1.25 for inmates in hospitals in 1970 (Jones, 1975: 29)

Washing all our Sins Away

Laundries were important features of colonies and hospitals where women inmates were usually employed (Potts and Fido, 1991; Walmsley, 1995). In an all-female environment, Mahood notes that laundries had a particular meaning to remind the women of their sins:

> Laundries were common features of female penitentiaries because they helped cut the cost of inmates' confinement. More importantly, laundry work served a symbolic function: through laundry work women daily performed a cleansing ritual. They enacted penance for their past sins and purged themselves of their moral contagion (Mahood, 1988: 55).

In other words, the structures used in penitentiaries had an overt Christian ideology. In the convent movement these structures were mediated, like other aspects of convent life, through the language of Catholicism.

The symbolic connections between spiritual renewal and washing are an integral part of the movement's understanding of its role in society from the time of its establishment. Mother Foundress explicitly drew the connection in her notes for a retreat, which she planned in 1885:

> He calls 'Mecum'. To go on with Me . . . Such a glorious thing to work harder for Him in evil days, but work for Him means – for me – self conquest . . . *Wash* me thoroughly. How I have really felt those words when the innocent, simple Sisters come for advice . . . (in Gilpin Wells, 1988: 180).

Although both Angel and Mother convents had commercial laundries, the ordering of activities was different to other work situations. The women worked in silence or were occasionally to offer communal prayers. Maria told me about the atmosphere in the laundry:

> *It was hard in the laundry, one crease in a sheet and back it would go and if it fell on the floor, you'd have to start all over again. And if you didn't finish you stayed there 'til you did. And no talking. We spent most of the day in silence. You'd be sent to Mother if you talked.*
>
> (MS:) Why couldn't you talk?

> (Maria:) *Oh, there were all sorts of rules like that, the Sisters would say prayers. It was to help us stay pure* (1992).

This is a marked contrast in atmosphere from other work environments described in oral history accounts of working class people (Mace, 1994; Phillips, 1994). Phillips describes how women on the shop floor would sing. He notes one informant recalling:

> I think they sung in all the factories. Now if they hear you singing, they'd think you're barmy. They would! But they used to sing, didn't they? Sing a lot, mate, in them days . . . (Phillips, 1994: 61).

The extent of control over the women's bodies in the convents would be surprising in a secular work environment. The meaning of this control needs to be seen in relation to the beliefs of the religion that permeated the work environment of the convents that had its origin in the teachings of the Foundress. Mother Foundress wrote to her Sisters in 1888, exhorting them to view silence as a sign of purity:

> Silence . . . to most people is a penance. The tongue itches to talk. When we have to say five words, we long to say twenty. Talking is the cause of almost all evil, sin and misery in the world. St. James says: The tongue is a fire, a world of iniquity . . . full of deadly poison, and Our dear Lord Himself, gentle as He is . . . (says) But I say unto you, that every idle word that men shall speak, they shall render an account for it in the day of judgment. (in Gilpin Wells, 1988: 217)

If work in the convents had been simply designed to supplement the income of the convents, then the rule of silence would not have been necessary. The rule of silence during work was a direct result of the teachings of the Mother Foundress, but it also signified control over the women's bodies. The women who lived in the convent had entered because of larger social moral panics about women and purity. The Sisters were representatives of Catholic values and society's moral guardians. What was being communicated through the rule of silence to both the Sisters and the women who lived there was personal restraint and containment, appropriate virtues for women (Davidoff and Hall, 1992). Work in silence created this restraint and contained the women's desires. The religion and the work they undertook became symbolic vehicles for transmitting ideas of appropriate femininity.

The majority of people in colonies and hospitals worked within the institutions often doing similar tasks to paid staff. In most mental deficiency, and later mental handicap, institutions, labour was allocated according to social perceptions of appropriate work for men or women (Potts and Fido, 1991), with traditional gender roles being played out in the way work was allocated. Men would work in the workshops and on the farms, while women worked in the sewing room and the laundry (Walmsley, 1995: 136). In the women-only environment of a convent, both laundry work and farm work were conducted by the women residents but aspects of socially defined male and female work practices were curiously maintained.

Clean and Dirty Work

As well as the laundries, both Mother and Angel convents farmed for food. From their time of entry, the women worked either on the farm or in the laundry and the occupations of each of the women were clearly ordered and hierarchical in nature. Laundry work was seen as '*clean work*' and farm work as '*dirty work*' (Martha, 1993). While there is obvious physical truth to these notions, they also hold the key to the symbolic meanings of work in the convents. Douglas suggests that:

> If we can abstract patholgenicity and hygiene from our notion of dirt, we are left with the old definition of dirt as matter out of place . . . It implies two conditions: a set of ordered relations and a contravention of that order. . . . This idea of dirt takes us straight into the field of symbolism and promises a link-up with more obviously symbolic systems of purity (1970: 113).

In an environment like a Catholic convent, which is so rich in symbols, the divide between clean and dirty work also came to represent the inhabitants' notions of purity and sinfulness. Women who came to the convents were often first sent to the farm (Martha, 1993), and women who worked in the laundry were given more privileges than women who worked on the land (Martha, 1992). The women were being expected to prove that they were capable of rehabilitation, of being able to 'wash their sins away'. To take the religious imagery further, once cast out of Eden, 'man shall toil by the sweat of his brow'. In other words, symbolically the women on the farm were sinners who, in Catholic theology, needed to earn their redemption.

The Sisters were in charge of the laundry while hired laymen supervised the farm work. There is a complex set of interrelations here. Women's work was inside, removed from the outside world. The Sisters could provide redemption, the men, being lay people could not. The world of the Sisters, the laundry, was clean. The world of the men, the farm, was dirty. The symbolic connections between cleanliness and femininity and dirt and masculinity were being drawn through these ordered patterns and were, as Douglas suggests, related to each other.

Women understood and prized being able to move to the laundry. Mary told me:

> *I wanted to work in the laundry, it was warm and dry in there. The farm was hard work and you were always dirty, but my mother felt I would get too pale working inside all day so I couldn't* (1992).

The distinctiveness of work in the laundry and on the farm was further highlighted by the ordering of tasks within the 'homes' themselves. Because farm work was seasonal and the laundry was not, the women who worked on the farm used the winter to participate in maintenance work on the 'home'. Mary told me that in the winter they would '*paint the walls, repair things and keep the house in order*' (Mary, 1993). All these tasks are reminiscent of traditional 'male' activities within a home. Farm girls were expected to fire up the coke furnace each morning, '*a very dirty job*'(Mary, 1993). The most prized and 'successful' aspect of laundry work on the other hand was '*washing and sorting the silks*'(Martha, 1992), the most delicate and feminine of garments. There was a clear hierarchy within the work structure. Although laundry workers worked all year round, they were also responsible for helping the Sisters in the chapel. Farm workers, on the other hand, were responsible for decorating in the winter and the more servile tasks of fetching and carrying water to wash dishes:

> *We had no running water in our dining room, so we had to fetch a big tin bath of water from the girls in the laundry to do the washing up. We took turns to get it but it was heavy.* (Mary, 1993).

Work arrangements in the early part of the twentieth century in the convents created a pattern of life that was all pervasive. It established order in the lives of both the Sisters and the women they 'cared for'. The routine created a sense of identity and a sense of place for the women.

Toiling by the Sweat of Your Brow – The Farm

In an attempt to keep costs down, most of the food in the convents came from the farm. Both convents had farms from early in their development until the 1970s when it was thought more lucrative to sell the land. The farms were most important during the war when food was scarce. Mary spent most of her working life on the farm:

> *Our farm provided most of our foodstuff – milk from six cows, eggs from our hens, and vegetables and potatoes from the farm. I dug the potatoes and cleaned out the cows. It was dirty work. The Sisters didn't run the farm, like they did the laundry. The men would organise the farm. We were not allowed to talk to them and when they asked us questions we had to say go and ask Sister. I remember once one of them asked me how I was and I said, 'Go and ask Sister.'*
>
> (MS:) How did you work if you couldn't talk to them?
>
> (Mary:) *Oh, it was easy. You just followed instructions. I liked the farm but I hated having to do the coke boiler, we had to clean it out every morning and it was so dirty* (1993).

Men supervised the work on the farm, and the women were not allowed to talk to any man, except the priest. They heard instructions and carried them out. The women were to 'follow instructions' and could not question tasks as this would appear to be 'talking to the men'.

Men did not come into the convent building. A 'men's room' was set aside on the outside of the residential home, reached by an outside door. The women would bring the men food to that room. Men represented the outside world and were seen as unclean and unable to enter the convent. The men would have muddy boots but the women were allowed to clean themselves and their boots and enter the convent. Punishments in the convents often consisted of harsh treatment using the dirty boots from the farm work. Mary told me of one occasion when she had talked to a man on the farm and had been punished by:

> *Having to wear my dirty boots tied round my neck all through dinner. I had to kneel in the middle of the dining hall with these smelly boots on so all could see* (Mary, 1994).

In addition to the cruelty of this action, the religious and moral significance is powerful. The connection between 'earth dirt', 'male dirt' and 'sinfulness' is being drawn as is the notion of dirt being something out of place. Dirty farm boots are for outside use, not inside the dining hall. Symbolically, having to wear the boots inside indicated Mary's behaviour as disordered, 'out of place' behaviour. She kneels for all to see, to be made an example of, and to denigrate further the dirt of farm work through connecting it with sinfulness and talking to men.

By physically separating the clean work and the dirty work, the Sisters were establishing an order that highlighted the importance of the avoidance of uncleanliness. By creating a closed space that was entirely female where men could not penetrate, the order exhorted a belief in feminine values of purity and suggested that maleness was dangerous, for men were connected with dirt and reminded the women of their sins and the need for the cleansing power of Christ, warning them of the dangers of dirty thinking and behaviour. It created a strict regime with a range of punishments including deprivation of food if rules were disobeyed. Elvera told me:

> *Oh, it was cruel sometimes. You would come into the dining hall and go to your seat and there, your plate would be turned face down and your heart sank. No dinner for you today. You had been a bad girl (1992).*

This set of meanings built on the labelling process of 'good' or 'bad' girls, which the women took on when they came to live in the convents, and was a powerful way of maintaining order and control in the convents. Actions such as deprivation of food as noted by Elvera and the shaming of Mary, making her kneel through dinner, have echoes of stories from other convent experiences such as Humphries (1998) and other accounts of institutional abuse. The meanings are all the more powerful because of their religious symbolism connects to the women's identity and sense of personal value.

The farms were extensive, not only growing vegetables and fruit but also keeping animals. During the difficult years of the war and the 1950s, they provided food for the convents, but as with the laundry most of the farm work was labour intensive and back breaking. Mary wrote:

> Now the potatoes we also did the old fashioned way. We set them over a hundred long rows by hand. (One of the men) and his tractor came behind us and covered the drills up. Then in

> the spring and autumn we picked the potatoes by hand into buckets and put them into fifty two pound sacks, and towards the end of the day two of us carried each bag up to a big cart (Adams, 1995: 29).

The farm work ended when the convent movements sold off some of their land. However, at Angel convent, chickens were still kept as late as 1984 (Adult Education tutor, 1996).

Unlike the laundry workers, the women who had worked on the farms did not have the same nostalgia for their work. The work held little status and signified to the farm women their lowly position within the convent structure. It was the farm women who were first able to go out of the convent grounds to do errands in the 1960s and 1970s and although some women said they enjoyed the outdoors, when the farms were sold off, the work was not generally missed (Jane, 1990; Mary, 1993). The homes were by then receiving financial support from the State and several Sisters told me they were glad to be rid of the bother of the farms:

> *Oh that* (the farm), *well now that became a waste of time. There were other things to be getting on with. Not that it didn't have its place, it did, but I was glad when we gave it up* (Sister Ruth, 1990).

Farm work also had its lighter moments. Mary wrote of her days on the farm in her autobiography:

> Many a time one of the cows went astray and went tearing down the high street . . . with us running after it. It was quite hilarious! (Adams, 1995: 30).

Despite the harshness of the work, farm or laundry, many of the women who worked talked of camaraderie amongst colleagues. The next section outlines how the women engaged with their work regime and how they supported each other.

Work and Support

Many stories of working women's lives in the last century emphasise mutual support (Roberts, 1988; Mace, 1994; Phillips, 1994). In the convents, similar stories could be heard. Industrial psychologists have recognised that people form a major element of their identity from their work (Grossman and Chester, 1990) and the women in the convents were no different. Elvera told me that the women helped each other to ensure they did not get into trouble for 'sloppy work':

> *You had to do a certain amount of work, but we would help each other out. When Sister wasn't looking we'd give the slower ones some of our pile that we'd finished so it looked like they'd done enough work* (Elvera, 1992).

For many of the older women, with the laundries run down and as they neared the end of their lives, they felt their lives were being devalued. Maria bitterly told me she had been '*forced to retire*'(Maria, 1992). She said:

> *I retired last year and I hate it. Nothing to do all day except TV. I pray a lot though. But they've run down the laundry, I don't know how they are managing. We brought in quite a bit of money* (Maria, 1992).

These older women, like Maria, Elvera and Martha and many other retired people, felt a loss of status when their work skills were no longer needed. From being the heart of the survival of the home they have now moved to being peripheral. From major 'breadwinners' in the 'family', they have become dependent on others. Staff working in the convents found Maria's response to having to retire 'amusing'. '*She's eighty years old. She needs a rest*' (Judy, 1996). Joanna told me that she had offered some of the women counselling in an attempt to help them make the transition to retirement (Joanna, 1996). Yet, what the staff were not acknowledging were the competing needs of residents in the convent homes. Work in the laundry had been high status but became unnecessary. The older women who had worked hard over the years in the laundry saw their own lives devalued in the same way as the laundry was now devalued.

As these women became more dependent and frail, the loss of their work and the destruction of the laundries shook their identities. The needs of the older members of the community were not the same as the younger women who saw a life outside the convent as potentially exciting. While their experiences in the first half of the twentieth century were harsh, the women found meaning in what they did and found spaces for pleasure and pride in their work. The younger lay staff and younger women who lived in the convents saw the work of the laundries as repressive and negative. A report on the laundry at Mother convent (1994) highlights this view:

> The washing machines were huge copper boilers taking over 100 pounds of washing which then needed to be fished out with long wooden paddles. The stone floor in the washhouse had gulleys to drain away the sudsy water during the transfer process into trolleys which were then wheeled to even more labour intensive rinsing and drying processes (Brown, Y, 1994: 3).

The laundries were oppressive sweat shops but somehow the older women did not see their lives in this way and felt abandoned and devalued by their loss in status.

The local wealthy members of the parish sustained the laundry in the early part of the century. Martha was in charge of the silks and all the most delicate items:

> *Oh I used to love those, so pretty and so nice to touch. I wouldn't want to wear them. No good for the likes of me, you have to be well-to-do to wear those* (Martha, 1992).

The hierarchy of activities in their work found echoes in their understanding of their position in the rest of society. For Martha, touching and working with the silks was sufficient even though she was never to wear them. Most of the women who talked about the laundry at either Mother or Angel convents had managed to get themselves into jobs which they liked. One woman, however, told me of the oppressive nature of the hierarchy in the laundry, between the women:

> *I was glad when it burnt down. It meant I could come to classes more. I wouldn't have minded if I'd been in the press room that was warm but I had to stay in the washing room. I tried to move and even Sister said I could but Siobhan came and said she would beat me up so I went back to the wash room* (Sara, 1990).

This story offers a more complicated picture of work in the laundry. The hierarchy between the women in both convents was extensive and it seems where you stood in the 'pecking order' affected what enjoyment you were able to take in your work.

The women told me of several occasions when there were quarrels over payment from customers. Maria told me a story about a woman who was convinced that one of the women had stolen the payment money:

> *One time one woman kicked up such a fuss saying she'd put the money in the basket and we said she hadn't paid. The men who brought the washing in told her it was the Sisters who took the money and they'd never steal, but she kicked up a fuss and said we were thieving bad girls, but when she got home she found the money on the mantelpiece and she had to apologise* (Maria, 1992).

This story was told with a great deal of relish even after forty years. Clearly Maria felt affronted by the woman's accusation and was still amused by the apology. Because there is a such clear morality within the convent, being called a thief for women who see themselves as good was an attack on their status and vision of themselves. All the older women accepted the moral perspective that led to them living in the convent in the first place. Gloria told me with great pride of her honesty being rewarded:

> *They sent the money in the baskets and sister would collect it. One time I was checking all the pockets and I found a five pound note and I took it to Sister and she sent it back and I got back one pound. Some would do that but others wouldn't bother at all. But it shows I was right, don't you think Mary?* (Gloria, 1993).

Getting customers for the laundry over the years became difficult. From being a laundry for wealthy private customers, the Second World War offered an opportunity to 'wash the uniforms of the soldiers billeted down the road' (Maria, 1992). After the war, the market for private washing diminished as washing machines became popular in private homes. Mother convent took in washing from local boarding schools, but slowly the laundries became less important financially to the homes than the payments from social services departments caring for women with learning difficulties. After Angel convent's laundry burned down, a smaller laundry for the private use of the home replaced the industrial one. In 1994, Mother convent's laundry was closed. Both events were emotional and many of the women told me they felt very sad to see them go (Siobhan, 1990; Yvonne, 1990; Martha, 1992; Maria, 1993; Elaine, 1993).

The Loss of Work and the Growth of Leisure

As the convents no longer had the financial need for industry and social attitudes to people with learning difficulties changed, work in the convents became focused only on household tasks. The women washed and cleaned for themselves and the Sisters. They prepared food and moved from farming to gardening. Domestic duties had always been part of daily life but had not been seen as work, rather as daily chores. Hence the work that the women did in the 1980s and 1990s was not seen as important. Leisure pursuits became more significant as the women had more time on their hands. During the 1970s and early 1980s, policy changed, encouraging education for people with learning difficulties rather than sheltered workshop training (*Better Services for the Mentally Handicapped*, 1971 and the *Jay Report*, 1977). Social Education Centres replaced the adult training centres that had provided work opportunities for people with 'severe learning disabilities' (Williams, P, 1995: 92). Adult education courses were being set up for people with learning difficulties across the country (Sutcliffe, 1990) and the women in the convents took advantage of these. New roles for some of the women emerged, such as acting as escorts for less able women or doing voluntary work in the parish. Most of these activities are not defined as work but favours and tasks. The women no longer had jobs and one woman told me that she saw £3 – £4 a week she received for her domestic service in the convent as '*pocket money*' (Sara, 1990).

The most common activity in the convent homes that I observed in the 1990s was watching television. At Mother convent Joanna developed a ceramics workshop and a charity shop where some of the women worked. Those who worked there were proud of the shop (Mary, 1992). Both convents attempted to provide more positive outlets for some of the younger women, including reception work in the convents. The majority of the women either went to adult education classes to fill their days or if they were more elderly remained in sitting rooms watching television. For these older women who took pride in their work in the laundries, their lives seem to have lost any meaning other than their religion. For younger women who have never worked except doing domestic work in the home, the idea of work was appealing. When asked what they would do if they won the lottery, one woman said to me, '*I'd get a job*' (Tess, 1995). When I explained that by winning the lottery she would not need to work she replied, '*I wouldn't need to but I'd like to and if I won the lottery I could buy a job*'(Tess, 1995). Here Tess highlights the status that work occupies in our society, which provides greater citizens' rights and adult status for workers than any other form of activity. For many people with learning difficulties, the goal of citizenship and adult status continues to elude them:

> The vast majority of citizens with learning difficulties will only be able to achieve full inclusion in society when educational, community and work places are re-structured to enable that to happen (Ramcharan, Roberts, Grant and Borland, 1997b: 256).

However, it is not just a question of re-structuring work places. As with debates about residential living, traditional work and training patterns such as the laundry and farm work of the convents were questioned by theories of Normalisation. Segregated living and segregated work were seen as part of the problem of services that created difference for people with learning difficulties (Wolfensberger, 1983). Even so, moving into the wider job market can also prove problematic. The closure of long-stay institutions and the shift from adult training centres that provided menial contract work (Murray, 1988) to social education centres affected the work experiences of many people with learning difficulties (Williams, 1995). People with learning difficulties who attend 'training' programmes seldom move into jobs. Colleges seldom see employment as a logical outcome of training (Lister and Ellis, 1992). Paid employment has also altered significantly over the last thirty years. In moving people into the wider society, global changes have marked the decline of British industrial base (Thrift, 1989). The nature of the paid workforce has changed from a largely male, full-time workforce to an increasingly female part-time (and insecure) workforce (West, 1982). One woman who had moved into the community and found a part-time cleaning job told me:

> *It's all very well working, but now I can't lose my job. Sometimes I get cross and my boss says, 'you do that again and you're out'. I'm frightened and the hours are no good ...* (Susan, 1991).

Even when women have moved into the 'real' world of work, it seems that they, like Susan above, have gained a double-edged form of citizenship, the right to lose a job and to live in poverty. Several theorists (Brown and Smith, 1992; Walmsley and Downer, 1997) have highlighted that Normalisation has not accounted for such inequalities and differences in society. 'Normalising' into an unequally stratified society therefore is more difficult and complex than has often been suggested.

For the older women in the convents, who had gained status through work, 'retirement' offers little. The social worker at Mother convent told me that when the laundry was closed, the women would 'just sit around':

> *The wasted space was quite incredible. These huge rooms with nothing in them. Great big high ceilings with nothing going on. It must have been soul destroying just to be walking around all day long. Or sitting in the lounge . . . Yes, the laundry would have been quite an inviting place, really, despite all my criticisms of it . . .* (Social Worker, 1996).

For most of the women the fracturing of 'work', the loss of certainty of their 'place' and the disintegration of the convent community into the larger community was a frightening experience. The harsh forms of control had gone but nothing had replaced it. Like many people in the wider community who experience unemployment, the women did not see a progressive future. As one woman said to me when her computer class finished for the summer break:

> *What am I going to do on a Tuesday morning? I've got nothing to do, just sit around* (Tess, 1994).

The development of supported employment schemes may offer some opportunities that recognise difference and could engage with people's right to work in a more creative way, but many of these schemes are failing as the culture of the schemes are rooted in caring and service rather than commerce, and they cannot effectively engage with the demands of private companies (Steele, 1993, 1996). While Ramcharan et al (1997b) are right to suggest that wider social changes are necessary to ensure inclusion for people with learning difficulties, this has to be seen in the context of a growing 'underclass' within the society at large (Murray, 1990). In our society there is not one but many communities, all working within power relationships. People with learning difficulties have not been included in a larger society, with rights to work in meaningful jobs but remain with other groups of people who equally have little access to society such as the elderly, disabled people, minority ethnic groups and the working class.

During the first half of the twentieth century, structured work activities dominated the lives of the residents and the Sisters. As the century progressed, residents' work became marginal to the running of the convents and the sense of self worth gained by the women who worked diminished as they spent their days with little occupation. The symbolic meanings that work offered the women, providing, on the one hand, a 'sense of place', and more negatively, a rigid and powerful hierarchy were difficult to challenge, where work and religion interacted but it gave the women a way of understanding their lives. The symbolism of work patterns built on the religious labelling process of good and bad girls, by creating clean and dirty work spaces. For some women who gained status from this hierarchy, the loss of the industry in the convents reinforced their sense of disintegration, as women moved into the wider community. The next chapter discusses the development of leisure time and questions whether the meanings placed on leisure offered a sufficiently positive identity for the convent residents to replace their work identity.

Chapter 5

Leisure and Pleasure: Repression and Incitement in the Convents

While work hours were long and arduous in many institutions, including the convents, there was always some free time. Stories of leisure activities are common in most accounts of life in institutions (Morris, 1969; Alaszewski, 1986; Potts and Fido, 1991; Cooper, 1997). Daily life was ordered in the convents to create clearly defined boundaries between work and leisure and this chapter focuses on the leisure activities organised by the convents and their meanings. It also discusses how the women found pleasure in their daily lives; not only in leisure activities but also through the friendships they developed with other residents in the convents. Leisure patterns changed over time and here I discuss the impact of these shifts from what was more a communal to a more individualised form of leisure by the end of the last century.

In several accounts of life in institutions (Potts and Fido, 1991 and Cooper, 1997), leisure is not always described positively. In her account of her experiences in St. Lawrence's hospital, Cooper states that holidays were tedious:

> If you went on holiday with the hospital you sat on the grass and didn't do anything. They just used to sit on the grass if it was a nice day. You didn't go to the beach or anything (Cooper, 1997:28).

Cooper is pointing out that leisure activities need not be pleasurable although they are often thought to be connected with enjoyment. To make sense of the value and meaning placed on leisure activities in the convents, some clarity on the distinction between leisure and pleasure is necessary.

Defining leisure and pleasure

The stories used in this chapter focus on both the structured times and activities organised by the Sisters outside of work, which I would define as 'leisure', and the 'fun times' the women experienced, which I define as pleasure. This distinction between time away from work on the one hand

and fun times on the other is important. There have been taken-for-granted assumptions in most of the literature on institutional care that organised leisure activities are an indication of a better service. However, any leisure activity, like any work activity, can be and often is controlled by those in authority. In Cooper's account discussed above, the hospital residents were not given the opportunity to do 'anything' on holiday except 'sit on the grass' (1997). The authorities were in charge of the holiday, taking any pleasure away from the experience. Recognising that leisure and pleasure are sometimes separate experiences suggests that, in planning services, it is the quality of the activity and the control over the activity that is important, not necessarily the nature of the activity.

Pleasure can be experienced on many different occasions including leisure times but can also be found during work activities, as well as in private moments. It can be subversive, reversing and challenging the authority of those in positions of power or it can be experienced by being part of a group that maintains authority. Some of the stories I was told highlighted how the women found pleasure by subverting the authority of the Sisters. The women also told me about the pleasure they gained from friendship groups and from contributing to decision making in the convents.

Many of the women in the convents were, at times, defiant and ingenious in their pursuit of pleasure and unlike other accounts of institutional life (Morris, 1969; Jones, 1975; Alaszewski, 1986; Atkinson and Williams, 1990; Lewis, 1997; Cooper, 1997; Humphries, 1998) the women seemed to find more opportunity to experience pleasure and friendship.

Friendship and Pleasure

> *We used to go outside and wave at the soldiers. We'd climb up on the roof and wave at them. They were kept in the brewery down the road. We'd wave and shout out. We'd make pretty sure no one saw us and we'd come in before the Sisters came* (Maria, 1993).

The women, who climbed the wrought iron stairway to see into the barracks of the soldiers who were temporarily billeted nearby during the Second World War, were in their late twenties. Most had been at the convent since their early teens. They were clearly aware of the subversive nature of the activity. To wave and shout at the soldiers, in the hope of getting their attention, was an act of defiance against the Sisters in charge of them.

This story provides an example of how the women in the convent were able to find space to enjoy themselves, despite, and to a certain extent, because of, the constraints that their environment imposed on them. Recounting the experience Maria described a complicated look-out system:

> . . . *One of us would stand at the bottom of the stairs and watch, someone who could whistle. Someone would always listen for the whistle, while the rest of us looked out for the soldiers. Oh, we had fun! We never got caught though* (Maria, 1993).

Maria spoke with a degree of pride and enjoyment. She used the story to explain to me how she had exercised some control over her life. It is an example of a pleasurable experience snatched from work time and in defiance of the Sisters. It is an example of how repressive circumstances can incite defiance and create pleasure, for if the Sisters had not established such a repressive regime within the convents the incident may not have had the same relish.

This story is one of many that centres on an attempt to make contact with men. It is also a story about girls' camaraderie and friendship. The women needed to plan together and to rely on each other. They were also having a good time together, despite the difficulties of their lives. 'Having a good time' despite adversity is a common theme in many older people's stories (Jerrome, 1992; Mace, 1994). In particular, the excitement of doing something you are not allowed to do with others who share your illicit behaviour can be an extremely pleasurable experience, both doing the activity (and getting away with it) and recounting it, as it indicates personal power over those in authority.

The women in the convents, the residents and to a certain extent the Sisters themselves, lived with repression; control over their personal attire, their behaviour and their food. They were constantly under surveillance and many 'ordinary' activities were considered taboo. Breaking even the most innocent of rules was a way of asserting their independence in defiance of the power of the Sisters. Working together in a friendship group as these women did gave them greater possibilities for pleasure, not only because they shared and understood the subversion but also because they shared the oppression.

In such environments, to succeed in subverting the accepted and correct way of life is more pleasurable than in less repressive circumstances.

In examining institutions for people with learning difficulties, it is easy to find the harshness and oppression of daily life, as it is so obvious, but finding people's experience of pleasure can be more difficult (Brechin and Walmsley, 1989). In the world that the convent residents inhabited, there was space to develop friendships and experience pleasure and the women fought to maintain that space. The next section outlines how that space was created within the world of a Catholic convent.

Culture, Leisure and Pleasure in the Convents

Like work, the leisure activities of the women living in the convents altered over time. While there were certain activities that were particular to the convents, the pattern of leisure activities that developed reflected some of the changing leisure patterns that many Britons experienced during the last hundred years. These included the development of privatised leisure and the growth of the European package holiday. The story of leisure in other long-stay institutions also suggests that particular forms of recreation can be traced to wider social developments. In several accounts of hospital life (Potts and Fido, 1991; Cooper, 1997), although separate from wider society, leisure activities also mirrored activities in the wider community. In Morris's extensive 1960s study of long-stay institutions, she pointed out that 'Thirty-nine per cent of patients sampled were in hospitals which made no provisions (other than films and dances) for patients' recreation' (Morris, 1969:185). She says that in private 'homes' patients had better contact with staff because there was less reliance on television as a form of recreation. In hospitals, there was greater potential for other forms of 'training' than in homes where residents tended to work. Jones (1975) points out that the *Better Services for the Mentally Handicapped* (1971) policy document encouraged the development of group activities like drama, music, and horse-riding. She also emphasises that the leisure activities that were developed were appreciated, but that there was a clear routinised pattern including a calendar of events such as 'the summer outing' or 'the Christmas dance'. Holidays were less frequently identified in these accounts but Morris suggests that in the hospitals where holidays were taken, most 'patients' were able to get away. Potts and Fido (1991) use life history accounts to chart the development of leisure in 'The Park', the long-stay institution they studied, pointing to the building of the hall in the 1930s as a key moment in offering leisure activities within the 'colony'. Rather than increasing the potential for leisure, however, the hall limited people's ability to go to the cinema and to church services outside the institution, which they had been previously allowed to do.

In another account of a mental handicap hospital, Alaszewski (1986) argues that meal times were not only structured events but were themselves moments for the enforcement and maintenance of the power hierarchies between patients and staff. The type of food eaten, the preparation of the food and who ate with whom all added to patients and staff knowing their 'place' within the structure of the hospital.

In any community, there develops a range of specific activities that helps to create a sense of shared identity for the community (Douglas and Nicod, 1974). The convents, like other communities, had their specific cultural activities. On entering a convent in London, Liverpool or Sussex, there was an atmosphere that enabled the visitor to recognise that the culture was similar to any other convent of the same Order. It was a powerful way to create a sense that life, in what was a relatively unusual setting, was immutable.

Catholic cultures are rich and offer a range of coherent meanings and symbols for community members. The religion uses art and dramatic pageant to reproduce its belief through a range of celebratory events, including, saints' feast days, Lent, a forty-day abstinence period before Easter, the Ascension, Advent before, and Epiphany after, Christmas. These events took up much of the time given to leisure in the convents. They took place each year, each one having a specific ceremony and ritual attached to the occasion. They were all so inscribed into Catholic belief that they were taken for granted. The experience of the 'Catholic calendar' was distinctive. It was a significant element in the life experiences of the women residents. One told me about the practice of decorating a particular resident's place at the table on their saint's feast day.

> *On feast days we would have something a little special. There would be flowers in the dining room and Father would sometimes say something. If it was your feast day sometimes there would be special flowers around your place at the table. It was all very nice* (Myra, 1990).

This sense of a cycle of activity that was reproduced yearly created a sense of security and a belief in the correctness of the activities of the convent. It enabled the residents to be certain of their place within the structure of daily life, creating an understanding of who they were and a sense of inclusion in the community of the convent. When the older women talked about how leisure had changed, the rituals that had disappeared were ones that they missed the most. Many of these activities that formed part of the Catholic calendar were viewed by the older women as pleasurable (Myra, 1990; Margaret, 1990; Maria, 1992; Martha, 1992 and Mary, 1993). The sense of pleasure was rooted in the security and personal value which the ritual offered. It was also rooted in maintaining the order of daily life and the hierarchy that sustained it, rather than the subversive pleasure described in the story of waving at the soldiers.

Because the women had such little contact with outsiders until the 1960s (including not having a radio or television, as well as the prohibition on talking to strangers), leisure activities were focused on the localised, physical space of the convents themselves. The celebration of a feast day for the women in the convent was a localised experience. The yearly event was focused on physical reality, their own dining hall, their own setting at the table. '*There would be flowers in the dining room . . . there would be flowers round your place at the table*'(Myra, 1990).

Being a home for women created a particular environment. It established a set of power relations between the inhabitants that was built around an ideal of motherhood and infantilisation, not unlike the initial experience when the residents entered the convents.[1] This notion of the convent family also affected the type of leisure activities that the women experienced. In the convents, the residents were seen as girls, daughters to the Mothers and Sisters who cared for them. One resident, Eileen, drew a picture for me of her twenty-first birthday party (Figure 5).

It is a bright picture, with a number of places set with a knife and fork with a large birthday cake placed in the centre of a brightly decorated table. I was told stories of balloons, party games like 'pass the parcel' and presents from Sisters that included 'teddies' and 'dolls'. Many of these sorts of practices are usually associated with young children, and 'teddies' and dolls are not presents usually given to adults. This process of infantilisation was

[1] see chapter three for a fuller discussion on entering the 'convent family'.

Figure 5: Eileen's Birthday Drawing

common to the experience of many women with learning difficulties (Noonan Walsh,1988). In this way, pleasurable activities re-enforced the women's position in the convents as 'the children'.

Leisure as 'Family Life'

In the later part of the nineteenth century, middle class women began to establish a particular style of family life. Homes came to be seen as places of relaxation and withdrawal from the world (Cross, 1990). Women were to create a home environment that was an 'escape' for the man when he returned home from work:

> In the nineteenth century, the home became the specialised place of recreation. The shock troops of fire-side happiness were mostly women in the rather distinct and new role of homemaker. Industrialization meant the removal of affluent

> married women at least from the workforce, and changes in the household and childrearing work of wives cleared the way for female leadership in the creating of a new domestic leisure. (Cross, 1990: 104)

The notion of the family home as the site of spiritual peace and reflection is also echoed in the leisure activities of the convents in the early part of the twentieth century. As indicated in the writings of the Foundress, the Sisters were to be the spiritual image of the middle class mother. Between 1913 and 1940, leisure in the convents had echoes of the description outlined by Cross, above. Leisure was restricted to two hours an evening, Catholic celebrations such as Christmas and Saints feast days, daily mass and a visit to a place of natural beauty on Sunday. Activities were highly structured and often conducted in silence or quiet conversation. In the evenings, women would '*sit in a sitting room or on a veranda and knit or sew*' (Martha, 1992). One of the Sisters would play the piano and sometimes the women would sing. These activities are reminiscent of leisure activities for most middle class women and girls in the nineteenth century. These controlled and so-called 'civilised' leisure pursuits were in sharp contrast to the hard and sometimes rough work of the laundry or the farm that the women engaged in during this period.

On Sundays, the women would walk in two's to mass. The regimented regime of crocodile lines marching to the local church, whether in Mother or Angel convent, often annoyed the women, even if they were religious. Some of them would attempt and sometimes succeed in avoiding attending mass. Elvera told me that she would:

> *... bring on a faint. We'd be all lined up ready to go into chapel. We were supposed to be quiet and I'd whisper to Laura behind me, "Wait for it. I'm going to go over now"* (1992).

Elvera was especially pleased that she was able to fool the Sisters into believing she had fainted. She would '*work on' her faint. I'd practice sometimes. It's just your breathing and going over at the right angle so you don't hurt yourself*' (Elvera, 1992). It amused her friends and, as she said, '*gave us something to giggle about. We were all a little naughty, my group*' (Elvera, 1992). Again it was the extent of the control that provided the pleasure, for if the women had not been forced to go to mass, there would have been no need to subvert the Sisters' authority.

After mass, whatever the weather, a walk on the downs or to a park or a visit to the beach was organised. Many of the women I interviewed complained about having to go out:

> *Oh, those walks on the downs. They were awful, every weekend and you know we sometimes had to go out without a coat* (Elvera, 1992).

One woman told me that one of the signs of positive change was the ability to '*stop going to the beach*'(Mary, 1992). The women saw their inability to choose their own activities as a symbol of their oppression.

Even after the Second World War, and into the 1960s, middle class feminine philanthropic values dominated in the convents. Leisure time was spent 'doing good'. Many of the women I spoke to had involved themselves in bazaars and fetes for the Catholic parish they lived in during the 1950s and 1960s, including knitting and sewing items for sale in their free time, selling tickets for entry to the bazaar and working on the stalls. In her poem for Sister Millicent, Elvera records:

> *. . . The spirit is still among us as we sew or knit or sell*
> *And the jumble sales we'd visit my word they'd make pounds swell*
> *When we could pick up ten dolls for just the price of two pounds*
> *Then up to the senior quarters where the dolls' hospital was found*
> *And without any anaesthetic an operation was performed*
> *Limbs and joints were reset a wonder to behold* (Elvera, 1972).

Both Sisters and residents were busily engaged in doing good for the parish. The pleasure evident in Elvera's poem hints at the feeling of mutual endeavour which the women and the Sisters experienced, an example of inclusion that was valued by women like Elvera and Maria.

In the 1960s, the Sisters allowed the women to talk to strangers. They were going out into the community and the community was coming in to them. Women who worked for the bazaars describe themselves as proud of their contribution to parish funds, seeing their time being used to some purpose (Elvera, 1992; Mary, 1993, 1994).

At the same time as the fetes and bazaars, the women met parish community members through amateur dramatics. Elvera recounts the long hours spent in preparing for the plays:

> *The nights we stayed up to practice to nearly midnight or more*
> *When you got down on your pattern cutting out on the floor*
> *Then someone would come in and say, your orders for breakfast please*
> *You knew not whether to be cross or pray she was such a dreadful tease* (Elvera, 1972).

This is another example of Elvera recounting activities that included the Sisters as much as the residents and where the Sister concerned was being treated by the women as 'one of them'. The pleasure gained from these events can be found in the sense of inclusion in activities with the Sisters, breaking down authority structures and creating a closeness with the women. The plays were highly significant events and only happened at Mother convent. Angel convent had no in-house performances until the advent of Adult Education in the 1980s. Mary describes the importance of the plays:

> *We also put on concerts consisting of a play, then singing and dancing. I always took part in the plays. We had Operettas, and funny plays. We had two days of giving concerts. The first day was for the parents and nuns from other convents and our own, even Mother General came to them when she was down our way, the second day was for the people from the parish and their friends to watch us. We started to practice in October and had the concerts in January. We had to practice in the evenings after our supper from round six pm to sometimes eleven pm . . . but it was great fun and we had many a laugh* (Mary, 1994).

It is also significant that the Sisters from the convents attended on the first day with parents while parishioners attended on the second day. This structuring of the audience symbolises the meaning of the relationship between the community and the convent members. The Sisters were family and saw a private rehearsal of the plays. Community members came once it was felt the performance was ready to present to a 'public'.

The Celebration of Christmas

Until the 1930s, the women were given an additional two days off work as well as Christmas and Boxing Day, making a four-day holiday. In many of the conversations, the activities of Christmas were described as important. The women were given small presents and a special meal was prepared. Most of the women were isolated from their natural families and spent Christmas in the convents. Often their mothers had died and after taking their daughters to the convent many fathers did not visit again. It was the Sister-in-charge who fulfilled the mother role, organising the meal and presents. The local priest, as the father, would spend the day with the women. He would deliver a pre-Christmas talk after celebrating mass.

> *In the morning we would go to mass, father would then give the pre-Christmas talk. Then we'd have Christmas dinner. Sister would always be working on that. Then in the afternoon, we'd get presents. Father would hand the presents out. One year I got a box of chocolates and, another year, some wool for knitting* (Joan, 1992).

While the father had great power by being able to reprimand 'family' members and exhort them to be good through his pre-Christmas talk, he is also a figure of ridicule as Elvera described in the poem below. In it she explained how the women worked on the parish newsletter with Sister Margaret Mary:

> *. . . But first we had to wait around for Father's weekly letter.*
> *He'd barely settled down to write when the telephone would ring.*
> *I'm wanted in the Presbytery, we couldn't do a thing.*
> *'I'll just be a few minutes', he'd turn to us and say*
> *But the time in Ireland differs a few minutes – means a day.*
> *We were always sure he'd forgotten.*
> *We picked up the phone, if rang,*
> *We gathered all around it and this is what we sang;*
> *'Why oh why are we waiting', we sang loud and clear*
> *And that great peal of laughter could be heard at the palace pier*
> *(Elvera, 1988).*

Christmas was a highly structured event with its particular rituals and it remained this way until the 1970s. While the presence of the priest and the Sisters gave Christmas in the convents a particular Catholic meaning, it also, like the rest of the leisure activities, reproduced many of the activities in the rest of society.

As a tradition, Christmas is often seen to be 'centred in the family and is largely controlled by women,' (Barnett, 1954:22). The convent residents' account of Christmas celebrations during the early part of the last century has echoes of familial attitudes. Unlike other times in the year, when the women prepared the meals, during celebrations and at Christmas, Sisters and residents cooked together, sharing responsibilities. Alaszewski (1986) describes how the structuring of meals, in his research on a 'mental handicap' hospital, encapsulated the power structure within the institution. Eating and preparing food is always a significant cultural and social activity:

> If food is treated as a code, the message . . . will be found in the pattern of social relations. . . . The message is about different degrees of hierarchy, inclusion and exclusion, boundaries and transactions across boundaries (Alaszewski, 1986: 249).

He saw a clear distinction between the patients and the nurses with the two groups having separate tasks in the hospital. The nurses prepared food and the patients ate the food. From their beginnings in the convents, the pattern was different. Most of the women were given food-preparation responsibilities. In Goffman's study of mental health institutions (1961), staff waited on inmates at Christmas creating a role reversal (Riggins, 1990). In the convents, on the other hand, activities were shared. The 'Mother' of the convent would always preside over the Christmas roast, emphasising her benevolence and the priest became a 'real' Father Christmas, when he give out presents to the women. Using the local priest in this role established patriarchal power within the female environment of the convent, precisely because his presence was unusual and therefore special. The distribution of the gifts by the 'father', although wrapped by the 'mother', symbolised his ultimate authority but also legitimated the role of the mother.

At Christmas, some of the residents were allowed to write 'mottos' or short poems about other women who lived in the convents. Those who wrote the mottos were often seen as more powerful, having been given more authority by the Sisters. They were often bound up in particular friendship groups. These groups establish 'boundaries which include some people and exclude others' (Jerrome, 1992:87). The women in these groups enjoyed convent life and several of them had gone to live 'outside' but had returned. Some even felt that they '*would have liked to be a nun*' (Maria, 1992). These women measured themselves against the Sisters, not each other; they were in effect 'sub-nuns', the real 'not quite Sisters' of the convents. The Sisters developed and perpetuated this power structure that created a kind of 'big sister/little sister' divide. Women told me that certain residents, like big sisters, were given 'home' responsibilities. They were allowed to 'care' for other women, sometimes giving them extensive control over the less able women, not unlike the 'trustie' system in other institutions (Potts and Fido, 1991). It was these women who were generally allowed to subvert the authority of the Sisters. They were more likely to be listened to and they were given more freedom in their own lives.

The Christmas mottos were read out after the Christmas presents were distributed:

> *Martha would read out the mottos, the Sisters would stand either side of the benches where we sat on the veranda. Elvera wrote the mottos. They were sometimes funny, but they could be a bit nasty. Martha would often tell her not to be unkind. But it was a way of getting back at some of them, them that had got out of their place.* (Laura, 1992).

Barnett suggests that Christmas rituals are a way of maintaining family group membership. Laura's story explains how the hierarchy between the women was maintained. By standing either side of the benches, the Sisters legitimated the role of the women who wrote and spoke the mottos. Laura said '*it was a way of getting back at some of them, them that had got out of their place*' meaning that the mottos were designed to re-establish each member of the convent in their own place in the hierarchy. Christmas is a powerful moment to affirm or challenge group members' identities (Miller, 1993) for, as Barnett says, activities at Christmas:

> . . .use domestic rites to preserve memories of previous Christmas celebrations and to recognise the roles of different members. This usually promotes continuity between generations and contributes unity to the kinship group (Barnett, 1954: 55).

As well as promoting unity, all these activities also re-establish power relations between siblings maintaining 'Mothers', 'Sisters' and the sub-nun group at the top of the hierarchy in the conventss.

The women were complicit in the lifestyle that the Sisters had established in the convents. They were complicit as many in the sub-nun group were both able to subvert the Sisters' authority and be part of its maintenance. This gave these women not only a stake in the way of life, but some power to shape its development. The convents were for most the only home they had; it was important for them to support its continuation and with that their place within it. This complicity is a significant reason for the enduring system that the convents developed and nurtured.

By 1994, Christmas at Mother convent was very different from the early accounts. There was no specific celebration on Christmas Day, '*just a nice lunch*' (Louise, 1995). Two parties were held early in December as in many other day and residential services. Individual residents were encouraged to invite friends and family members. I was invited to attend one such celebration, to observe and participate in the proceedings. Joanna, the lay manager, and her deputy manager, Andrew, organised a buffet of international foods, including satays and guacamole, set out in a large room with tables and seating areas. Some people, including the manager, sat on the carpet. People came and went as they pleased. There were few Sisters present and no priest attended. Music played quietly on a cassette recorder, creating an informal atmosphere. There were no moral speeches, no mottos to satirise and put down the women and no small presents. While the convent residents had a great deal more variety, several of the older women did not attend the parties. '*Oh, I couldn't be bothered to go down. It's not the same as the old days*' (Maria, 1994).

The Christmas celebrations of 1994 were as much a product of their age as the Christmas described by Laura from the 1930s. The changes that occurred in the celebration of Christmas in the convents also represent a change in the rituals and belief systems of Catholicism as well as changes in institutional homes for people with learning difficulties. The new celebrations do not infantilise the women. The new lay culture also did not overtly allow women to dominate each other, however bullying between the women continued outside of the sight of the care staff, despite the ending of practices such as the 'mottos'. The care managers lived outside the convents and had lives and families separate from their work and therefore 'Christmas' was celebrated early to fit in with their lifestyles. While there are more obvious benefits from the changes from the more openly hierarchical celebration of earlier times, the real issue of authority did not alter. Despite the clear differences, the provision of a greater variety of food, a more relaxed atmosphere and the removal of religious connotations, leisure time in the convents was still controlled by those in authority.

As Christmas celebrations in the convents altered over time, so the practice of taking holidays changed from being largely a communal religious event to a more individualised activity. How the women felt about holidays is discussed in the next section.

Getting Away – Holidays During the Twentieth Century

Since the 1920s when time off from work became a feature of ordinary people's lives in wider society, the idea of the holiday away from home changed, for many people, from being a week at an English seaside resort to a package holiday in Europe or beyond (Urry, 1989). For people with learning difficulties who lived in institutions, holidays also changed. Potts and Fido (1991) note that in the mixed sex institution they studied, men tended to be more likely than women to go on holiday and that after the Second World War more people can 'remember going on holiday' (Potts and Fido, 1991:95). As early as the 1930s, in the convents many women would spend a week at another convent in a different part of the country. Maria loved to visit other convents:

> *We used to visit the other convents, for our holidays. It was nice really getting to know the other Sisters and seeing other people* (Maria, 1992).

For some of the women like Maria, these holidays were enjoyable. She felt it was like '*visiting friends*' (Maria, 1992) where you share the same values and practices. This was particularly the case for the sub-nun group. These women felt secure and powerful in the convent environment. As one woman said to me, '*There are worse places to spend your life*' (Martha, 1992).

After the war, several of the women travelled abroad to Lourdes in France or Knock in Ireland for 'healing holidays'. Louise described one visit to Lourdes:

> *My holiday was a great success. I went to Lourdes with the Sisters and the girls. We went by plane and we stayed in a nice*

> *hotel. I liked the trips best. We went to Bernadette's house. I went to the churches* (Louise, 1995).

With the Catholic commitment to pilgrimage, many of the women had the opportunity to travel abroad before most other people with learning difficulties were able to.

By the 1990s, the women were encouraged to take European holidays in small groups, to see other cultures, and experience different ways of life. Care staff working with women in the convent would argue that this practice was consistent with normalisation theory. By encouraging 'clients' to participate in the 'ordinary' pleasures of our leisure culture, people who themselves have been defined as different, were given an opportunity to become part of the community. How the women understood their new found 'freedom' was complex and often individual. For Athena, whose mother was Greek, the opportunity to visit Rhodes in the summer of 1993 was a poignant and significant moment. Athena used her two-week package holiday as a way of re-forming her identity as an Anglo-Greek woman. She participated in the usual tourist activities, '*We ate a lot of Greek salad. I love my salad. We went to the beach*' (Athena, 1993), but she was using the holiday to find a part of herself that had been denied through living in the convent. She told me, '*I'm Greek you know and now, I know where that is*'(Athena, 1993).

For other women such as Mary, a visit to Malta paints a familiar picture of a package holiday:

> When we arrived in Malta a Mini Bus was waiting to take us to our Apartment in St. George's Park Complex at St. Julian's Bay. By mistake we were dropped at the Hotel Entrance and we had to make our way to the Apartment entrance about 300 yards away in almost complete darkness, but eventually we arrived there. We found our apartments and to our horror one of the apartments was without electricity, the one with lights we had to undress in and by torchlight we got into bed and went to sleep. The temperature was 100 degrees Fahrenheit. Very Hot! (Adams, 1994a: 5).

Holidaying 'within Catholicism' as the women did earlier this century kept them within a segregated world, not of hospital or institution but the particular community of Catholics. However, although included in the

Catholic community, the effect of the earlier holidays was to create further separation from the wider community. The change to holidays provided greater access to that wider community as Mary discovered. For women like Athena, taking a holiday to Rhodes gave her a deeper awareness of her own background. In other words, holidays in the earlier part of the century maintained Catholic beliefs and community identity, but in the 1990s the women's individual experience of different countries developed their individual identities. The next section takes the idea of growing individualised leisure and examines how this has affected the women's lives.

From Communal to Individualised Leisure

With the arrival at Mother convent of a new care manager, Sister Ursula, in 1972, the women were given more freedom. She had been '*told by her superiors to give people their independence*' (Elvera, 1993). However, changes were also underway at Angel. Alice told me '*it was in the 1970s that we were able to go out more, the Sisters said it was good for us*'(Alice, 1990).

The most significant change for many of the women in the convents was the advent of television. Mary described the coming of television in this way:

> Before the 1960s we never had a radio or TV – just a piano . . . In the mid-1960s we had our first TV, . . . that could only get BBC1 and it was in black and white (Adams, 1992).

Television watching in the 1990s formed a central part of many of the women's lives in the convents. Most women enjoyed soap operas such as East Enders and Coronation Street, like many other people in British society.

The meanings that many of the women placed on television programmes they watched were developed in relation to their own experiences. For example, the activities of the characters in East Enders were seen as different to the women's lives, as Louise's comments on the soap illustrated:

> *. . . that's what makes it interesting, 'cause I'd never meet anyone like that. It makes it interesting you see, 'cause then*

you can think, thank God I'm not like that. I wouldn't want to live like that. All that fighting and that, oh no. (Louise, 1994).

The women had become voyeurs on the rest of society's entertainment. They did not engage with the world of paid employment and did not experience the most common social relationships, like going to the pub, as the characters in Coronation Street or East Enders do. The majority of the women, like the Sisters, saw themselves as different to the rest of society despite the changed environment.

The arrival of television also marked a structural shift in the organisation of leisure activities. By the 1990s, the women in the convents' experience of leisure was largely unstructured and activities were individual. Not only did they not have to go to the beach on Saturdays and Sundays but they were able to go out as they pleased. Many chose to go shopping. Their shopping trips were usually to buy toiletries for themselves and their friends who were not able to get out. I asked several women if they ever stayed on after they had finished their shopping to have a cup of tea in a cafe. Most did not, although having suggested it in an interview, one woman did come up to me the following week and said she and a friend had '*stopped at the tea-shop and had a cup of tea and a scone. Thank you for the suggestion, Mary*' (Alice, 1990).

Figure 6: Tess's CD Drawing

Many of the women had televisions and cassette recorders in their rooms and tapes of their favourite music. Their taste in music varied, some preferring Irish folk music and some pop music. A few enjoyed classical music, like Tess, who owned a CD player (Figure 6). She told me:

> *As a child I always liked music. I liked the melody. I'd listen to the records at home . . . I especially like Puccini, La Traviata, Carmen and Faust* (1995).

Roberta drew a design of her room (Figure 7) which includes a picture of Elvis Presley, a television and a tape recorder. Unlike the dormitories of the earlier part of the century, rooms were personalised and indicated aspects of the individual's identity. The women could engage in private entertainment and could have choice about which television programmes to watch or what music to listen to. On the other hand, they no longer invited each other into their rooms, so if an individual was watching television, she did so alone. Leisure became much more private, a similar experience for many other people in society.

Meals were no longer taken in large dining halls. Both convents' buildings were adapted into 'flats' with four or five women sharing a small kitchen where light meals and snacks could be prepared. This allowed for more choice but it also created isolation. Many of the older women were not very mobile and were unable to visit others outside their particular unit. Maria

Figure 7: Roberta's Bedroom

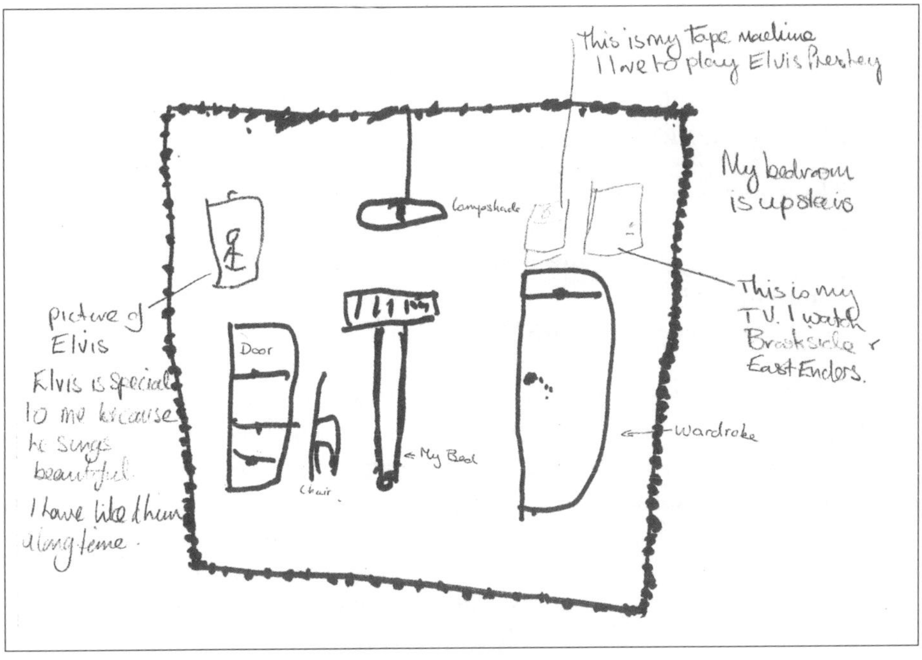

spent most of her time in her bedroom watching television. She did not like the women who shared her unit and had no one else to talk to. With the individualisation of leisure, many of the women experienced difficulty in finding space for meeting with others and sustaining contacts. Many leisure and pleasure activities depended on friendship for their affirmation and continuity, which, as activities have become more individual, was more difficult to sustain. The final section of this chapter explores how this process of individualising leisure affected the friendship groups described earlier in the chapter.

The Loss of Camaraderie

Most of the literature on friendship relating to people with learning difficulties paints a depressing picture. Richardson and Ritchie state that many adults with learning difficulties had 'a very limited range of real contacts and connections' (1989:20). In Jones's study of long-stay hospitals she says that:

> Group formation was nebulous, and usually consisted of an identification with staff and an attempt to please them . . . many patients were virtually islands each one for himself or herself (1975: 27).

Walmsley notes that the majority of the literature on friendship and people with learning difficulties emphasises friendships with people not labelled as having learning difficulties:

> The emphasis in Normalisation on the value of relationships with people who are not disabled tends to devalue disabled people. Yet the reality of life in institutions or in the community is often that relationships with other disabled people are very important (Walmsley and Downer, 1997: 39).

Bayley (1997) argues that service structures do not allow people with learning difficulties to develop 'stable' relationships. He argues for developing strategies for inclusion to enable relationships between people with learning difficulties and people who do not have learning difficulties. Inclusion is a laudable aim but relationships between people with learning difficulties should not be devalued by policy makers. The literature on people with learning difficulties therefore has perhaps not 'heard' the stories of friendships in the few life history accounts that have been written

(Walmsley, 1995; Adams, 1995; Cooper, 1997; Lewis, 1997). In the convents, friendships were extremely important, illustrated by Elvera's comments:

> *I've been out you know, several times. I've had several jobs but I always came back. I missed my friends. I missed the fun times we had together. It can be quite lonely out there, you know when you don't know anyone* (Elvera, 1992).

This comment by Elvera re-enforces the importance of female solidarity discussed earlier in the chapter. Elvera spoke of how she came to be leaving the convents. The Sisters first got her a job working in an old people's residential home in 1938:

> *Oh no, that was terrible. I only stayed one night, Mary. There was mess on the sheets and they expected me to clean that and I said, "No thank you, I'm not doing that" and I walked out and was back here like a shot* (Elvera, 1992).

Her second job was working as a domestic for a family in Croydon after the Second World War:

> *The work was all right, but I was alone so much. I stuck it quite a while, but then Christmas came and they all went out and told me to cook the dinner for them, for when they came back, and I'd never done that and I was all alone. I had no friends you see, so I phoned and I asked Sister could I come back, and she said all right, so back I came. And I'm happy here, . . . I was settled here with friends* (Elvera, 1992).

In 1990 there were nearly sixty residents in Angel convent and fifty in Mother convent. Friendship groups tended to be no larger than four or five women. The size of the institution did not prevent residents from forming groups that were meaningful to them. Groups of friends would plan activities together like Maria's account of waving at the soldiers. Friendship groups were mechanisms for protecting each other against the punishments of the Sisters. Martha told me of how Laura defended her against the Sister-in-charge when she laughed during work time:

> *We were larking about during work. We had no mirrors you see, so one day Laura looks in the window at the laundry and*

> *she can see herself see, so she says, 'Oh Laura, you look beautiful today' and I laugh and Sister says, 'who was that?' and I own up but Laura says 'No Sister, it was me what made her laugh, so don't punish her' so she never. Laura got me off* (Martha, 1992).

To illustrate how friendships in the convents were not fully appreciated by the staff, I examine the story of Laura and Martha from Mother convent who I interviewed and observed together in many different situations.

Laura and Martha had known each other since 1922 and had shared most of their lives, working and living together. In her nineties, Martha was generally quiet and reserved except when Laura came to see her. She became animated, laughed and talked a great deal, indicating that through Laura, Martha could still see her past self. Staff had not placed the two friends in the same flat, but had separated the more and less able older residents suggesting that their concern had been to think about ease of care activities rather than the residents' whole experience (Dowson, 1997). Laura would visit Martha when she could and being more able she would do Martha's shopping for her. When they were together they would reminisce about past events. Martha was concerned about Laura 'going'. The staff had plans to move Laura into a home for older people but she died in 1994 before she moved out. Laura had spoken to Martha about the potential move, but staff had not considered the possible impact on Martha. When Laura died, Martha had to ask to go to the funeral. Her own grief had not been acknowledged until she cried at the ceremony. Martha lived on in a small unit with women she said she did not like. She died nearly a year after Laura in May 1995. Potts and Fido (1991) tell of friendships, within the colony they studied, that were destroyed by friends being separated after the closure of the hospital. As the convent resident grew older, some members of their friendship circle died or were removed. Seldom did care staff recognise the significance of these friendship groups.

In Western society, this is often symbolised by older family members being placed in care. In the convents, to move to the senior wing where the older women lived could provide a symbolic abandonment, especially when prior life experiences were ignored. Family members who are the centre of family life become more peripheral as they grow old (Jerrome, 1994). Maria had been living upstairs in the 'senior wing' for a number of months, and talked about never seeing anyone:

> *No-one comes to call. I'm just up here you see, and with my bad leg, I can't get down to see them. But I guess they don't want to be bothered with the likes of me, not any more* (Maria, 1992).

From being central figures in convent life, these women were abandoned to live retired, individualised lives, not unlike many other accounts of older people's residential care (Peace et al, 1997). Yet it was not only the older women who experience loneliness. As leisure and work activities became more individualised, there was little space for any of the women to share activities, and the camaraderie and mutual support that sustained many of the older women no longer found the space to grow and develop in the convents.

Leisure time shifted from being peripheral to daily life to becoming the main focus for activities as the laundry and farm work disappeared from the convents. For some of the women, access to society's leisure pursuits offered a greater sense of self worth, but equally for those who gained power and pleasure from their friendship groups, the move to individualised leisure undermined their potential for fun. The authority of the Sisters was challenged and subverted through the development of powerful 'girls' friendship groups' that fell into decline. The significance of these groups in sustaining the women residents through the oppressiveness of convent life was clear from the stories they told me. This points to the importance of friendship in creating pleasure in these women's lives and suggests that friendship between people who share the same experiences of services should not be undermined or ignored but nurtured.

Choice in leisure activities may have been more extensive in the later part of the twentieth century, but the proliferation of individualised activities removed the camaraderie that the women experienced earlier in their lives. Pleasure was gained through these friendship groups and the group activities that sustained them, but as communal activities dwindled, loneliness replaced pleasure. The next chapter follows the theme of pleasure and explores issues of sexuality in the convents.

Chapter 6

Motherhood and Infantilisation: The Paradox of Women's Sexuality in the Convents

Throughout the twentieth century, women who had been labelled as having learning difficulties were subjected to a range of policies and practices to 'curb' their sexuality. Eugenicists argued for not only segregation from the mainstream of society but also for sterilisation of women. In 1931, the Sterilisation Bill was introduced into Parliament and although unsuccessful, many women with learning difficulties were subjected to sterilisation against their wishes even into the 1980s (Craft, 1987; Brown and Craft, 1989). Sterilisation was the culmination of the moral panic about 'feeblemindedness'. It grew directly out of the earlier Mental Deficiency Acts (1913,1927) which recommended institutionalisation for women who were sexually active but unmarried. While this pervasive and oppressive form of control particularly affected working class women as Jones (1986) details, the convents provide evidence that controlling women's sexuality in this way affected women from all classes, as many of the women who were institutionalised in the convents were from middle class families.

While women with learning difficulties experienced more external control over their sexuality than other women, the stories recounted in this chapter show how the desires and experiences of the convent residents echo many other women's experiences. Being institutionalised or having a learning difficulty does not prevent desiring to be loved or wanting sexual pleasure. The effect of sexual morals and sensibilities that led to women being put into institutions in the earlier part of the twentieth century has also led to professionals seeing the sexuality of women with learning difficulties as somehow different from other women (Conneally, 1988). The differences that have existed are rather more about how women's sexuality has been controlled.

For the convent residents, the closeted environment of a nunnery created particular limitations on sexual expression. Catholic doctrine was opposed to eugenics but Catholics practiced segregation as part of a particular value system that idealised images of women, either as a wife and mother or as a celibate woman of religion removed from worldly temptation. The morality of Catholicism in Britain was 'obsessed' with 'the sins of the flesh' (Hornsby-Smith, 1987: 90) during the twentieth century and the practice of segregating 'childlike' (Kelly, 1988: 166) 'daughters' from the rest of the world highlights this obsession. Even after the changes of Vatican II, Catholic doctrine on sexuality was extremely restrictive.

At an international symposium on sexuality and people with learning difficulties in 1975, Monsignore Assopardi advocated total abstinence from sex for people with learning difficulties. However, Assopardi also advocated abstinence from any form of sex, except procreation in marriage, for all Catholics, indicating a particularly limited view of sexual expression for any practicing Catholic. In this climate, the women in the convents nevertheless attempted to express their sexuality. The rest of this chapter explains how convent residents dealt with their sexuality.

Mothers and Grown up Sisters – Mature Sexuality

Catholic belief in appropriate sexual behaviour emphasised the 'permanence and inviolability of the marriage contract' (Hornsby-Smith, 1987: 90). In a Catholic definition of appropriate sexual expression, sex is necessarily an adult behaviour, as it is confined to procreation, leading to the care of children within a family environment. Sexual practices were regulated and contraception and forms of abortion or sterilisation were considered sinful (Coman, 1977). This created a complicated relationship between Catholic doctrine and women's sexuality because the religion sees sexual activity as intrinsically connected with procreation. Hence, for Catholics, appropriate sexual expression was a mature sexuality maintained within the privacy of the home. As Hornsby-Smith points out:

> Women's place was very definitely in the home and this view was regarded as being not only natural but also legitimated by rather narrow interpretations of the role of the Holy family of Nazareth (Hornsby-Smith, 1987: 90).

Other forms of sexual expression, homosexual or lesbian sex, masturbation and so on were to be confessed and restrained. Mother Foundress pointed out that her Sisters had a special relationship with Mary the mother of god:

> Consider that each Order has a special devotion, and ours is to Our Lady, bearing Jesus within her. Thus the indulgence prayer that we say daily, 'oh, Jesus, living in Mary' is so especially our own. Now this devotion ought to have an effect on our lives. The Angels at least ought to see this mark upon us, and men also should see it (in Gilpin Wells, 1988: 212).

The Mother Foundress wished to work to save 'fallen' young women and, as already noted, one of the convents discussed here, Angel convent, was actually founded as a 'safe haven' for Soho 'girls'.

The Sisters of the Daughters of the Mother of God were to be pure but they were to take their inspiration from their 'special devotion' of 'Jesus *within* Mary' (my emphasis). Calling Mary 'the Mother' was significant both for the work of the movement and its relationship to the development of women's sexuality.

The relationship between nuns and God or Jesus has always had sexual connotations. The ceremony that confirms a postulant as a nun symbolises a holy marriage between the new nun and Christ and his church (Bernstein 1976, Campbell-Jones, 1979). Historically, the idea of religious ecstasy has highly charged sexual overtones, particularly noted in the 'blessing' of St. Teresa (Knox, 1982). However, the idea of Mary the Mother is also imbued with sexual meaning. Mary was 'covered by the Holy Ghost', a miraculous form of intercourse. For the 'Daughters of the Mother of God', the special devotion was 'Jesus within Mary'. If man and the angels could see this 'mark' of spiritual pregnancy, then they had reached their fulfillment as Sisters. They had grown up. They were complete. As Mother Foundress herself pointed out to one of her Sisters:

> Mother: Do you think you have made any sacrifice?
>
> Sister: Yes, from the world's point of view, but not one I have ever regretted or could regret.
>
> Mother: Then you don't know yet what the Faith is worth. Nothing is sacrifice that is given up for it (Gilpin Wells, 1988: 190).

Living a life of 'Jesus within Mary' is not a sacrifice because it is the fulfillment of womanhood. It is the 'natural' outworking of femininity.

Sisters were expected to develop and mature as mothers. The mature sexuality of motherhood required a demeanour of acceptance and self-control. Mother Foundress told a new superior:

> Don't go about like someone who wants to frighten people. Act in a modest kind manner. Don't cock your head in the air. Our Lady would not do that (Gilpin Wells, 1988: 200).

The Sister was still learning to be mature. 'Cocking your head in the air' was seen as an act of defiance, of sexuality and an expression of childishness. This is the opposite of the correct expression of mature womanhood. Celibacy was a calling, a holy fulfillment (Gilpin Wells, 1988). Sisters learnt their maturity through service. It was seven years before a Sister took her final vows (Bernstein, 1976).

Being a 'mother' in the convent movement did not allow real motherhood. The Sisters did not actually have children, but they were to look after the sick, the poor, the aged, and the repentant. The women who came to stay in the movement's houses were referred to as 'our girls' (Gilpin Wells, 1988: 155). The Sisters were responsible for the women and, as I argue in Chapter Three, the experience of coming to live in the convents was like becoming a child again, a sort of re-birth. The Sisters had their children. These children were the women they 'cared for'.

Chodorow argues that women grow to be women from their relationship with their mother. She says girls learn 'what it is to be womanlike in the context of this personal identification with her mother and often with other female models' (Chodorow, 1978: 176). The women who came to live in the convents were expected to see the Sisters as role models and to identify with the Sisters to help them grow up. These principles that the Mother Foundress established at the end of the nineteenth century were still the teachings of the movement in the 1990s. The Mother General of the movement drew out this point when she wrote in a recent biography of the Mother Foundress:

> She (the biographer) has been able to see the timelessness of the Church behind the changes of its outward face-changes which, for a less perceptive author, could have obscured the continuity of the Divine light which has guided the Church and the Foundress of religious Orders through so many ages (Sister M. St. Pius, 1988).

In other words, she is emphasising continuity of belief within change, continuity of the beliefs of the 'Foundress of Religious Orders'. The effect of constructing the Sisters as role models for appropriate 'motherhood', through 'Jesus within Mary', created an infantilisation of the women they cared for. The only possible way to escape this infantilisation process was mimicking the maturity of service-work as the Sisters did.

Mimicry and Motherhood – Almost but Never Quite Sisters

> If you were a Catholic and were a model of goodness you were awarded a neck braid and a medal about every six months until you became a Child of Mary. First you had a yellow braid, then six months later a green one, then a brown one, then a pink one, then a red one, then lastly . . . we were given an Aspirants ribbon for two years . . . After two years we were given the Child of Mary's ribbon . . . I was very happy when I got mine, but I lost mine almost at once through being naughty (Adams, 1995: 35).

The Sisters formalised the symbolic process of maturing for the women who lived in the convents, reproducing a similar set of procedures to those developed for postulants. The women took three years to gain their Child of Mary's ribbon, about half the time required for a nun. Once gained, these women were given responsibility within the convent. The ribbons were tentatively given. Any woman seeking to be a 'Child of Mary' had to be 'a model of goodness'. If they were 'naughty' they would lose their ribbon and have to start the process again. 'Being naughty' consisted of similar activities to 'cocking your head', in other words, things like talking back to Sisters or, more seriously, not fulfilling your responsibilities. Mary wrote about how she lost her ribbon through an outing to the fair:

> This happened because we had a resident here who was absolutely man mad . . . she was one of my group of four. Most of us wanted to go on the big wheel but she did not want to, so we left her standing near by. When we came off she was standing talking to a man whose name was Keith . . . He took her off on his own, and she told me to keep quiet about it but one of the other residents . . . reported it to the staff in charge (Adams, 1995: 36).

Mary was expected to act as a mother and as she did not fulfill this role correctly, she lost her sign of maturity. Women such as Mary were always aware that their ability to be accepted and trusted by the Sisters was uncertain. The process of 'growing up' was a process of 'not quite growing up'. The women could lose the powers given to them. Unlike the Sisters who, on reaching their goal, after seven years, could be called Sisters or if they were even more successful, finally 'mothers', the women could only ever be 'a child of Mary'. This 'not quite' a sister or mother is akin to the process described by Bhabha (1986). He argued that black people in British colonies were 'almost British subjects' but 'not quite', almost but not quite white. Keeping black people as almost British subjects in this way re-affirmed the value of being British, because recognition was difficult to obtain and became a prize worth seeking.

Adapting this concept to the convents, the women became almost, but not quite, the grown up mature Sisters. They were forever almost, but not quite, mature women. Keeping the women they cared for as 'children' also helped provide a security for the Sisters. As women, the Sisters were also almost, but not quite, mothers. In other words, in the convents, both groups of women, the Sisters and the residents' identities were insecure, 'almost but not quite' because of their differences from the rest of society.

Women often have ambivalent feelings about maturing. Sayers (1986) and Chodorow (1978) suggest that girls do not necessarily easily move into an acceptance of motherhood. Chodorow says:

> . . . Children seek to escape from their mother as well as return to her. Fathers serve in part to break a daughter's primary unity with and dependency on the mother (Chodorow, 1978: 195).

The Sisters needed the women to remain as 'not quite' to assure them of their own femininity. Elvera's poetry is filled with exploits from convent girls, sometimes making fun of the Sisters and sometimes just having fun with friends. In one of her poems she talks about several young women buying bras which were prohibited in the convents, not worn by Sister or resident, more or less until Vatican II. She recounts how these women saved up their meager wages to buy rocker-style padded bras:

Do you remember the days when padded bras came to the shops
You had some fashionable youngsters here that liked to be top of the pops
They saved lots and lots of pennies till they had enough to buy

And they stalked to the back of the chapel with a twinkle in their eye
But you knew only too well
They knew that you were there – maybe saying your beads or very fervent prayer
With grey beret perched on the side and their chests like Doris Day's
You chased them out of the chapel to put on calico stays (Elvera, 1966).

In this poem, Elvera paints a vivid picture of these young women attempting to explore their sensuality, to look sexy and to take pleasure in their figures. She contrasts their childish 'twinkle in their eye' and their berets 'perched on the side' with the mature Sister, 'saying your beads', devoted to God, saying 'very fervent prayer'. The Sister would not have 'a twinkle in her eye' but 'knew only too well' what was going on and was able to take control, making the girls put on calico stays again. This incident reaffirmed the Sister's authority but also reaffirmed her maturity. Nevertheless, by creating the residents as 'children', the women were paradoxically more able to relinquish responsibility and seek pleasure. Being considered children enabled them to 'play' as children, not needing to take responsibility for their actions and it was in this space that several of the women experimented with sexual feelings and emotions.

Sexual Silences

Sexual relationships between any of the women in the convents were not permitted. It was generally not discussed and, even as late as 1990, if some women expressed an interest in men, it was usually in the context of being a wife and mother, living what they understood to be the norm for women outside the convent. Most of the older women I spoke to seldom described their feelings about men or sex beyond this. For the women, sex equated to 'getting married'; sexual pleasure could not be thought about outside of conventional heterosexual relationships.

Walmsley (1995) interviewed several women with learning difficulties who had lived in institutions and outside of them. She highlights that discussion of sexuality was infrequent with her informants, but this may have had to do with the nature of her study, which focused on friendship. Booth and Booth (1994), who interviewed parents who had learning difficulties, by contrast heard many stories including tales of abuse and rape. Potts and Fido (1991), who interviewed people with learning difficulties from one long-stay institution, recount stories of love relationships. From my research in the convents it was clear that several women did not equate their sexual pleasures with 'sex'. There was a kind of silence around the word sex if not the experience of it.

In some cases women simply did not have the language for the experiences they had undergone. Even discussions of menstruation were taboo in the convents, creating an environment where the women were not certain what menstruation or the menopause were. Maria told me that at her convent orphanage no one had ever explained to her that women bleed:

> *I'll tell you something. Well I was late to see it, you know what I mean, my period. Well, I didn't know what it was. We were staying over in the laundry for a few days while they built the girls' wing. Well, I had all this blood and I was screaming and everyone said, 'what's the matter, what's the matter?' And I said, 'there's this man and he's stabbing me' and they said, 'there's no one here' and I said, 'I'm being stabbed' and the nuns came and said, 'what's the matter?' And they said, 'Maria says she's been stabbed' and the Sister said, 'I'll take her, I know what this is' and she gave me a towel and I put it here.* (pointing to her chest)

I wanted to clarify the point. I asked if this was because she didn't know where she should put her sanitary towel:

> *I didn't know anything about it, no one had told me you see. When I was about eight or nine I saw one of the towels hanging out to dry and I said 'Sister why don't you give me those to wash and she said, 'no those are special.' And I asked what they were and she said, 'you won't be having those till you're grown up.' Now you won't put that in your book will you?* (Maria, 1992).

Maria's story is not uncommon. Some women saw menstruation as a form of punishment for their sins. Our interview continued. I told her I wouldn't use the story if she didn't want me to, that I understood it is a little embarrassing. I said: 'it happens to all women, and we've all got stories a little like that. I've come on at embarrassing times.' She replied:

> *Oh yes, it's part of us isn't it, since time began, since the garden of Eden, since Eve gave Adam the apple. Yes, you can tell that story and you can say, I like apples!*

Maria's conversation did hint at an interest in sex ('I like apples') but she did not want to explain further.

> *I'd rather not talk about that. There's some that have run away. They'd talk about it, but I'm a good Catholic woman and I like it here* (Maria, 1992).

Maria was keen to emphasise that she was a good Catholic and therefore did not talk about 'it'. Women who 'ran away' from the convents, she thought perhaps would talk. I respected her desire for silence about sex and attempted to find other ways of investigating the subject.

As has been argued elsewhere (McCarthy and Thompson, 1994; Smith and Stuart, 1995), sexuality is more than sexual activity and includes a range of experiences and sensual feelings. People with learning difficulties have seldom been given the space to explore their sensual experiences to enable them to develop an understanding of their desires because of historical fears of their sexuality (Conneally, 1988; Williams, 1992). I decided to focus on sensual feeling rather than sex and found this line of investigation more fruitful.

One woman showed an ingenious device for clitoral stimulation. She had tried a number of other dildos but had settled on this one. It was a cleaned out, empty roll-on deodorant bottle. She said it gave her a lot of pleasure:

> *I tried it before I washed it out, but it hurt, so I washed it and it's quite good. I like the way it makes me feel. I use it at night and sometimes in the toilets. No one knows. If Sister caught me I'd be in for it. It makes me feel funny. My knees shake. It's nice.*

I asked why she thought she would be 'in for it' if the Sister caught her. She said:

> *I don't know. She doesn't like us touching ourselves down there. When I want to go to the toilet, she says don't hold yourself, it's not nice. She wouldn't find this nice* (Susan, 1990).

It is unlikely that Susan was clear about the terminology or that her pleasure is defined by society as being connected with 'sex'. Her understanding of Sister's displeasure was connected with social etiquette.

The meaning of the activity for Susan was that she enjoyed the 'funny feeling' but she was aware that the activity was something to keep quiet about.

Even though the convents were women-only environments, there seemed to be little direct evidence of sexual activity between the women. Some women did care very deeply for each other and might have expressed this through holding hands or the odd kiss. However, women seldom felt free enough to speak about relationships. Nevertheless, there were indications of some sexual fantasy, as Elvera's poem about her play acting shows:

> *We loved to perform and be dressed up*
> *And especially change our name from girl to boy.*
> *Oh what a joy, but alas it was only a play.*
> *I was often chosen to play the part of a boy*
> *But I loved to get into trousers*
> *It was such a pride and joy* (Elvera, 1966).

When I asked her what she meant by this poem, she said she often dreamt of being a boy. Segal (1994) identifies a common female fantasy about having a penis. Perhaps Elvera was constructing her own version of this fantasy but as a consequence of the silence about sex in the convents her fantasy was played out in 'getting into trousers'.

Lesbian activity is perhaps more censored in convent life than any other. If there are obvious expressions of lesbian activity, these are heavily controlled. Below I explore how various aspects of sexuality have been controlled, not by the Sisters but by the women themselves.

The Policing of Sexuality – Talk and Repression

During 1991, a young woman came to Angel convent who confided to me that she had had some sexual experience. Her name was Claire and she made friends with Siobhan. Claire and Siobhan would go for walks together. Siobhan told me '*Claire is the first real friend I've ever had. I like her a lot.*' (Siobhan, 1991). Rumours amongst the other women in the convent began to circulate that Siobhan and Claire were lovers. Several residents told me they were seen holding hands in the garden. Siobhan was seen with her arm around Claire while they watched television. I was told they would creep into each other's bed at night. The other women were watching the couple and there was an air of excitement about their so-called 'love relationship'. Eventually Sister was told and Claire was called in and reprimanded. Claire ran away and Siobhan was blamed for causing her to go. Siobhan was very upset for quite some time. She said to me, '*Now I have no one. I am quite alone.*' (Siobhan, 1991). Siobhan never confirmed or denied that she and Claire were lovers. Given the strong consensus about what was appropriate behaviour, and the extent to which the women policed themselves, it is unlikely that she would have been prepared to do so. Thompson argues that:

> To be heterosexual, all a woman needs to do is to fall unthinkingly in with what everyone does . . . To be a lesbian . . . requires some measure of self-reflection, or at least self-consciousness (1993: 170).

Siobhan did not make that sort of decision and did not name herself yet she was self-reflective about her sensual desires as her comments about being alone after Claire ran away indicates. The way the incident developed highlights the extent of surveillance in the convents, even as late as the 1990s, as the women acted as a control over each other. Siobhan was not liked by many of the women in Angel convent. They would move away from her when she came into a room, avert their eyes when she spoke, often becoming silent in her presence. Telling Sister about the relationship between Claire and Siobhan was one way of getting at Siobhan and it also shows the extent to which sexuality was still a taboo area for the women who lived in the convent in the late twentieth century.

There were acceptable ways of 'not speaking' about desire. The following is one example of how the women expressed their feelings without being exposed.

There were particular stories about a care worker who was reputed to '*spend time with a number of women*' (Jane, 1991). There was never any public display of affection. She was popular and stories about her were associated with pleasure and warmth. She would take people to the cinema or sit and talk to them at night if they were frightened in the dark. During a creative writing class several of the women chose to write a poem about her. The following is the result:

Talking about U.

She is fairly tall and pale.
She wears glasses.
She has short black straight hair.
She wears blue jeans and white shoes.
Some people think she looks like a boy.
I was waiting at a bus stop once
and I was talking to U
And this woman asked me if I was talking to my boyfriend.
I laughed and so did U (Creative Writing Group, 1985)

The poem begins by describing U, her body shape, her hair and her clothes. The poem then hints at her sexual difference, 'some people thinks she looks like a boy'. The 'male' character was, as I indicated above, the only symbol that was charged with 'sex' in the initial discussions I had with the women. Although three women composed the poem, the next few lines move into the first person singular. This makes the event of the bus stop personal and quite sexually charged. The 'boy' has become 'boyfriend' and the shared laughter suggests shared knowledge. It has a sense of excitement and fun and whether U was actually having affairs with the women or not, she was clearly, from this poem, an object of desire. I would not suggest that the women who composed the poem would necessarily see this desire for U as relating to sexuality. The 'talk' within the poem is veiled and is conducted in the safe environment of a creative writing class. Unlike Claire and Siobhan, the feelings were not discussed or relayed to the Sister in charge, creating an interesting mix of talk and silence, where boundaries were known and taken for granted.

Erotic images did occupy some of the women's thoughts and some also explored aspects of sexuality that would be considered 'perverse' by many in society. The sexuality was unnamed and the talk was veiled. In the next section I argue that if adults with learning difficulties continue to be infantilised, they could experience sensual pleasure like the women in the convents without an appreciation of how it is understood by society or even understanding the potential dangers attached to the activity. While there are aspects that are appealing for women about the opportunities that unnamed silent sexuality offers, it also creates great vulnerability. I will explain how this appeal and vulnerability operated in the convents by discussing a number of abusive relationships that the women discussed during my time at the convents.

Fascination and Vulnerability

Since the 1970s, there has been a growing desire amongst professionals working with people with learning difficulties to see 'valid' and 'appropriate' sexual expression supported and encouraged (McCarthy and Thompson, 1994; Smith and Stuart, 1995). Craft's groundbreaking book, *Mental Handicap and Sexuality* (1987), sets out six basic rights that she saw as central to the development of a sexuality for people with mental handicap:

> The right to grow up . . . The right to know . . . The right to be sexual and make and break relationships . . . The right not to be at the mercy of the individual sexual attitudes of different care-givers . . . The right not (to) be sexually abused. The right to humane and dignified environments. (Craft, 1987: 26)

This charter of rights was a useful starting point for a group of people who have been historically denied sexual expression (Craft, 1987). In addition to a belief that people with learning difficulties should be able to be active sexually, concern has been expressed by practitioners and researchers that people with learning difficulties are often vulnerable in sexual encounters. In particular, Brown and Craft (1989) exposed some of the sexual abuses that people with learning difficulties have suffered:

> People with learning difficulties have been ignored as victims and the implications of traumatic sexual experiences minimised because the service has not been able to deal with its own ambiguity (Brown and Craft, 1989: 76)

In the convents, the issue of abuse was often hidden. Siobhan was always keen to express her sexuality and did discuss some of her feelings with me. As well as her feelings for other women she would occasionally attempt to form sexual relationships with men she met in the street. She would sometimes spend time near men's public toilets. When I asked her why she would do this she said:

> *It's all I can get. It's hard to meet men, especially if you're like me and it's all I can get. I get excited there. My mum says I mustn't want men, and Sister, but I want it. I can't help it if it makes me feel nice. It's funny. It smells funny. It's sort of dark and the walls are all smooth and cold.*

I asked her if she would like to have sex somewhere else like a bedroom. She replied:

> *I'd like to get married and do it. That's what you're supposed to do* (Siobhan, 1990).

Siobhan was barred from going out of the convent grounds for some time after being caught in the men's toilets at the local shopping centre. Her story is a mixture of conflicting messages. She says 'doing it' makes her feel nice but she also reproduced the traditional vision of sex in marriage in her conversation with me. It is difficult to tell if she liked the atmosphere of the men's toilet or the more direct excitement associated with sexual activity itself. Siobhan comments on the feeling of the walls as 'smooth' and 'cold', which might be related to pleasant feelings. The smell of the toilets is not described as unpleasant but 'funny', indicating that she does not regard the environment as offensive.

She also says 'it is all I can get' and describes herself as less able or attractive, 'especially if you're like me'. Begum says of disabled women's body image:

> Through the countless images of beauty that find their way into the daily lives of women, the message that they must have a certain appearance to be admired and loved, particularly by men, is internalised. Certain aspects of disability can make it difficult for a woman to incorporate her physical characteristics and her daily needs into this concept of attractiveness (1992: 77)

Perhaps Siobhan felt she would not be able to form a more stable and permanent relationship, because she had, as Begum suggests, 'internalised conventional images of beauty'.

Taking Siobhan's actions out of her context, where the activity made her 'feel nice' and she got 'excited', would suggest that she was being exploited by the men in the toilets. Her carers saw the situation in this way and 'gated' her, forcing her to stay in the convent grounds for several months. What the men felt or thought about Siobhan is impossible to know and is not the issue here. For Siobhan, the men were all she 'can get' but she was also struggling to express her own sexuality within severe limitations. Her interpretation of events shows she was aware of her own sensual desires even if she was not aware of how the consequences would affect her. At this level, it was Siobhan who was using the men. The repression of desire by her mother and 'Sister' created even more desire to act and it is possible that Siobhan was gaining pleasure precisely because others considered her activities outrageous.

She was obviously not acting responsibly but it is difficult to see how she could be expected to do so, given the extent of 'care' and 'control' that others had over her life. In other words, choice was extremely limited and responding oppositionally to others' decisions about her life was all that was left to her, a state of childish reactive behaviour. While this state of childhood potentially offers women spaces in which to engage in active sexual pleasures, it also increases their vulnerability.

Siobhan's activities made her vulnerable to a range of potential dangers. In several of the other stories, it became clear to me that because the Sisters saw the women as children, they did not believe their sexual stories thus leaving the women even more vulnerable. Many people have complicated feelings about sexuality in Western society and, as Brown and Craft say of carers, they have 'not been able to deal with (their) own ambiguity' (Brown and Craft, 1989: 76) about sex. The adult education tutor at Angel convent told me that she had often spoken to the Sister-in-charge about sex:

> *It used to amaze me the up to date knowledge Sister had on sexuality . . . We used to talk about some of the parents, about their sexual problems. She knew it all . . . It used to make me think – just what is going on in your mind?*

However, she also felt that she did not want to be 'up to date' with the sexual activities of the women:

> *I don't think she wanted to know. I think she thought that she ran that convent like clockwork and underneath all that clockwork was all this mechanism going on. People leaping in and out of bed with each other and doing their own thing. As long as Sister didn't know about it, then everything was going to be all right* (Adult Education Tutor, 1996).

Clearly her attitude was inconsistent, possibly related to an ambiguous attitude towards sex and sexual feelings for herself and the women residents, as the next illustration suggests.

There were few men who worked at the convents but in Angel convent Thomas the gardener was often referred to in conversations with the women. Most of the women disliked him but one woman, Yvonne, told me she was going to marry Thomas (Yvonne, 1990). Yvonne was always talking about Thomas and how he took her to the garden shed. While I was facilitating an adult education course on women's bodies, Yvonne told me she wanted to kiss Thomas. Other members of staff would dismiss her comments as fanciful as Thomas was 'in his sixties'. On one occasion when we were discussing menstruation, Yvonne began shouting abuse at me and left the room. When I was able to speak to her on her own, she told me Thomas would put his hand '*down my knickers*' when she had her period (Yvonne, 1990). Yvonne said she knew it was wrong and '*that's why I shouted at you*' (Yvonne, 1990) but that she liked him doing it.

Having discussed with Yvonne how she wanted me to proceed, I raised the matter with the Sister-in-charge. She dismissed the story out of hand, saying that Yvonne was always making up stories about her period and that she had an unhealthy, silly interest in Thomas. While the Sister agreed to remove Yvonne from garden work, she did not believe Yvonne's story. Yvonne was also removed from my class.

The Sister was attempting to create a wall of silence about the incident. Several months later I heard from another woman that Yvonne had been sexually assaulted by Thomas with a garden spade and had to go to hospital to have stitches (Jane, 1991). What I feel is significant about this story is not whether in fact Thomas did put his hand down Yvonne's knickers, although that is a serious issue, but the effect the relationship was having on Yvonne. There was a combination of fascination and fear at work in her story. Yvonne was frightened about what she was doing. She knew it was 'wrong' but she was also gaining pleasure from the experience.

Yvonne wanted to marry Thomas and clearly he was engaging with her in some sort of sexual way. She wanted his touch and his attention and had romantic notions about him, but the final incident with the spade was a horrifying conclusion. The whole story emphasises the need to recognise women's sexual desires and confessions and to treat them seriously. Ignoring them or seeing them as childish fantasies created greater vulnerability for the women. My attempts to raise the matter were unsuccessful and I am still unsure and, at times, unhappy about the course of action that I took.

Clearly, the power relations between Yvonne and Thomas were enormously unequal. However, the relationship, as many abusive relationships in which women participate (Benjamin, 1983), was fulfilling a need in Yvonne. Despite the obvious abuse and physical violence of the final incident, Yvonne expressed desires for Thomas and these should have been treated seriously and explored with her.

As with Siobhan, Yvonne wanted to express her sensuality. These two women were fascinated by the possibilities of pleasure, complex and problematic as that may have been. It is important to understand the context of these women's attempts to gain pleasure. The difficulty they were experiencing was not at the level of their desire or the conditions in which they found themselves but rather the power/dependency dynamics (McCarthy and Thompson, 1994) that were at work both in the relationship with the men concerned and the power/dependency relationship with their 'carers'. As Shakespeare states:

> We need to remember that power is a feature of relationships between all subjects, and there are various hierarchies in which people are multiply positioned . . . When disability comes into play, conventional relationships of gender, age, sexuality and power may become more complex and nuanced (1996: 213).

In other words, simply seeing unequal power relations in sexual activities is not sufficient to explain behaviour and feelings and the context in which people express themselves requires further analysis. Examining sexual activities will only provide the basis for understanding sexual feelings. Examining the meanings, the social context and the complexities of different power relationships within the sexual encounter provides a fuller picture of sexual experience. For example, in Yvonne's case her ambivalence about Thomas led her to ask me to speak to the Sister in charge about her relationship. Yet, her 'carer' did not take her comments seriously, in some sense allowing the relationship to continue unacknowledged and without limits. This lack of recognition made Yvonne highly vulnerable. However, the carers themselves were struggling to address conflicts arising from social and moral attitudes about sexuality as well as their own feelings about sex.

If some of the residents crossed the boundary of acknowledgeable and acceptable sexual attitudes, they fell into another more dangerous realm of 'silence', a space where activities were not only denied but ignored, as with

Yvonne. This silence created, as Benjamin suggests, 'a fear of boundlessness; women involved in activities however disturbing or perverse . . .(that) express deep yearnings for selfhood and transcendence' (Benjamin, 1983: 281). Yvonne was unsure about the boundaries of her relationship. She felt limits should be placed on her involvement with Thomas, and by talking to me, she attempted to set boundaries. She liked Thomas's touch and she wanted some sort of acknowledgement and recognition of herself. She was also unclear about the activities she was engaged in and, by those in authority ignoring her desire for clarification of right and wrong, Yvonne was placed 'beyond' safety in a boundless world where abuse was possible. Acknowledging her desire would have created boundaries and would have made her less vulnerable.

In an attempt to establish themselves as sexual beings, women like Siobhan and Yvonne were placing themselves outside the acceptable, the spoken about. The convent's denial of desire and bodily pleasure only enabled its expression in marginal conditions and left the women vulnerable. Joanna told me that such stories were common in her experience:

> *People shouldn't be surprised at that* (Yvonne's story) . . .*it was quite common, people would be paid off. One woman was having a relationship with one of the men that worked at Mother. She was sent away for a termination and came back. He just carried on working there, no discipline or recourse* . . .
>
> *Yeah, that was another peculiar area when you think about the morality of these things, . . . it was also to do with a reverence for men. Men got away with all sorts of things, the gardener was allowed to stay* (Joanna, 1996).

Silence was more important than speaking. Cover-ups were more acceptable than having to face the complex of sexual practices that the convents produced. Equally, Joanna highlighted a broader point about who has the right to be heard and valued. The men in these accounts, as with Thomas, were able to continue working in the convents while the women were ignored and devalued.

Yvonne's story is itself complex and is more than a description of an abusive act. Yvonne's own desire for Thomas needed to be acknowledged and her understandings of the situation valued. In the final section of this chapter I argue that particular difficulties highlighted in these stories about sexuality in the convents have wider implications for the development of sexual identities.

Paradoxes and Dilemmas: Sexual Connections between Women

The stories from the convents reveal a number of significant points that feed into current debates on sexualities at the turn of the century. Plummer argues that 'sexual stories (that are) categorically clear can no longer hold and in their place come stories of deconstruction'(Plummer, 1995: 134). Our perceptions of ourselves as one particular 'type' of person are no longer possible as life stories have become more complex. Women's bodies have been historically 'the battleground on which quite other struggles . . . have been waged' (Jacobus, Fox Keller and Shuttleworth, 1990: 2). In other words, women's sexuality has often been at the centre of a definition of appropriate social morality and, as noted at the beginning of the chapter, this has been especially the case in Catholicism.

The convents are in many ways a symbol of the dilemmas of many women today. The fixed category of a mature sexuality, like taking on a role of 'mother', limits the potential for pleasure for women by emphasising a demeanour of modesty and a set of values that focus on self-control and acceptance. While it is valid to suggest that motherhood does offer women power, it does not offer them an active sexuality because it is based on the principles of denial and control (Chodorow, 1978). However, the possibilities for play in a childish sexuality can engender difficulties, as seen in the relationships of Yvonne and Siobhan.

Carers and services still find it difficult to imagine a sexuality for people with learning difficulties. As McCarthy and Thompson say, 'it is easier to see signs of exploitation than of mutuality'(1994: 46). The complexities of vulnerability and abuse set against personal pleasure are difficult to resolve especially with groups of people who have historically been seen as 'children' and 'in need of care'. This is not to condone abuse. However, focusing on the extent of desire and choice in sexual practice offers a more subtle understanding of sexuality. Recognising the validity of Siobhan's desire for pleasure and the reality of Yvonne's feelings would provide a better starting point to explore sexual safety than ignoring their experience.

Working on the area of sexuality was the most problematic aspect of my time with the convent residents as I constantly felt unable to make appropriate decisions about disclosure, and felt that my involvement was sometimes a negative one, altering the delicate balance of talk and silence that prevailed in the convents about sexual desires and practices.

The women watched over each other. Often the Sisters ignored activities, thus creating a lack of safety in an environment which ostensibly provided a haven. For the Sisters, ideas about sexuality itself was complicated by their own contradictory attitudes. The experience of the Sisters echoes many other services for people with learning difficulties where decisions about acceptable sexuality between service users is still seen as a contentious issue. The history of provision for people with learning difficulties has been bound up by concerns about sex which remain unresolved even today. It is, therefore, vital that carers are able to engage with this debate, acknowledging the complexity of their own feelings and recognising the continuing influence of past moral values. Only then will they be able to develop an acceptance with people with learning difficulties of their right to sexual expression as Craft (1987) argued nearly fifteen years ago. For Catholics, the role of women in society was intrinsically connected to procreation or celibacy in service to God. This dichotomy created ambiguity in attitudes to sex for the women in the convents. Many of the convent residents found themselves in abusive, but also sometimes, in pleasurable relationships. The convents often ignored the women's sexual activities, to the extent that they were placed in highly vulnerable situations. This was partly to do with the contradictory feelings towards sex that the Sisters experienced themselves, highlighting the need for greater clarity about sexual practice and sexual experience. Yet, the women's feelings about their sexual practices were also contradictory and were, as with other aspects of their lives, not just about victimisation. The realm of sexuality highlights the complexities and problems in trying to speak with one voice about people with learning difficulties. It is clear there are many stories to hear and many voices with different perspectives.

The meaning attached to the experience of sexuality is vital to an understanding of the complexity of sexuality for women in general and especially for women in positions of vulnerability. While support for sexual expression and 'pleasure and joy' (Smart, 1996) is an ideal, prescriptive attempts at defining a sexuality for women with learning difficulties remains elusive. One solution could be to work towards a 'moral pluralism' (Weeks, 1986) where there is an acceptance of different desires leading to an 'intimate citizenship' (Plummer, 1995) which enshrines rights to intimacy.

The current debate on sexuality and people with learning difficulties has become stuck in a deterministic view of 'appropriare behaviour', still influenced by ideas of 'passing' as 'normal' (Wolfensberger 1972). However, sexual expression in our society is diverse and thinking more creatively about the 'proper balance between private pleasures and public policies' (Weeks, 1986:120), may lead to a greater emphasis on rights. Women with learning difficulties have been particularly scrutinised over the last century and a half (Jones, 1986; Craft, 1987; Brown and Craft, 1989). Perhaps now it is possible to be less rigid about sexualities and to enable women to express their sexuality safely and without prejudice.

Chapter 7

'In the world but not of it': Community Care and the Convents in the New Era

The NHS and Community Care Act (1990) made sweeping changes to the nature of provision for people with learning difficulties and this chapter focuses on the convent movement's response to this legislation as well as the residents' experiences of that response. It discusses the process of closure of Mother convent and the movement into community-based housing for women from both Mother and Angel convents. It identifies the upheaval and trauma experienced by the closure of Mother convent and different responses to living outside the care of the convents. It charts the development of more inward-looking policies at Angel convent, contrasting these with Mother convent's embracing of life in the community. Using specific women's stories, the chapter examines the experiences of different groups of women who moved into the community. These stories express different attitudes to living in the wider community and indicate differences that exist between people who carry the label learning difficulties. The chapter begins by contextualising the social position of the convents in the new era of community care.

A New Playing Field

The NHS and Community Care Act (1990) formed part of a process of change from 'incarceration' for people defined as 'feeble-minded' towards people with learning difficulties living 'in the community'. The picture of 'community care' is complex and cannot be reduced to a functional notion of service plans within social services and health authorities. Even institutional care, which could be seen as a part of a particular era of public planning, affected people who were defined as having a learning difficulty in different ways. Institutions come in different forms and have different meanings, for both the residents of the institution and for the wider society. The effects of the 1990s' legislation was far reaching and forced public sector institutions, such as social services, to justify their existence and re-think their identity. The Act created quasi-markets where public services were to distinguish their role as purchaser of services from those as providers, creating a part market-driven service provision. Direct payments, whereby users could buy their own support, challenged the traditional paternalistic role of welfare. User involvement was encouraged in the planning of services and in the evaluation of quality, although how real this involvement is has been questioned (Dowson, 1997). However, questions of 'choice', like definitions of 'institution', 'culture' and 'care' discussed earlier in the book, are taken for granted within much policy literature. How user involvement and choice of lifestyle can be implemented within a service model, which continues to be determined by 'needs', rather than wants, is problematic. As Ramcharan, Roberts, Grant and Borland point out, 'by conflating the two (needs and wants) the power for identifying services on the basis of needs assessment is transferred from the service user to the professional' (1997a: 176).

As well as these moves to greater consumerism, the Act sped up the closure of institutions. Some studies have noted that smaller households, once seen as the correct place for a life in the community, are reproducing institutionalised environments (Collins, 1992; Cambridge, Hayes and Knapp, 1994), for example by continuing to determine who people live with, what time they go to bed or where they go during the day (Dowson, 1997: 106). Yet, many people who have moved out of institutions report being happier in their new lives in homes in the wider community (Cambridge, Hayes and Knapp, 1994: 103; Hatton and Emerson, 1996). The experience of living in 'ordinary settings' is still being debated and the principle of normalisation, as I discussed in Chapter One, is being re-evaluated (Brown and Smith, 1992).

As well as public sector provision, the voluntary sector has been active in developing services for people with learning difficulties throughout the last century. The 1990s legislation placed greater emphasis on the role of voluntary sector organisations and they too had to adapt to the new social environment (Atkin, 1996). Some of these organisations had an explicit religious or spiritual intention (Emerson, Hatton, Cullen and Cross, 1996), such as the L'Arche or Steiner communities (Segal, 1990). While organisations like these communities were affected by changes in public policy, their own internal beliefs and values had as much impact on their changing identity as public decisions like 'care in the community'. These beliefs and value systems structure the strategies and plans of spiritual organisations differently to state organisations. Some theorists (Vanier, 1982; Robinson, 1989; Segal, 1990; Brown and Smith, 1992) argue that such spiritual communities have a special and perhaps 'better' way of life to offer residents than the materialistic post-industrial world that we live in. Wolfensberger (1983) has also argued that provision in public services is imbued with materialism. Such work suggests that community care emphasises consumerism and materialistic demands and does not therefore provide a value system worth emulating.

Debates on this theme are keen. Paul Williams (1995) and Rouix, Bach and Crawford (1997) argue that segregated communities mitigate against 'citizenship'. For, by choosing segregation, the responsibilities of citizenship to engage in and contribute to the society are withdrawn. However, as Ramcharan, Roberts, Grant and Borland point out:

> Whether inclusion should be an end in itself, whatever the effects on the individual, poses another vital question which, if ignored, could lead to further oppression of society's most vulnerable citizens (1997b: 256).

In other words, the principles espoused by notions of citizenship, rights and 'ordinary living', are problematic and 'choice' in lifestyle is still a contested debate. These debates contribute to the re-evaluation of normalisation. Using the convents as a case study, the section below examines the experience of 'place' for the residents in the convents indicating that feeling part of any community is important to personal identity and that making 'choices' about lifestyles is more complicated than is often suggested.

The Community of Religious

Once the women entered the convents, they were given a role. They became part of the convent community. The community member's role could be, and sometimes was, a demeaning one but the residents could still see themselves as part of the community because they had a place and a role in that community.

Both the Sisters and the women they cared for were outsiders to the wider British society. They shared a sense of otherness. While writing her life story, Mary reflected on being allowed to talk to 'outsiders' for the first time:

> *It was very strange at first, because people thought that the residents were either nuns or lunatics, but slowly they began to realise we were just like other people . . . (Mary, 1994b: 16)*

Experiences were common to the Sisters and the residents, including celibacy, attendance at mass, observance of silence and early rising and sleep times. Work and leisure activities were conducted within a clear hierarchy where the Sisters were in charge of decisions. Power relations were constructed with parallel structures for advancement for Sisters and residents and while some of the women became 'sub-nuns', they never crossed the divide to become Sisters. This hierarchy not only operated between the Sisters and the residents but, amongst the different groups of women, each group had its own hierarchy. Both residents and Sisters shared a common religious faith and only a few residents were not Catholic. This shared faith made the women part of a larger Catholic community within Britain and the larger international community of Catholics presided over by the Pope in Rome. Although at face value all the women could claim membership of a range of other communities, most had been abandoned by these communities. The community of the convent, and with it, the religious community of the Sisters, was the strongest allegiance that most of the women had. Yet, one of the major philosophical roots of care in the community was that:

> . . . care receivers should be able, wherever possible, to live in normal houses in local communities, supported where necessary in meeting their needs. They should be able to be integrated into local activity – in short, should enjoy an ordinary life rather than a life apart (Dalley, 1989: 201).

For some of the women living in the convent, this notion was problematic. What they knew was convent life and this was the world that had given them a 'place'. As Martha told me, '*there are worse places you could spend your life*' (Martha, 1992). Hence, for both the Sisters and the residents, views about 'normalisation' were contradictory.

For some of the Sisters and some of the residents, the Catholic doctrines espoused at Vatican II[1] could offer a theological basis for care in the community. However, Catholic belief in 'community' is rooted in the

[1] For further explanation of Vatican II see Chapter One.

religious parish, not the wider secular world. Within these particular cultural beliefs, the language of 'choice' and 'community care' may well have different meanings to lay professionals. These contradictions created tensions within the movement itself and led to very different solutions in different convents. The next section explores these conflicts by comparing the different stories provided by the convent residents with accounts from other people who have lived in long-stay institutions.

Living with What You Know

For the residents, attitudes to living in the convents produced conflicting emotions about the outside world. Sometimes these feelings reflected the Sisters' world view and at other times were different to their perceptions. Several of the women had very mixed feelings about possible lifestyles that might be available to them. Alice had lived in the convent since her sister decided that she was unable to care for her after she finished boarding school. Alice was a friendly woman who was considered a sub-nun and who was given responsibility for a number of the other women. She lived in one of the cottages within the grounds of Angel convent and was openly critical of some of the practices of the Sisters:

> *They never pay us enough. We work so hard and we just get pocket money. Sister Ida's the one you have to watch out for. She's got a stick.* (Alice, 1990).

Sister Ida walked with a stick and Alice told me she would sometimes use it to hit women on the backs of their knees. After complaints about Sister Ida's behaviour, she was retired in 1994.

Alice attended a range of courses designed to assist independent living at the local adult education centre, including cookery, community studies and budgeting. She had developed the confidence to travel on her own. She became a regular Saturday shopper, spending her 'wage' of £3.00 per week on toiletries and the *Radio Times*. Despite what would be regarded as good preparation for 'moving into the community' and her criticisms of the Sisters, when I asked Alice if she would like to move, she told me, '*No, I don't think so. I like the cottage, you're safe there*' (Alice, 1990). This comment surprised me but it was clear that Alice felt she knew the convent and, to a certain extent, believed that she was safer there than in the wider community.

This sentiment was repeated by a number of women interviewed in both convents. Moira, who lived in Mother convent, told me, '*If we have to move out, we have to. I'm facing up to reality, although I don't want to go.*'(Moira, 1993). Other older residents said, '*No, I'm settled here. They left it too late. I've only got a few years left. I'm settled*' (Elvera, 1993) and Martha, '*I chose this Catholic life you see. I like the old ways*' (Martha, 1992).

These views of some of the women in the convents are echoed in some other life history accounts of people with learning difficulties who were institutionalised. In *Know me as I am*, Bill Challis of Leavesden Hospital, Hertfordshire comments:

> May I . . . express with absolute horror the very thought of being put into what is termed a community home? Having reached the age of nearly 70, I am well settled here. I am of informal status, which means I am able to discharge myself if I so wish. But I want to remain where I am. I have friends all around me. The world outside does not bother me any more. I have been indoctrinated through a system, which destroys all freedom of thinking . . . I do not want too much freedom, just enough to let me know that I can come and go if I desire (Atkinson and Williams, 1990: 99).

There are a number of common elements shared between this viewpoint and some of the ones that I encountered when interviewing the women in the convents. The women had established a way of life with friends, routine, and, they said, safety. Those who wanted to stay in the convents were older, usually those over sixty.[2]

While there are common elements between the convent women's stories and the comments of Bill Challis, above, there are notable differences based on the Catholic convent community and its language of symbols that the women used to make sense of their lives. The idea of change frightened these women but some also felt they had embraced convent life successfully. This world view was not always appreciated or understood by

[2] The question of age and people with learning difficulties has not been fully acknowledged and is one factor that affects life choices (Walker, Walker and Ryan, 1996). Further discussion on issues of older women in the convent can be found later in this chapter.

care staff or social workers who came to the convents. While their concern to remain in the convents could be seen as the women having been 'indoctrinated through a system which destroys all freedom of thinking . . .' (Challis, above) it should also be recognised that the Catholic religion itself has significant symbolic and personal meaning for some of these older residents. Martha, who died at the age of ninety-seven in 1995, told me:

> *The staff are all right, but they bother me when I'm praying. They don't seem to realise what I'm doing . . . said to me, get off the floor, you'll catch your death', but I was praying. You have to do that on your knees* (Martha, 1992).

For some of the women, in particular the older women, rather than focusing on the negative aspect of 'indoctrination', as Bill Challis experienced, felt their beliefs and convictions were a positive reason for staying.

Recognition of spiritual values echoes the ideas expressed by Vanier (1982) and Brown and Smith (1992) about the L'Arche communities. Many secular care workers do not understand religious belief. The lay care manager of Mother convent wrote after she resigned:

> I had at the point of taking up the post, no particular conviction or interest in religion (Brown, Y, 1994).

This view is common amongst secular care workers and while it is possible to value spiritual beliefs without an 'interest in religion', it is difficult to understand it. Whether the reasons for staying were religious belief, as with Maria, or a feeling that what you know is better than what you do not, as with Alice, these women were certain that they wanted to live in the convents, suggesting that 'choice' is problematic in developing 'community care'.

The convent movement's response to care in the community had been to establish an advisory board that reported to their movement's social care board. The advisory board argued that they should provide communities within communities:

> As a Congregation, we would promote a policy of care in the community, working in close collaboration with local authorities so as to avoid duplication in services (SMG, 1992).

A range of recommendations ensued, including the appointment of a social worker for each resident, the extension of day and respite care, greater choice in activities, the appointment of a lay co-ordinator across all the services and the development of professional training for Sisters. The movement would continue to offer a residential service where this was demanded in 'cottages' in the grounds of convents, or 'flats' in the main buildings. Women who wanted to live in the 'outside' world would be able to board with approved families from the wider Catholic community that would provide a sort of safety net to help them maintain their friendships and practice their beliefs. Aspects of the community care provided in the convents during the 1980s and 1990s was rooted in the principles of Vatican II with the Religious community working with the laity.

At Mother convent, a female lay care manager was appointed in 1989. She extended day services, encouraging service users from the locality to come into the convent. For a time, this policy was highly successful. Staff were able to transform the old residential site imaginatively, offering on-site cafés, some part-time work for residents and ex-residents, an art studio and a charity shop. At Angel convent, Sister Ruth developed links with a range of local authority community opportunities, including adult and further education and leisure services. Day-care and respite for non-convent residents was also established here.

At a national level, the new lay co-ordinator for the care services of the movement, found, as some other voluntary organisations discovered, that working with local authorities was more complex than the movement had imagined. Reading comments that despite the possibilities in the NHS and Community Care Act for voluntary organisations, smaller organisations, such as the convents, were not benefiting:

> Public authorities are likely to prefer one large contract to a plethora of smaller ones, and even when small organisations are successful, they will take on the features of larger agencies (Reading, 1994: 25).

Despite local successes, the new Foundation found developing different services for people with learning difficulties problematic to organise and, as a result, facilities were reduced. The culture of the convent movement clashed with secular social services, usually over the reluctance of the Order to change traditional practices, including controlling how local Sisters operated particular care homes, as is highlighted in the closure of Mother convent. The impact of this decision affected the women who lived there differently as I discuss below.

Good and Bad Practice for the Convents

> On the 25 November 1994 Mother General came down from London with her assistant in the care home department, to have a meeting with all our staff. They were at the meeting for nearly two hours. After they came out, they told us to go to the dining room. When there we were told that Mother was going to close down in two years time. You could have heard a pin drop as there was a stunned silence for at least ten minutes, then the tears came (Adams, 1995: 50).

The announcement of the closure was expected by the people who had been following developments at Mother. Later, Mary says: 'I had already guessed it was going to happen – I am no fool you know' (Adams, 1995:50). The convent movement was struggling to maintain its position in the field. Fewer women have chosen to become nuns since the 1960s and the care work could no longer be maintained only by the Sisters. Joanna, the lay care manager of Mother, told me:

> *I'm sure it's to do with a recognition of not being able to do the jobs they always wanted to and they haven't got the numbers to continue, they haven't got the numbers to continue control. They will have to be handing over to laity and they don't want to do that so better get out really* (1996).

Financially, the Sisters did not receive pay, but convents had to budget for their salaries which went directly into the movement's central funds. As the number of Sisters declined, so too did their financial base. The lay care manager found that her decisions were not always final. If the Order wished a Sister to move to another convent, the lay care manager had to accept their ruling. As financial tensions also increased, the Order decided to close Mother convent:

> *I have to say the biggest problem overall was my financial management 'cause most of the money had always previously been creamed off and gone to head office . . .* (Joanna, 1996).

Joanna altered the practices within the convent considerably and was not prepared to work within the religious framework of the convents that required obedience and silence. Initially she was popular with the Generalate, having put forward a plan to expand day services in the convent. I asked her why she thought attitudes changed:

> *No idea . . . yeah . . . well my idea was always to close it anyway, eventually, but to ensure that there was a stable core unit of perhaps a half to a dozen people to take account of the elderly people and also to offer the back up where people could come back if needed . . ., it basically went wrong when the relationship broke down over what was technically a totally unrelated issue . . . they realised how far things had gone out of their control with no way of clawing it back so the only way of dealing with it was to get rid of it . . . You know it was an experiment and it failed* (Joanna, 1996).

It is probably because of the distrust that developed between the Order and the lay care manager that the closure was announced without any further discussion allowed. The implementation of the closure and the effects on residents over the following two years, until the convent finally closed in October 1996, were equally difficult.

When I interviewed Joanna, she told me:

> *It was done in exactly two years and as you say a lot of people have died . . .*
>
> (MS:) How long would you have wanted (for closure)?
>
> (Joanna:) *I think I estimated five to eight and that was overall so in some ways six years was in that boundary but I don't think I would have done it . . . I think yeah, I wouldn't have done it in such a pushy way but . . . (they were) under pressure to do that. It denied a lot of people choice. We have a lot of people who are out of county now . . .not everybody has had those choices and nobody has checked about the care and as to whether they are doing okay there hasn't been a follow up . . . and that is what I find so crazy that there wasn't an option for them . . .Yeah how do people make choices if they don't have options and experiences? How can you make a decision*

> *without actually trying something. It's no good going to tea somewhere, you need to experience living there* (1996).

The new lay care manager, Andrew, who took over after Joanna left, brought in social workers to support people in making their choices about where they wanted to go. This was better practice than in many other environments (Brown and Smith, 1992: 153). However, the ultimatum of closure meant that women were not able to take sufficient time to decide their future lifestyles. This has been noted in many closures (MacDonald, 1990). When discussing relocating people from residential accommodation, Brearley et al. states:

> Change creates hazards and potential dangers and good preparation, planning and support can help reduce these hazards and dangers (Brearley et al, 1982: 9).

Six of my informants at Mother convent died before the closure was complete. Many of the older residents in the convent found the proposed closure terrifying. Gloria commented:

> *. . . And what about Martha? She'll be ninety-seven soon. This is her life. I don't mean to be cruel or anything, but I hope she dies before they do it. She's so unhappy. If I have to go, I will but I want to stay somewhere in the area to be near my friends* (1995).

Before the announcement of the closure, Gloria 'tried out' a placement with a family in the local area, but decided she did not want to live there. Gloria felt she would be able to save for her holidays better if she stayed in the convent's residential accommodation (Gloria, 1993). After the closure was announced, there was more pressure placed on residents to move. The Generalate had designated October 1996 as the month for closure and by that time over thirty women had to be placed in new homes.

In May 1995, Gloria agreed to move away from the local area to a different county about 150 miles from her friends. She agreed to this move because it was a residential facility for older people run by the same convent movement. When Gloria died at the end of 1995, she had been unhappy in her new residence. Martha died in September 1995. Some research (Brearley, et al, 1982; Lawrence, et al, 1987) has suggested that relocation may be connected to high mortality rates and although it is difficult to be certain of the reasons for the numbers of deaths during the closure period, perhaps the experience at Mother convent could provide further evidence of this connection.

Maria also said to me:

> *When he asked me where I wanted to live and I said, 'here, I want to live here'* (at the convent), *he just said that wasn't possible . . . but I like the convent, so I said, 'well then it would have to be another convent 'cause that's what I know and I'm quite religious'. There's nowhere else for me to go. No one else would want me* (1995).

Maria's feelings are complex. She does not think she would be 'wanted' in any other community but also feels positive about her religious beliefs. Maria is one of the women who said she would have liked to have been a nun, *'but it wasn't possible'* (Maria, 1992).

She felt she belonged to a community within the convent and was frightened about what other life she could have had in any other community, or, as Brearley et al suggest, 'loss disrupts our ability to find a continuity of meaning in our experience' (1982: 20). Maria died in April 1996, just before the closure. Elvera was still alive in 1997. She moved into a small house in the local area that was run by the movement with six other women from Mother convent.

During the period of closure, there was extensive pressure to find new living accommodation for women who had lived in the convent for many years. The women were generally quite clear about one aspect of their new living arrangements. Like Gloria, they wanted to remain in the local area. Tess and Louise felt strongly that they wanted to be with their friends:

> *I would like my friends to come and have a cup of tea and a chat and listen to music. I would buy a new kettle for them if I get to move and go to a church for mass on Sunday morning with my friends* (Tess, 1995).

> *I want to stay in the area. I have lots of friends. I've lived here for forty-one years* (Louise, 1995).

Louise died before the convent closed and Tess was moved to another county. In reality, it was difficult for staff to find appropriate homes. If the women were out-of-county placements, which many were, it was often necessary to return them to their original area. If families were keen for the women to live nearby, it was necessary to take their views into consideration. Given the time limitations surrounding closure, it was not always possible to find accommodation in the local area that met the women's physical needs. Guidelines on choice were abandoned to meet the needs of the timescale. The picture in Figure 8 was produced by Roberta who wanted to live near her father who was in a nursing home in East Sussex. In 1995, she moved into a group home that was in the same county but was 25 miles from his accommodation.

The social worker involved in supporting people through the closure told me:

> *Again I think we failed people, because if they are off our books they are off our books, and we haven't got the time or resources to chase them up . . . I think they should have*

Figure 8

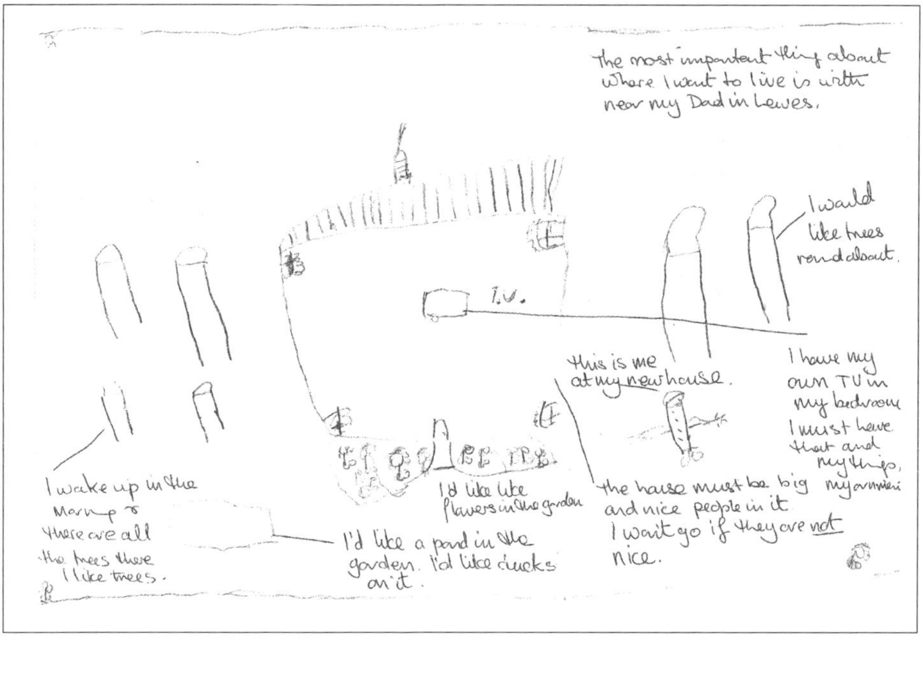

> *changed the timescale. They kept bringing the timescale nearer and nearer which meant staff began to panic, thinking 'I need a job'. I would do that myself but it means there are less and less to offer a service to the women left* (Social Worker, 1996).

Visiting Mother before it closed was depressing. The large buildings seemed empty and the few women who were left had less support as staff found other jobs. By April 1996, there was only one member of staff and a Sister on duty at night for ten women where previously the ratio had been one staff member to five residents. There were several break-ins and an agency was asked to supply a temporary staff member for sleep-ins. Inevitably as with any proposed closure, staff left to find other work. The Sisters whose numbers dwindled had come to rely on employed staff and as these staff saw their employment disappearing they left to find other work.

The women who had been abandoned by their families initially were now being abandoned by the convent movement itself. The familial identity was destroyed, and, symbolically, the 'daughters' were being forced to leave home. It is not that Mother convent had necessarily even been the 'right' place for the women, but even if individuals had seen their entry as a 'choice', as Martha had, most had been encouraged by family to live in the convents at an early age. The women did not have the experience of the outside world to make informed choices about their future lifestyle. It is difficult to see how the notion of 'choice' could be simply applied in this milieu.

At Angel convent, the repercussions of the closure of Mother convent affected the developments that had been underway since the 1970s. Sister Ruth was moved to a smaller residential facility in 1996, and a different Sister was put in charge of the home. Contact with adult education was limited and the women who lived in the convent began to have classes in the convent itself. There was a general view amongst staff that the movement as a whole would close down all its learning difficulty facilities. Joanna told me:

> *I think with them appointing a director of social care I think that's galvanised their ideas. I mean they're making lots of money on the private hospitals . . ., and they are ever so good at terminal care for people who want to be in that kind of situation, wouldn't suit me, but yes, if you're a very strong Catholic and it's quite nurturing there and the recognition that*

> *people with learning difficulties don't need nurturing they actually need to be stretched and given lots of opportunities, and they recognised that they couldn't fulfill the role that most of them had joined for* (1996).

Here Joanna is suggesting that 'nurturing' was a significant element of what the Sisters wanted from their vocation. Current social policy states, as she said, that 'people with learning difficulties don't need nurturing', hence the Sisters' role as mothers had become obsolete.

Nurturing in the context of the convents was about having a protected and controlled space with limited opportunities, but as the care manager states, people with learning difficulties 'need to be stretched and given . . . opportunities'. The culture of the convents created a care environment with punitive and protective 'mothers' and infantilised 'girls'. Care in the Community, with its emphasis on 'ordinary lives' in 'ordinary houses' (Kings Fund, 1988), highlights the role of adult status and citizenship within society. This created a conflict for the convent movement that became too great to reconcile.

The wider political decisions of the convent movement and the wider social policies affected the lives of several women negatively, particularly those who felt they had had a 'place' in the convents. However, while many of the sub-nuns were keen to stay in the convent community, they were not the only voices. The next section examines the stories of a number of convent residents who did move into the community and describes their different experiences.

Leaving Home – Finding a New Community

The residents in the convents who moved out all had their own individual feelings about their experiences. However, three distinct attitudes to living in the wider society were identifiable. There was one response which saw the convent as a prison. The women who held this view were keen to move out; most were young and had expectations of life outside the convent. There was another group that I have called the sub-nuns, who wished to remain within the convent and saw the changes which had taken place as a threat to their way of life. There was also a third group that wanted to move out of the convent buildings yet wanted to maintain the support of the staff and the contacts and friendships they had developed over the years. Each of these attitudes is represented in the following stories. The first example is of a young black woman who wanted to leave Angel convent and successfully re-negotiated her life.

Jessica had lived in a cottage in the grounds of Angel convent until 1990. She was then encouraged to move out. She was confident in her use of money and attended a local Further Education College studying word processing. When the move was planned, I asked her how she felt. She said:

> *I'm really pleased to be going. There is racism here. Some of the girls call you names. I'm getting on now and I'll be held back if I stay. I'm looking forward to making new friends* (Jessica, 1990).

Jessica moved out and stayed in a boarding house. She was not completely unsupported and when a problem developed with paying her rent, the Sisters found her a new home. Jessica was keen to break her ties with the convent and told me when I interviewed her six months after her move:

> *I wouldn't mind seeing Jane. We used to be friends, but I don't want to see the others. My life is different now. I like college and hang round with them* (Jessica, 1991).

She went on to tell me she had become involved with the black students' group at the college and was finding out about her past. Jessica's ability to find another community to relate to seems to me to be an important factor in her success in living in the community. Her story highlights the need for other community ties beyond the convent to enable successful community inclusion. As Ferns states:

> As is the case with other Black people, Black people with disabilities need to meet as a group to strengthen their own identity . . . (1992: 146).

Jessica was able to do this by becoming involved in the Black students' group where she was able to develop new friendships, claiming affiliation to a community who recognised her and offered her personal esteem and adult status. This is not always the case for people with learning difficulties. Ramcharan, Roberts, Grant and Borland point out that for most people with learning difficulties 'full inclusion in society . . . (will only be possible) when educational, community and work places are re-structured to enable that to happen' (1997b:256). However, as indicated in the case study above, cultural and community affinity is also potentially a factor in 'inclusion' and for some of the other women in the convents, this was not possible. The following story highlights the loneliness that some people moving into the community experience.

Susan was a young woman in her early twenties. She lived in Angel convent for six years. She was always keen to leave and told me, '*I don't believe in all this God stuff. Mass is a real drag. I can't wait to get out. I want a boyfriend like my sister*' (Susan, 1990). She was an able, articulate woman, who worked part-time as a cleaner. She moved into a hostel in London for young people with learning difficulties in the autumn of 1990. She made friends with one of the men in the hostel and became pregnant two months later. The man involved did not want to form a permanent relationship and Susan was distressed. She said to me, '*I wanted a boyfriend, now I'm having a baby and he's gone and left me. I know what the Sisters think. They think it serves me right*' (Susan, 1991). Susan moved to a group home and her baby was adopted. She continued to shift between part-time jobs and different relationships but told me when we met the next year, '*I've learnt now. I'm on the pill so it's okay*' (Susan, 1992). At this final interview, I asked her how she felt about the convent now and she said:

> *When I was there I wanted to leave. I still wouldn't want to live there but there were some good bits. It's a bit frightening living like I do now. They've cut my benefit so I have to work now, but sometimes I don't feel like it and I like the boys but I've learnt they don't always treat you right. Sister always used to say that . . . But I'm not unhappy, just a little lonely. Do you still see Tembe? I'd like to see her again. Where is she? Do you have a phone number? I'd like to call her. I don't have many friends* (Susan, 1992).

Susan is not unlike many young working class women working in part-time, insecure jobs afraid of greater poverty. Susan was involved with a number of men but did not feel able to establish a permanent relationship with any of them. She was very lonely and, because she had lived in the convent in her late teens and early twenties, had never developed the friendship networks which sustain many women. She had no community ties to draw on and therefore, despite living in the community, she was never able to find her place.

Amanda is an older woman in her nineties. She moved into a group home in 1988, after leaving a long-stay institution where she had lived since 1954. Before then she had lived in Mother convent from 1914. I met her at Angel convent where she attended a reminiscence group. She would come along to the convent and seemed to enjoy the company. When I asked her how she liked her new home, she became tearful and told me, '*I want to come and live here. I want to live with the Sisters*' (Amanda, 1990). She found the group home difficult and did not enjoy living with men for the first time in her life. '*They smell and are dirty. They say filthy things*' (Amanda, 1990). She missed going to mass: '*No-one will take me*', she said. Her care worker told me that Amanda's difficulty was that she had been used to going to mass regularly in her previous home but her current staff did not have the resources to get her to a service that frequently. When Amanda was asked where she would like to go for her holidays, she asked if she could stay in Angel convent, '*then I can go to mass every day*' (Amanda, 1990). The years she had spent in the long-stay institution, after she had moved out of Mother convent, had not changed her view of the importance of convent life. Thirty years on, with experience of a number of different lifestyles, she still wanted to live in a convent. The traditional preparation for 'independent living', cookery, money management, and so on, did not offer Amanda the preparation she needed to move from a female-only environment to a mixed-sex environment that was based on a secular modern world. If independent living is to be successful, the beliefs and value systems which individuals have used to make sense of their world need to be understood and valued.

The final story of community living comes from Mary Adams, who I introduced at the beginning of the book. Mary was a devout Catholic but never thought her Catholicism should mean 'a life apart' in a convent. She had always wanted to leave but had been forced to remain by her parents who felt she was '*too sensitive*' to cope with '*real life*' (Mary, 1992).

When I first met Mary in 1992, she was already being 'trained' to move out. Figure 9 is a picture of Mary in the grounds of Mother convent in 1990. In 1993, Mary moved from the main convent building to a flat owned by the movement down the road from the main convent site. She was very happy and she blossomed. Her religious belief could be expressed through her local parish community. She had been involved in parish work since the 1970s and was the first resident to go out into the wider community to sell raffle tickets for the bazaars. She was also an active member in the parish women's group. In 1993, she was elevated to being a

Figure 9

'Eucharist Minister' (Adams, 1995:48) in the church. Mary's attitude to living in the community was positive, '*I really do like being independent*' (Mary, 1994). The independence which Mary developed was supported by a number of opportunities. The convent gave her a part-time job as a receptionist for the day centre they had developed, which she found '*interesting*' (Mary, 1994). She attended a number of adult education classes: 'I am doing my final term at the University of Sussex using the computer, and have really enjoyed doing it.' (Adams, 1995:48).

Mary was a 'community care' success story. In September 1994, she moved into a bedsit of her own in an unsupported home. She became assistant tutor on adult education courses in local history and computing and co-led a reminiscence group with me. As Mary said in her developing autobiography in October 1994, 'I go up to the convent every day from Monday to Fridays to do my charges so you see I am not lonely and it suits me fine' (Adams, 1995:48). She had a range of support networks and shifted between friends and contacts in the parish community and the convent.

Mary visited her brother for Christmas holidays in December 1994. After staying a few days, she complained of stomach pains. Her brother took her back to the convent where the staff offered her a bed and cared for her and he returned home. Although she was living independently, the staff at the convent remained her 'family' in times of need. Mary continued to feel ill and had to cancel an interview appointment we had arranged. She told me, *'I don't know what it is, the doctor says I've been eating too much, but I don't know . . .* (Mary, 1995).

Mary was taken to hospital in the middle of January 1995. She was diagnosed as having cancer with a maximum of a year to live. When I visited her later that month, she was saying her rosary, a set of Catholic prayers. She told me as we discussed her condition; '*That'll teach me to do so much, to expect so much.*' I argued that she shouldn't see the disease as punishment. She continued:

> *I wonder if I should have said the things I've told you and there's the autobiography. I don't know . . . I wonder if this is God's punishment. I mean I feel ashamed of what I've said. The Sisters are good people. I've been thinking about the mass I went to for the Order last year. I remember all the things the priests said about the Sisters, all the wonderful work they have done with the poor and people who have got problems and I feel ashamed. I wouldn't be good enough to be a nun. I believe I'm going to God you know. It's a comfort. I'm glad I have that to believe in* (Mary, 1995).

Mary did change some of the stories in her autobiography. She said in the final version:

> I came to realise what wonderful people the Sisters had always been to everyone who were poor and had problems and I began to feel ashamed of myself (Adams, 1995: 49).

Mary died in March 1995 and her funeral was held in the local Catholic Church. Despite the building holding over two hundred seats, the priest had to squeeze in extra chairs. At the service, people spoke of Mary's dedication to the parish and her work for the convent. It was an emotional service and she was later buried in the grounds of the convent.

Several of the people who had known Mary were surprised at her burial place. A member of the local social services department said to me at the funeral, '*Even in death she was unable to get away from this place*' (Social Worker, 1996). Yet Mary had asked to be buried in the grounds of the convent. In her last few weeks, she had felt guilt about her challenges to the convents. She needed to come to terms with her life and illness and this was one way she felt able to express her complex emotions. Talking with her in her last few weeks made me more aware of the complex psychological experiences that convent life had given many of the women.

Difference and Different Lifestyles

The women in the convents made sense of themselves through the language and culture of the convents. The powerful cultural and religious practices from the time of their entry into the convent and throughout their time there affected their sense of self and their view of the wider society. The women like Mary and Susan, who wanted to leave the convents for quite different reasons, found that convent life and the religion shaped the way they saw themselves. In other words, these women had developed identities that included the meanings inscribed in the Catholic culture of the convents.

The guilt that these women felt had negative effects. While Susan's behaviour was not uncommon amongst many young women, she saw her behaviour through the eyes of the Sisters. Equally Mary, at the end of her life, measured her success as an inability to appreciate the 'goodness' of the Sisters. The way Mary internalised guilt for her feelings against convent life perhaps has implications for other 'spiritual communities', indicating a need to examine moral values and their impact on community members. Spiritual belief patterns can have profound effects on people and can lead to justifications of behaviour that would not be considered acceptable outside of such communities and this risk of the powerful impact of value systems should not be ignored. This issue also has implications for other service provision, where taken-for-granted service practices will also shape the identities and available options for residents (Dowson, 1997). On the other hand, Mary also found dignity through her religious beliefs. Her conviction that there was a life after death gave her strength through a difficult and destructive illness.

The deeply held religious beliefs of the women also affected their preparation for living in the wider community. As they moved out of the convent environment, the women needed to learn more than independent living skills. They left the convents with personal and cultural understandings that made sense in the convents but did not make sense in the wider community. Preparing people for transitions to live in the wider community requires an awareness by carers of the range of different experiences with which people have lived.

Writing about the oppression of people with learning difficulties, Williams points out the importance of difference within groups:

> Integration policies may, intentionally or otherwise, serve to devalue rather than enhance the characteristics of those whose integration is sought . . .By stressing the rights of the oppressed group to have access to the opportunities and life-style of mainstream society, this could lead to an underrating of the specific needs the group may have, and perhaps, their right to be different (1989b: 258).

The picture of the convents painted through these stories is fractured, and individual women felt differently about leaving the convents. Convent values affected the experience of all the women but much of this impact was ignored by care staff, whether social workers or convent staff. For example, Mary's Catholicism and her relationship with the local parish played a vital part in her being able to enjoy her last years outside the convent.

The closure of Mother convent offered many women the chance to live in 'ordinary houses in ordinary streets' (Kings Fund 1988). For many this was a positive experience but others found the stress painful and difficult to deal with. It is of course difficult to measure the impact of moving on the number of deaths which took place during the upheavals of closure of Mother convent as many of the women who died were elderly. However, there is some evidence that relocation can create added stress and lead to higher mortality (Brearley et al., 1982; Lawrence et al., 1987). Those women who successfully found networks and support groups in the community enjoyed their new found freedom. For those who did not, there was little to live for.

Often taken for granted, the notion of community and community allegiance are more difficult, especially when individuals can lay claim to membership of a range of communities (Bornat and Walmsley, 1994). Future service planning for people with learning difficulties requires not only a concern with 'the community' but a deeper understanding of attitudes and specific beliefs within different communities.

The on-going debate about the 'right' lifestyle (Segal, 1990; Williams, 1991; Collins, 1992; Groves, 1996), in the form of 'normalisation' or 'social role valorisation', or 'caring communities', often ignores the very people for whom services are provided, focusing on particular forms of provision and not on experience of lifestyle. The taken-for-granted notion of choice in lifestyle and provision needs to be unpicked. There is now a greater recognition of the need to value different experience (Brown and Smith, 1992), but often the complexity of experience that lies within different groups is not always seen. For example, at the level of choosing options, for some of the women in the convents 'choice' would have been to remain within a convent environment while for others 'choice' was to live independently. Choice is not only about options, it is also about rights. Different experience also plays a significant part in shaping identity which is seldom understood. The convent environment was saturated with constant reminders of morality; being good was a vital part of being successful. For women like Mary, being 'good' was wrapped up in her sense of self. She had longed for such recognition and was keen even in the last few weeks of her life 'to be good'. For many people with learning difficulties, the continued limited experience of opportunities prevents the development of a more positive sense of self in society, often making them fearful of change and their continued experience of denial of rights makes implementing choice difficult. The life stories from the convent residents' point to the complexity of developing a truly inclusive provision for people in the community.

Conclusion: Stories of Shame and Esteem – Women with Learning Difficulties and the Right to Tell Tales

> *'I want people to understand my feelings'* (Jane, 1989).
>
> *'Even though I will never meet the people who'll read this – I want them to know I'm a real person'* (Susan, 1989).

The women who worked with me on the development of this book were keen that their stories should be heard. Most felt that they had been locked away from society and forgotten and they wanted to rectify that. This project is an attempt to provide a brief glimpse into their world. *Not Quite Sisters* is about women who shared a lifestyle, whether Sister or resident, but the power structures within the convents meant that the women were often at odds with each other. The book is not meant to pass judgement on the 'care' provided for the women who lived in the convents. Rather, it attempts to show that particular conditions create particular outcomes. The stories told here are built on the life stories of the women who worked with me in the convents. It is their vision of their lives, but, as I was writing down this story, I became aware that there were different versions of daily life in the convents.

In the first chapter of the book, I argued that life history accounts from people with learning difficulties have only recently been recognised as authentic accounts of their lives. We also need to recognise that individual life history accounts do not speak for all people, even when there is a degree of shared experience. In this final chapter, I reflect on how we tell our stories to help us make sense of our experience and how people use this process to give themselves a sense of self-esteem. My, and others', involvement with these women also affected how the women told their stories. I use the life stories of two of the women who lived at Mother convent, Mary and Elvera, whose contributions to the account of convent life in this book are particularly significant. They told different stories about convent life, sometimes with their own internal contradictions.

The support, which Mary and Elvera's accounts received from different people, reveals how we 'hear' people's stories, both in wider society and within communities. Their stories provide an opportunity to examine how different styles of storytelling can change the perceived social value of a life history, which could affect how people with learning difficulties' life stories are heard.

While working on gathering the stories from the women in the convents, I was struck by a sort of hierarchy of storytellers. Some women felt they had the authority to tell stories while others did not. For example, the women who did not use speech to communicate were often ignored by both the Sisters and by other residents. These issues raise more general questions about life histories and their role as 'documents of the past'.

Many of the accounts from people with learning difficulties that we do have provide detail about life in institutions that has hitherto been unknown, but some accounts receive greater attention and exposure than others. As I pointed out in Chapter One, there are few published accounts from women or people from minority ethnic groups and even fewer from people who lived outside publicly funded institutions. It is quite clear from my research that this bias in the record is not because women with learning difficulties or people from minority communities do not want to tell their stories. On the contrary, Mary's commitment to writing her life story led to the publication of her autobiography (1995). Mary's tale provides a valuable illustration of how people's life history accounts develop over time in relation to their present experience. Below, I discuss how Mary acquired the status of 'representative' for the women living in the convent.

Unique and Typical – The Role of Authorship

In the time I knew Mary, between 1991 and 1995, she was keen to study. She took up word processing in 1992 and became an adult education assistant in a computer class for people with learning difficulties in 1993. Mary was aware of 'research' as an activity, having already begun work on her family history, reading books and asking questions of family members. She was keen to contribute to my research. She would work with me, bringing me information, going over points when she had thought about a question, further providing me with many insights into her world. She also worked with me on a reminiscence project, until she died in March 1995.

Mary wanted to 'write her life'. This desire separated her from the other women I interviewed. Most were happy to discuss their lives but many declined the offer of working on a book of their reminiscences together, saying they preferred to just talk to me. Mary was one of the first women to move out of the convent, embracing the new drive to living in the community. She was also a devout Catholic as were many of the other women. Atkinson points out that the stories of people with learning difficulties who have lived in long-stay institutions can:

> . . . actually mirror the major changes of the century . . . (therefore shedding) light on the details of past policy, provision and practice through their day to day experiences (Atkinson, 1997: 102).

In other words, individuals like Mary in this study can be both unique and typical providing a specific, rich source of information. In 1993, Mary began working on her autobiography. I encouraged her to set down her memories. Later, through local contacts with a community publishing company, QueenSpark, Mary's story was submitted to the manuscript group for publication. Mary was seen by the lay care staff to be 'at the heart of this insular world' (Saunders, 1995: 3).

Through this statement, Mary is being recognised as an 'author'. By being at the heart of convent life, she is able to speak about the world. Unlike the other materials I collected in reminiscence books, for the women's own use, Mary's story was published. This sets it apart from all the other work produced by the women in the convent. Mary, therefore, became a mythical figure for people in her convent. She was no longer just 'one of the women'; she had passed a rite of passage into the external world. This moved her beyond the realm of an 'interviewee' to the realm of a social character in her own right. She was an author. The process of becoming an author is not just about telling your story, it is about social recognition. To become an 'author' in our culture requires a series of rites of passage through different levels to authorship, beginning with the right to tell a story through to the social recognition of publication.

As well as writing her autobiography, I interviewed Mary on several occasions and she was also interviewed for a training video for social workers. Examining the different versions of her story enables some comparison. Her story developed over time. She apparently learned to come to terms with painful experiences which in early written versions and interviews she skims. Her final published autobiography has many more emotional touches than her earlier work. As Jones, the QueenSpark worker who supported Mary to re-write her autobiography, states:

> What the Manuscripts Group wanted to be added to the original draft was a sense of Mary's feelings, . . . In order to help Mary to make the amendments requested, therefore, I had to ask of her some very difficult things (Jones, 1995: 6).

To become an author required Mary to examine her life in relation to her feelings about her experiences. Mary was proud to be a member of the manuscript group and proud that QueenSpark wanted to publish her story. She was ambivalent about some of the changes the publishing group wanted her to make. At one stage in the process, she thought about abandoning the whole project but in the end found a compromise that satisfied her, leaving out some detail and changing stories that placed some of the Sisters in a bad light. She notes in the autobiography that in the end, 'I have made a few alterations to this book, but not many' (Adams, 1995:49). There are many questions here, questions about feeling able to speak, and dilemmas in ownership of knowledge. The experience of working with Mary has implications for working with people to develop their stories in a social arena. Reflecting on my role in this highlights a number of dilemmas. I encouraged Mary to develop her story and as a 'researcher', I had status in her eyes and in the eyes of the care manager at the convent. I suggested contacting QueenSpark in the first place, and it was through the interviews with me that Mary began to question her experiences further. I was not, of course, the only person doing this, the care manager at the time also encouraged her, as did her computer skills tutor and the QueenSpark writers' group.

Mary's life story became a social icon. Social workers and care staff who work in the field who did not know her have read the story. This story gained an external existence, being used in a range of contexts, including this book. The process of developing a story provides clues to the meaning of a published product and this is seldom acknowledged or understood in studies of biographical writing (Stanley,1991). The process of constructing Mary's story had both positive and negative qualities, which I shall take up later. The next section explains how Mary's authority developed and contrasts her role with the roles of another storyteller in the convent, Elvera.

Contested Stories – The Power of Communities

Focusing on particular storytellers raises the question of how culture is translated between generations. Mary was given the status of storyteller at the time when the convent was changing. For the first time in its history, a lay care manager rather than a Sister-in-charge was appointed in 1989 and the old regime of care based on the rule of religious Sisters began to disappear.

In the convent, as well as Mary being recognised as possessing the authority to tell the stories of life in the convent, there was also another woman who had this status, Elvera. She was older than Mary and had been a powerful figure in the convent. Elvera and I met when I first came to Mother convent. As we walked down the corridor to the manager's office, she was keen to stake her claim as a storyteller. She showed interest in my project and told me there were 'a few things' she could tell me (Elvera, 1991). Over the years that I worked in the convent, Elvera would often appear while I was talking to another resident and join in the conversation. She brought me tapes of her poetry that she had recorded. She had been producing stories about the convent since she had moved there and had a collection of tapes that she was keen for me to use in my research.

Despite her interest in my project and the wealth of information she had, the manager did not suggest Elvera as a useful informant. Over time I became aware that Elvera was not happy with the changes at the convent and was not always complimentary about the 'new ways' (Elvera, 1993). Elvera was telling stories about glowing happy times in the past, 'golden days' as she called them.

Mary, on the other hand, told a range of stories about the past, including negative accounts of punishment and bullying which highlighted the need for change. She welcomed the developments that were introduced in the 1990s. Mary had studied and was re-working her story in response to current wisdom about people with learning difficulties. She understood that society thought that people with learning difficulties 'were not to be seen to be mixing with normal people.' (Adams, 1995:40).

This suggests that Mary had understood the process of labelling, and the impact of this definition on her life. This reflexivity enabled her to appreciate the positive meanings of the changes that the convent was experiencing. She had gained status with the changes. Elvera, on the other hand, was losing authority, as her romanticised version of the past was no longer seen as acceptable. Elvera wrote about her past:

> *Golden days, golden days in the sunshine of our happy youth*
> *Golden days full of innocence and full of truth*
> *Looking back through memory's haze*
> *We knew life hath nothing sweeter than in spring time*
> *Golden days when we were young*
> *Golden days* (Elvera, 1990).

Her framing of her youth in the context of 'golden days' 'spring time' and 'innocence' is reminiscent of a romantic tradition. Elvera was a keen performer and played the lead role in *The Student Prince,* one of the convent productions. The poem above has echoes of the romantic story of musicals and films of that time. Yet in her poem about 'growing up', she says:

> *'Twas the year of 1918 I came into this world*
> *The month and date the 16 June*
> *My hair they say was gold*
> *Barely a year went by when to an orphanage I went*
> *I was too young to ask why*
> *And here, seventeen years I spent.*
> *. . . And then in 1935, to headquarters I was sent*
> *And at the lovely age of 17, to(the) convent I went*
> *'Twas from the frying pan into the fire*
> *They were so strict, no mirrors allowed on the walls*
> *My long mane to admire*
> *The scissors soon came in sight and I was chopped above the ears*
> *I sobbed and sobbed all night long*
> *'Twas the start of all my fears* (Elvera, 1966).

While this is written in the heroic tradition that I discuss later in the chapter, it is a much harsher picture than the one painted by 'golden days'. Elvera grew up in an orphanage, never knew her parents and moved directly to Mother convent from the orphanage, which she describes above as 'from the frying pan into the fire'. While Elvera determined to compose romantic versions of the past, she also acknowledged the harshness of her earlier life. In her writing about caring and caring roles, Opie argued that it is possible in our attempt to present a clear argument to destroy complexity and contradiction in people's stories. Examining caring for elderly relatives, she used a feminist analysis that highlights the exploitative nature of the caring relationship. However, she found within people's texts other selves surfacing which could not be ignored:

> Interspersed through a number of texts are different moments which speak of love and affection and regard, which mitigate temporarily the tensions of the role . . . (Opie, 1992:53).

It is our complexity that makes us what we are and allowing for difference within individuals creates a rich and textured story. Elvera's poems reveal a complex set of emotions about her life, not just one account of her experience. Yet her insistence on 'fun times' despite adversity, common in all her tales, and her reputation of being a Sister's favourite, meant she was less popular with the new style of care. She refused the label 'learning difficulty' or 'slow learner', completely, while Mary used the term of herself with a critical understanding of its social definition. Elvera had come to claim that life in the convent was preferable to life outside and this re-working of the past was discordant with the prevailing policy of living within the wider community.

Mary's account in her published autobiography had more currency as 'The story' of the convent in the minds of people working in the field of learning difficulties in the local area than any other because it was published. However, different versions of a group's history can be told jointly as is revealed by the accounts of convent life. Mary and Elvera told different versions of the past and, curiously, the contradictions between their versions seem to lie at the heart of the experience of the residents in the convent. In some ways, the past was both awful and secure, full of friendship and fun on the one hand and drudgery, mistreatment and bullying on the other. Humphries (1998) found convents could be harsh environments. In this study there were a range of perceptions. Some of the women were keen to emphasise their own ability to find pleasure and friendship while others reflected more on the oppressiveness of their experience. These contradictions make it necessary to evaluate stories from the perspective of the author and their role within a community rather than placing an external evaluation on the accounts. As Stanley argues:

> The past like the present, is the result of competing negotiated versions of what happened, why it happened, and with what consequences (Stanley,1991: 7).

Different voices, offering contradictory interpretations of the past, if they are social and politically located within the community, can offer a more subtle picture of life within that community.

Written and Spoken Words

Mary and Elvera's stories competed at different levels. It was not only that they told different tales, but their styles were also different. Elvera's work was largely developed as performance. Although she could read and write, she did not write down her poetry or stories, preferring to speak or tell them. She gave me copies of her poetry on tape, which she had produced for celebrations such as feast days. Being able to speak at such an event marked you as a 'leader'. Elvera's work was unique, immediate but also historically focused, as she told the story of the past in her performances. As with any history, her poems told the history of the convent in relation to the present. Her performances included poems for special occasions for nuns who were care managers. In these poems Elvera recalls all that these Sisters achieved as care managers and through these tales she told the history of the convent.

Finnegan (1992) argues that within oral cultures the role of performance is powerful. She suggests that the structuring and execution of performances provide insights into the meanings of a culture. Elvera was also allowed to recall tales that placed the Sisters in comical situations. These tales usually related to the transgression of rules and reveal a convent culture being maintained through regulation but also sustained through transgression. For example, she tells how one Sister, Margaret Mary, broke the rule of silence herself:

> *The golden rule of silence was kept by each and all*
> *But one day going into mass a mouse was on the floor*
> *With your skirts tucked high around you and your call,*
> *'silence please*
> *The thing is not going to hurt you'*
> *And you let out a great big squeal* (Elvera,1972).

In 1972, when Sister Margaret Mary retired, it was only Elvera who told the tale of her time at the convent and Elvera's performance therefore gave her version of the past 'authority'.

The power attached to speaking the story of the convent at feast days was diminished as their status was undermined by lay staff who were more concerned with a secular service culture. Unlike Elvera, Mary wrote down her stories. She enjoyed writing and her tales became recognised by others outside the convent, as they were accessible as written text. Elvera's role diminished because the medium of her storytelling was limited to the convent while Mary's written accounts gained more status beyond the walls of the convent.

The Demands of Genre

For Elvera and others like her, stories of the times before lay staff were employed portrayed life as comfortable and continuous. Elvera lifted the daily grind of washing, eating and cleaning into the realm of the heroic. In her tales, certain Sisters were particularly praised for their kindness and sense of fun and she celebrated friendship and camaraderie. Some of the women were seen as cavalier heroines, subverting authority and enabling others to benefit from their daring adventures. For example, Elvera told me the story of the apples, which highlights some of these mythical qualities of 'Girls Own' adventures. In the tale the women had:

> a) *picked apples off the trees in the orchard and stuffed them in our clothes, bras, knickers, and all that . . .* b) *and Sister caught us . . . Sister said we had to go to confession,* c) *but I put it on a bit and cried and he* (the priest) *said the orchards belonged to all of us,* d) *so we could all get apples after that* (Elvera, 1992) (my lettering and brackets).

In this story a group of friends, Joan, Elvera and Martha had an adventure sneaking off into the orchard that was out of bounds. None of these women worked in the orchard so it was not their place to be there. They had stolen the apples, challenging the rule of the Sisters. Although they were caught they were able to win the day and enable all the women to take apples from the orchards if they wanted to in the future. The narrative structure of the story is a classical moral adventure tale:

a) Heroic group goes out on adventure, takes what is rightfully theirs.
b) The group is challenged but manages to beat the nasty rulers

c) by cunning.
d) The conclusion being a 'happy ever after'; life is better for everyone.

Patterning stories in this way does not deny their inherent truth, but indicates that storytellers in communities weave events through a set of conventions. It is a creative process that often reproduces archetypal opposites in a tale. Here we have heroines in Elvera and her friends, villains in the Sisters, and malleable, but powerful, men who help the heroines. The structure follows the classical pattern of a) disrupting a settled environment to create change, or putting something 'out of place' (Douglas, 1970), b&c) battling over the disruption and d) concluding with a new settlement. In her poetry, Elvera indicates similar myths. She is often talking about challenges to the authority of the Sisters. Atkinson highlights this mythical theme within life stories:

> The telling of life stories through the oral tradition brings us close to the use, even the development of myths. This is because oral narratives . . . are ideally suited to convey moral values in the process of recounting actual events (Atkinson, 1997:131).

This point is illustrated by the poem performed by Elvera at the retirement of Sister Margaret Mary. In the poem, she recounts a story about the Sister's clumsy behaviour:

> *Many years of your religious life you spent in (Mother convent)*
> *And you've many happy memories, which we know will never fade*
> *But did you know dear Sister that for many years,*
> *Your dear self and your helpers were called the three musketeers*
> *The years of entertainment we gladly gave to all*
> *Often caused lots of laughter when off the bench you'd fall*
> *With one hand you clutched the cross beam*
> *And you were suspended in mid air*
> *You started out to help but alas no one was there*
> *. . .To see a nun suspended without a flying trapeze*
> *To opportunity knocks would have brought a glorious scene*
> (Elvera, 1972).

This section of the poem highlights the importance of the re-telling. The poem subverts the authority of the Sister by telling of an embarrassing incident when others would laugh. It also shows the Sister's helplessness, suspended from the cross beam. 'Alas no one was there', could not be true or else how could Elvera tell the tale? It suggests that the women watched but did not help immediately, perhaps because they were laughing so much or else because they did not want to. Elvera also reveals how the Sister was seen by other women in the convent: 'your dear self and your helpers were known as the three musketeers'. These ritual events, where authority is supposedly subverted in fact re-establish power. Goffman noted in his study of the 'total institution' that at Christmas time inmates would perform 'satirical skits that lampoon well-known members of the institution, especially high placed staff members' (Goffman, 1961:94). He noted that this process re-enforced the order of the institution, allowing for a form of misrule at certain times. Certainly this seems to be the case with this poem of Elvera's. It is affectionate and warm towards the Sister. The performer expects the Sister to enjoy the stories as they are told. She has permission to undermine the authority. However, the rightful power is re-established by the end of the poem when Elvera tells of the women giving the Sister in question flowers, and states:

> *for it is just our loving way of saying many thanks to you for all the care you gave us* (Elvera, 1972).

Elvera uses traditional poetic form, as in her use of 'Twas' and 'art', utilising the heroic tradition and working within the demands of a specific poetic genre. Overall, Elvera's stories are more mythical than Mary's which tend to follow the more modern structure and genre of the written life course, which focuses on an evocation to 'reality'.

Mary developed her writing style from working in the tight constraints of 'family history' writing. She began her family history about a month before she met me. She told me that she was '*getting more interested in it now*' (Mary, 1992) as:

> My great grandfather wrote a book called the *Family Atkinson's Country* . . . and I copied it from the book, but from my father and mother downwards, I wrote that myself (Adams, 1991).

The style of Mary's writing follows the pattern of the work she had copied from the book. She wrote about herself:

> (I) . . . was born March 30th 1930 in The Dingle Nursing Home, Wake Green, Moseley, Kings Norton, Birmingham. Went out to Ghana with my mother but came back as I was seriously ill out there. Went to pre-prep school accommodation at the age of four . . . (Adams, 1991).

This style mimics the writing about her aunt that she copied from the original book. It is terse, clipped and matter of fact.:

> The title Dame was conferred upon her, and she inherited an estate in excess of £72,000.00 when her husband died (Adams, 1992).

Mary's impetus to place herself in this family tree was a sign of her desire to be a part of her own family. She noted later in her autobiography that she felt deserted by her parents:

> I was sent to a pre-prep school at four years old attached to the main prep school, as a boarder. I was brought there by my parents. . . . My parents thought it was a good idea to leave then, but I clung to mother screaming my head off and would not leave them . . . I was devastated and very unhappy. It was then I started to feel that I was not wanted by people (Adams, 1995: 11).

This emotional separation is not hinted at in her original of her family tree:

> Went to a pre-prep school accommodation at the age of four, at the Madonna, Letchworth, Herts, then went up to main building when I was seven (Adams, 1991).

It is both the constraints of the genre of such writing and her need to feel her story was equally a part of the family tree that encouraged her to write in this dispassionate way. Mary was giving herself a place and a status that had been denied by her family by writing herself into the family history. The genre had enabled her to construct herself as a valid part of the family.

As indicated through an examination of the style of Elvera's and Mary's stories, genre can facilitate and elucidate the meanings of particular stories, but it also places specific demands on the construction of the story, which creates particular meanings. Hence, in an analysis of people's life stories, the style or genre chosen will be important in itself and can reveal meanings within stories told. The final section of the chapter moves from the social to the personal context of storytelling and its relation to histories. It explores the connection between Mary's developing autobiography, the interviews I had with her and how she used the process of constructing her story to re-evaluate her life.

Writing as a Process of Healing?

Mary's early life is an account of a developing 'cycle of shaming' (Scheff, 1994, 1996). Like many of the other women who lived in the convent, she was placed there by her parents because she, like these others, was, '*too delicate*' (Maria,1991) '*needing protection*' (Myra, 1992) or, as Mary said, '*sensitive*' (Mary,1992). The process of becoming timid or sensitive can be clearly seen in her autobiography as a process of shaming. Mary illustrates the process described by Scheff as the 'signs of the state of a system. . .of one's bonds to others' (Scheff,1994:16).

Scheff explains the process in this way:

> . . . the original stimulus for shame, say a comment that one takes to be critical of self, may be only the first step in a long shame sequence. Once ashamed, one can be ashamed of being ashamed, each shaming state serving as a stimulus for further shaming (1994: 18).

In Mary's case, the experience of being abandoned was repeated at the end of every school holiday, and finally when she arrived at Mother convent. For Mary, being left was a sign of not being wanted, from the first time she was left at the age of four through the years at the different schools she attended before coming to the convent which she describes in this way:

> After dinner I told some of the ladies I was going to find mother, only to be told that she had left. I cried then and thought how horrible of her not to say good-bye to me. I felt so hurt, there again was the repetition of the time she left me

> when I was four years old. I thought, there it is, her showing me she did not want me to live with her, and I felt I had been badly let down again by both parents (Adams, 1995: 24).

It is difficult to know how her parents felt about the continual separations but for Mary they were moments of pain. Her arrival at the convent brought back the original emotional experience of feeling unwanted and shamed. The bonds with family were threatened by the continual separations. In her video interview, Mary talks quietly about her past, staring quite fixedly at the interviewer. Scheff (1994) argues that although shaming is hidden it is expressed in a variety of ways, lowered voice and staring fixedly at another are common. Mary particularly lowers her voice when discussing her parents. She said:

> *My mother was really fussy . . . I asked several times if I could leave but no, father was worse, very strict* (1992a).

Lewis (1971) suggests that shaming makes people feel they have been stupid or wrong. This sense of being wrong haunted Mary, expressing itself in her being over anxious. At the end of her video, she says tentatively, '*I think I've been a bit hesitant?*' (1992a)

The interviewer told her that she hadn't been and she turns to the camera for the first time in the interview looking more relaxed and smiling faintly. She needed the reassurance of 'doing the right thing'. Her sense of uncertainty about herself required her to check she was being accepted by others continually.

While Mary was at school, she was bullied by other children, which, she said, made her cry. She found this detail difficult to talk about and in early interviews glossed over her early life, presenting it rather like the account in the family history. Potts and Fido suggest that 'pretending not to feel or not to mind must, for some, become an automatic and effective method of coping with the pain of neglect' (Potts and Fido, 1997:42). However, in her final autobiography she recounts how some children treated her:

> There were two girls in our form who used to torment the life out of me, and when the teacher left the room they made me, by pinching me, stand on the table and pull my knickers down so that the children would jeer at me. I trembled often with fright and burst into tears (Adams,1995: 16).

This process of shaming children is common in many stories and arguably affects the sense of self esteem that an individual has (Simons, 1992). Mary told me she had cried a lot as a child. Her crying was used by her parents as one of the reasons why she needed to stay in the convent. Her own emotionality was shamed by making it her fault rather than the fault of her peers. Although Mary indicates that she 'enjoyed and was good at English and History', when it came to exams, Mary had 'difficulty remembering things' . She told me she had:

> *. . . quite a low IQ, mind you it's only since I've come here at the convent that my brain has woken up and I've realised I have potential (1992).*

As well as her 'brain waking up', Mary describes how over the years the Sisters gave her tasks and roles. Being successful was rewarded and she became the chief ticket seller for the convent's bazaars. As she moved out of the convent and took on new roles, including being invited to teach in several adult education classes and child minding for families in her local parish, her self esteem grew. Having her manuscript accepted for publication gave her a great sense of pride and achievement. In her family history, Mary wrote:

> I have become intellectually better, and have become very independent, but at the moment, I have had the temptation of going it on my own, but still holding back a bit (1991).

At the time, Mary equated 'going it on my own', or moving out, with 'temptation'. For Mary, whose parents had told her she would only leave the convent '*feet first in a coffin*' (1993), moving out was a big step. She had promised her mother she would not leave and Mary felt she should keep her word. However, she came to rationalise and re-evaluate the move for by the time she wrote her autobiography, she was able to say:

> If my parents were alive today they would be greatly shocked, but in time I am sure they would be very proud of me and of what I have achieved. Anyway, . . . It is my own choice, and I have the ability and confidence to do everything that I have taken on (1995: 48).

It was no longer a 'temptation', but a 'choice'. Mary had finally been able to shake off the rule of her parents. Gaining authorship had given Mary the self esteem she needed to value herself for what she was, or, to put it another way, as Mead says:

> The self . . . develops in the individual as a result of his (sic) relations . . . to other individuals within that process (1934: 136).

Mary had been originally 'named' as a 'slow learner', who was *'timid'* and *'would be taken advantage of'* (1992, 1993). However, this changed. As her years in the convent progressed she was recognised as successful. She wrote in her autobiography:

> It was in the 1970s that a nun came who showed me a lot of affection and trust. She started me on the road to independence, which I had been fighting for years . . . Everything changed then and I was looked up to and respected (1995: 45).

Mary needed the social recognition to build her esteem and to counteract the earlier shaming she had received.

The process of writing did offer Mary an opportunity to re-evaluate her life, to find some sort of meaning for the difficulties and to state clearly her feelings of hurt about being left by her parents. The process of being able to write and re-write her story in a structured narrative provided her with space to deal with her pain.

Reflecting on Telling Tales

Social recognition for storytelling is not just about uncovering history or personal therapy but also about the connection between the two. Constructing our social past and the role of individuals within this process continues to offer challenges for life history work. The authority and status of storytellers in communities are directly related to the development of a community's history. Despite the fact that the residents in the convent had been labelled and excluded from society as a group, their stories reveal diversity of experience amongst the women, even within the same environment of a convent. Here, I set out to gather stories from a range of women, including those who did not communicate effectively using speech. I have had some limited success, but the book does still concentrate on the stories of the most articulate. The weight of Mary's material in this book is significant. Her voice is heard above all others, except perhaps Elvera's. This is partly to do with her interest with my work and partly to do with her determination to write her autobiography. While it is possible to gain a sense of different people's perceptions and experiences by including the accounts of people with learning difficulties in our understanding of services, it is those who are given authority whose voices will be most clearly heard. As Walmsley and Downer point out, perhaps it is those who 'shout the loudest' (1997:35) who are heard by researchers and policy makers. Of course we need to celebrate the inclusion of the voices of people with learning difficulties in accounts of our social histories, but we also need to ensure that we do not expect them to speak with one voice.

The end of an Era – A Personal Conclusion

After the closure of Mother convent, the site was taken over by another voluntary sector project for young people. As part of my work, I attended a meeting on community development in the area and found the architecture, the long passageways and dark corners, brought back memories of previous visits. In the grounds, some remnants of its convent past could be found including the grotto with the statue of Mother Mary.[1] While our meeting continued, children played on the lawns outside the window. I asked people at the meeting if they knew what the place had been before it became a youth project and their response did not surprise me. Some knew that the building had been a convent but no-one knew anything about the women who had lived there.

I found the experience quite difficult. On the one hand, it was positive that the building was not being wasted and that the women who had wanted to live in the community were now able to do so, but the social history of those women's lives has been lost, even to people who worked in the local health and social care fields. That is why I wanted to write this book and why I hope we will be able to re-claim a more diverse understanding of our social history. Women who have been labeled as having learning difficulties have only recently gained the right to tell tales of their past. As they speak up we hear contradictory accounts of shame and esteem, sometimes, as in the case of Elvera, within the same narrative. This does not negate the

---

[1] See the photograph of Mary in Chapter Seven where she is standing beneath the grotto.

account or suggest inaccuracy; rather it adds nuance and subtlety to the reality of the complexity of people's lives. I hope that I have been able to do some justice to the remarkable experiences of the women who gave so generously of their time to help me develop this book and I hope that the desire of the women such as Susan to be known as 'a real person' has been, in some way, fulfilled.

Appendix 1

Short Biographical Details on the Women Interviewed

MOTHER CONVENT

Elvera

Elvera came to Mother convent at the age of seventeen in 1935 having lived in a Catholic orphanage since she was one year old. She was 'tried out' for living in the community on several occasions, working as a domestic worker in Croydon after the Second World War and as a cleaner in an old people's home in 1938. She disliked both and returned to the convent working in the laundry until 1989. When the convent was moving people into smaller units during the 1990s Elvera moved into a cottage in the convent grounds with two of her friends, Joan and Elizabeth. She stayed in the cottage until the convent closed in October 1996 and moved to a staffed group home with the six remaining women from the convent.

Gloria

Gloria came to Mother convent in 1948 at the age of eighteen. She was placed there by a social worker. Her mother had fits and was unable to look after her. She came from Nottingham. She was a very capable woman who worked in the laundry most of her time at the convent. One of the Sisters traced her sister during the 1970s but after spending some time together, Gloria decided to stay at the convent as they had 'different lives'. As part of the closure of the convent, Gloria moved out of Mother convent in April 1995 to another of the movement's homes, 150 miles away. Although she had asked to be transferred within the movement's homes, she was unhappy there and did not make new friends. She became ill and died in February 1996.

Maria

Maria came to Mother convent in 1925 from the same Nazarene orphanage in Bermondsey, South London as Elvera. She was fifteen at the time. Maria was the only woman of my interviewees who was sectioned under the Lunacy Act of 1890 under the term idiot. She worked in the laundry when she turned sixteen and continued working there till she retired in 1989. She had a fall in 1992 and walked with a frame or stick for the rest of her life. Maria died just before the convent closed in October 1996.

Mary

Mary was born in Birmingham, but went to live in Africa where her father was a schoolmaster. She returned to England due to ill health and went to a boarding school at the age of four. She came to Mother convent in 1947 at the age of seventeen and lived there until 1991 when she moved to a flat with two other women. She later moved to her own bedsitter with minimal support. She died of cancer in March 1995. Mary was placed in the convent because her parents felt she would not manage in the real world, she had been labelled as a 'slow learner'. Mary worked on the farm until it was closed in 1970. Between 1970 and when she died in 1995, she was an active member of the community. She organised the selling of bazaar tickets for the parish fetes, performed in plays at the convent, and became a Eucharist minister in the local Catholic church. She also worked with me as a co-tutor on a reminiscence course, learnt word processing and taught on a computer course. She wrote her autobiography which was published shortly after she died.

Martha
Martha came to Mother convent in 1913 at the age of sixteen. She was born in South Kensington in London. She was the oldest resident that I interviewed. She came to the convent of her own free will but on the advice of her father once her mother died. Martha worked in the laundry and had a senior position within the convent. She retired from the laundry in 1972. Martha died in May 1995.

Athena
Athena was born in Cyprus and her mother came to Britain during the invasion in the early 1960s. Athena was placed in the convent at the age of twenty-three in 1965, as her mother was unable to care for her. She lost contact with her mother some time after her arrival. Athena spoke a little Greek and remembered a number of traditional dances. She went to Rhodes for the first time since leaving Greece in 1963, in 1993. Athena moved out of the convent in 1995 and lives with a family in West Sussex.

Beth
Beth came to Britain in 1927 to attend a girls' public school. Beth was born and brought up in Grahamstown, South Africa. She came to Mother convent in 1941 and remained there, after an unsuccessful time at school. She worked in the laundry in the sorting and packing. She lost contact with her family by the end of the war. Beth became very silent in her later years and suffered from arthritis. She left the convent in 1993 to go to a home for frail elderly people.

Eileen
Eileen came to Mother convent in 1986 when she was eighteen. She had attended a variety of special schools and came from a middle class family. The family wanted her to board in a convent and thought that Mother would be a good place for Eileen. Her sister worked for the BBC and Eileen was very proud of her. Eileen left Mother convent in 1995 and went to a group home.

Joan
Joan came to Mother convent in 1933 at sixteen after leaving the Nazarene orphanage. She had spent several years out of the convent doing basic domestic work but returned as she said people 'picked on her'. She worked in the laundry most of the time, retiring in 1980. Joan moved to the group home in October 1996 with Elvera.

Laura
Laura came to Mother convent in 1922 on the advice of her father at the age of nineteen. She worked in the laundry and was particularly friendly with Mary. She was respected in the convent and had authority. She retired in 1975. Laura died in June 1994.

Louise
Louise came to Mother convent in 1951 after her mother died. She was twenty-six. Louise worked largely on domestic work in the convents, helping out in the kitchen. She became frail and had many falls during the 1980s, retiring from work in 1983. Louise wanted to stay in the locality when the convent closed and it was planned that she would move into the small group home with Elvera and Joan but she died in September 1996 before they moved.

Moira
Moira was born in 1933 and lived with her parents in China. Her father was in the foreign office. During the war, she and her mother and brother and sister had to flee China. Her father was captured and she returned to England. She was bombed out twice and was separated

from her mother. Moira was traumatised by the experiences and did not speak. She went to a 'Deaf and Dumb' school where she 'started to learn'. They had been encouraging. In 1943 she went to another school where she was bullied. In 1948 her parents found her again. After two years Moira got a job at the local priest's house. She worked as a domestic until 1970 while she lived at Mother. Moira worked in the community in domestic work while living at the convent and moved out to her own flat in 1995.

Roberta

Roberta came to Mother convent in 1966 when she was twenty-two. She remained in contact with her family and would return home for holidays and special occasions on a regular basis. She was particularly close to her sister whom she visited on a regular basis. Her father was in a nursing home in Lewes, East Sussex and she visited him when she was able. Roberta could talk but found communication difficult. Roberta had done a variety of work in the convent, including domestic work and cooking. She attended a range of adult education classes and enjoyed pottery. Roberta moved to a group home in East Sussex in 1995.

Tess

Tess was born in Surrey in 1946 and came to Mother convent after leaving her parents who were elderly in 1970. A social worker organised the placement on the advice of her parents. She maintained contact with her family and would occasionally go 'home' from the convent. Tess had done some work in the laundry. She left the convent as part of the closure in April 1995 moving to a group home in her home county.

ANGEL CONVENT

Alice

Alice came to Angel convent in 1943 at eighteen. She had been born in India where her parents were part of the English Rajah. Her parents died when she was 4 and she was shipped back to England with her brother and sister. She was sent to boarding school where she learnt little. After arriving at the convent, Alice worked as a domestic worker in a number of places including nursing homes and other convents. When adult education classes became available, Alice became very keen and did light domestic duties at the convent so she could attend classes. Alice moved out of the main building in 1986 and lived in the gatehouse at the entrance to the convent till she died in a car accident while out shopping in October 1992.

Jane

Jane was born in Romania while her father was working for the BBC in 1940. She returned to Britain almost immediately. She attended a grammar school until she was eleven. She then went to boarding school till she was sixteen. She tried to get work but was unsuccessful and went to Mother convent when she was eighteen. A social worker had arranged the move after discussions with her mother. After two years, in 1960, she moved to Angel convent to be nearer her mother. Jane remained in close contact with her mother and had a range of interests in Shakespearean theatre and Italian food. Jane lived still in Angel convent in 1996.

Myra

Myra came to Angel convent on the advice of her father when her mother died in 1923 at eighteen. She had lived in Newhaven in Sussex. Her mother was French and she remembered her with affection. When she came to the convent she worked in the laundry and retired in 1965. She enjoyed life at the convent and was religious. She died in 1990.

Siobhan
Siobhan came to Angel in 1979 at eighteen. Her mother remained in close contact with her and while Siobhan wanted to move out of the convent her mother blocked any change in her living situation. Siobhan attended adult education classes and worked in the kitchen at the convent. Siobhan was moved to a hostel in 1992.

Tembe
Tembe was born in Nigeria in 1971. Her mother emigrated to Britain while she was a child and Tembe went to school. After attending a special secondary school, Tembe came to Angel convent as her mother had returned to Nigeria leaving her and her brothers behind. Tembe was an active participant in adult education classes and left Angel convent in 1990 and returned to live with her mother who had returned from Nigeria. She went to study fashion design at Kingston College and moved into her own flat in 1991.

Yvonne
Yvonne lived with her mother in a flat in North London till she died in 1968 when Yvonne was twenty-four. Yvonne had been bullied at school. After leaving school she attended a social services day centre which she enjoyed. When her mother died, family relatives wanted her to live in a Catholic home as they were Irish Catholics. Angel convent was suggested and Yvonne went to live there. She lost contact with her relatives and still lives in the convent today.

Amanda
Amanda was born in London in 1890. She came to live in Mother convent after she had had an illegitimate child at the age of fourteen. She later moved to a large long stay hospital, Darenth Park, in south east London, at the age of fifty-four. The hospital was segregated and many of the Sisters continued to visit Amanda. When the hospital closed in 1985 she moved to a small group home. She was not happy and would come to Angel convent whenever possible as it was close to the group home. She wanted to spend her 100th birthday party at the convent. I do not know if Amanda is still alive.

Anne
Anne came to Angel convent in 1951 at sixteen. Anne's mother died during the Second World war. She lived with her father in the Forest of Dean. Her family were committed Church of England members and were landowners. Anne was raped by a cousin and her father felt unable to look after her and asked a social worker to find an appropriate home for her. Anne worked as a domestic in the convent. She moved to a cottage in the grounds of the convent in 1989 where she still lives.

Claire
Claire was from an Irish 'tinker' family. Social workers had encouraged the family to let Claire be taken into care as she had had to have two pregnancy terminations in three years and the family were under scrutiny for a range of social offences. Claire came to live at Angel convent in 1990 at the age of twenty-five. Her family were keen for her to live within a Catholic home. Claire ran away from the convent after an incident with another woman and returned to live with her traveller family in 1994.

Diana
Diana came to Angel convent in 1988. She was eighteen and had just finished attending a Steiner School in Sussex. Her parents found her behaviour too difficult. It was planned that Diana would eventually move into the community. She was articulate and very keen to learn, attending as many adult education classes as she could. Diana became involved in an integrated theatre company's project in London and hoped to develop her acting skills.

Diana was found a part-time receptionist's job but she found it boring and developed a pattern of absenteeism. She returned to the convent. Diana was moved to a hostel in 1994.

Jessica

Jessica was born in Jamaica in 1961 and lived there till her family emigrated in the early seventies. Jessica lived at home until 1979 when she was told she had to get a job as her parents were returning to Jamaica. She had a mild learning difficulty and found it difficult to get work. Her parents, on the advice of their social worker, sent her to the convent in 1980. Once in Angel convent her family left Britain. Jessica moved from the convent and boarded with a local family in 1991. She attended the local further education college and became active in Black student politics.

Lucy

Lucy came to live at Angel convent in 1970 at the age of twenty-three. She could not speak and had little other specific forms of communication. She had been cared for by her mother until she died in 1970. She came from Liverpool and was not visited by any other family. Lucy lived in the convent until 1997.

Margaret

Margaret came to Angel convent after leaving a nursing home where she had given birth to an illegitimate baby. Her parents had insisted that the baby was adopted and she was 'judged by the doctors to be best suited to going to the convent'. Her father had been a merchant seaman and she had lived in the East End with her mother and brother. She came to Angel convent in 1933 and remained in contact with her family. She had worked in the laundry until retiring in 1975. Margaret still lived in the convent in 1997.

Sara

Sara came from a large working class family in East London. She moved into Angel convent in 1963 at the age of eighteen. Her mother found it difficult to care for her as she became physically disabled. Sara returned home most weekends and had extensive contact with her elder brother whom she worshipped. Sara worked in the convent on domestic work and spent several years working in the kitchen. Sara went to work in a restaurant but found the demands too much and became aggressive. Sara still lives in the convent.

Susan

Susan came to live at Angel convent in 1983 at the age of eighteen on the recommendation of a social worker. Her family could no longer accommodate her. After moving to the convent she maintained a troubled relationship with her mother but felt unwanted. Susan had mild learning difficulties and worked outside the convent doing a range of domestic work. She was moved to a hostel in 1990.

Zarina

Zarina came from Somalia with her mother in 1985 at the age of sixteen. The civil war had affected the family's wealth and Britain was seen as a refuge. Her parents moved between Somalia and Britain and were advised that the convent was an appropriate home for their daughter. Zarina's dream was to return to Somalia to live with her grandmother who had largely raised her. Zarina still lived in Angel convent in 1997.

Appendix 2

1. A Selection of Elvera's Poems

Golden Days
Golden Days in the sunshine of our happy youth
Golden Days full of innocence and full of truth
In our hearts we recall all those that are,
Days of youth,
Days of youth and love
How we art with a deity that had no stain
Looking back through memories haze
We knew life had nothing sweeter than in spring time
Golden Days when we were young, Golden Days

A Tribute to Dear Sister for the Many Years she Spent at (Mother)
There are twelve months throughout the year from January to December
But October, 1974 is one we want to remember
When you arrived at our front door
Not knowing what was in store
You rang the front door bell, the rest only fate can tell.

Your community greetings over
You wanted some help with your cases
Willing hands were near and many smiling faces
First impressions are lasting
There's a saying that's very true –
Maybe your heart was lonely but the smile came shining through

'Twasn't long before you settled and learnt each one by name
But your first and last resolution was to treat us all the same.
'Twas very hard for some of us, who down the long hard years
had never known such kindness but only fear and tears.
But you covered that rude world
To be fair, 'Twas the only way
And no one could say
You broke it during the many years you stayed

For God's little chosen ones
A spot was in your heart
They often went for a cuddle
And this to them you would impart
We were a very big family
Over eighty or even more
But you coped with all quite happily
And never closed the door.

What I Remember of Growing Up
'Twas in the year of 1918 I came into this world
The month and date the 16 June
My hair they say was gold
Barely a year went by when to an orphanage I went
I was too young to ask why
And here seventeen years was spent.

I do remember very well my young and tender years
But what I know I will tell remembering many tears
I was the one the Lord did bless with the wonderful gift of brains
And even to this very day this gift with me remains
At lessons I was very bright and helped the other children along
But alas, it was because I was tall I would be blamed for all that went wrong.
A tale I now will tell which to us was great fun.
But often the strap fell on me when I was caught by the nuns
High on the classroom wall we had a cuckoo clock
But they did not like the chime, it was hardly wound at all
But soon as the teacher left the room the class would shoulder me high
To get the hour striking and back to our desks we'd fly.
She left each day at a quarter to ten to have her coffee break
She barely opened the classroom door when I know my life was at stake
And precisely on the stroke of ten the clock would strike its chime
And then the cuckoo would pop out and repeat its song ten times
Cuckoo, Cuckoo, Cuckoo, Cuckoo, yes it repeated it ten times
She glanced at me and shouted you take one hundred lines
And when I cried and pouted she doubled them three times more!

Performing
We learnt our prose and song and dance next to the stage we went
We loved to perform and be dressed up
And especially change our names from girl to boy
Oh, what a joy, but alas it was only a play
I was very often chosen to play the part of a boy
But I loved to get into trousers it was my pride and joy
I knew I had the figure and I knew I had the height
But so many hoped to be chosen, we were often in a fight
We often had an exercise book, to learn page by page
I loved these talking parts but, alas others got in a rage
Be it fare from me to boast aloud, but my praise I duly deserved
At least I could shine out at one thing, my voice the best ever heard.

Tricks on Sister
Do you remember the days when padded bras came to the shops
You had some fashionable youngsters here that liked to be top of the pops
They saved lots and lots of pennies till they had enough to buy
And they stalked to the back of the chapel with a twinkle in their eye
But you knew only too well
They knew that you were there – maybe saying your beads or very fervent prayer
With grey beret perched on the side and their chests like Doris Day's
You chased them out of the chapel to put on calico stays.

Remember the end of the berets, it was on the summer holidays
You took the girls to Victoria, by coach
It was the only way
When you returned in the evening we had to come in by the back
One beret on the floor in the cow-shed
The rest gone in the rag man's sack.
But Sister you really did say when we got out the summer clothes
'Now we've finished with the berets, you can get rid of those'
What you meant was the season was at an end
And as soon as we got your back turned round to the rage house we went!

It was you who started us on our outings to the sea
You even made our costumes which covered us from neck to knee
One day when the waves were extra strong
The stitches all gave way
The top had left the bottom so we joined our hands to pray.
There was no way we could come out till all the beach was clear
So we just kept under water but some safety-pins were near
We pinned tops to skirts, oh no trousers were not allowed,
We must have looked a picture in this pitiful wet scroud!

2. Mary

An early autobiographical account written by Mary Adams

I came on Saturday, 15 September, 1947. The home was self supporting at the time and had no money from the government. In our quarters we had four dormitories furnished with iron beds and small lockers in which to keep our things. Except for our recreation time, we kept silence most of the day. We went to Mass every morning at 7am. We had no money given to us except just before Christmas, and also once a year for a day's outing when we went to some place like Chesssington Zoo.

We had no running water in our dining room, so we had to fetch a big tin bath of water from the laundry to do the washing-up.

We took turns washing everything – crockery and cutlery – for perhaps a week or a month. We even did our own decorating, beginning at 5am – 9pm – that was in the winter. Our farm provided most of our foodstuff – milk from six cows, eggs from our hens and vegetables and potatoes from the farm. I worked on the farm for some time. We were very dependent on the staff.

Gradually things started to change in the 1960s. Before that, we were never allowed to talk to strangers outside the Convent. We were not allowed to travel on the bus. Holidays were still only one week a year and we got just two days at Christmas. We went to the beach every Saturday, and on Sunday afternoon we danced in our hall but in summer we went to the beach. Before the 1960s we never had a radio or TV – just a piano. We went out in groups of five or six. Some of the ladies used to run away a lot.

In the mid 1960s we had our first TV, a screen that could only get BBC 1 and it was in black and white. About then, our money was increased and we were allowed to go shopping on Saturdays. We still had only one week's holiday. We were cared for by resident staff. We were told where to go, and we always had to ask permission to go anywhere.

One good thing about the 1960s was that we were allowed to go out to sell draw tickets for our parish fete and bazaar. I was in charge of that. I started in 1960 and just this year I retired from it. I had charge of getting the tickets printed and of selecting a group to sell them. I am very good at memorising names of roads, etc. ., so I directed the selling group where to go. The folding of the counterfoils and counting the money was also my charge.

In the late 1960s some of us had our money increased to £6.00 per month. We also started going to dances, to the pictures, etc. ., and colour TV was provided.

In the 1970s we really started moving. We had hired staff coming in to do domestic work, the farm was no longer worked and money for our support was supplied by Social Security, but we were still looked after and our clothes, shoes, etc. ., were still got for us. Holidays were now ten days at Christmas and ten days in the summer. Some of us still had to go to some other Convents for the holidays.

It was in the middle of the 1970s that the staff sister in charge of us started me on the road to independence. Instead of going out herself she sent me out on shopping messages and to the bank. She also encouraged me to book my own holidays which I did. Some others and myself were also sent on courses.

We had a bungalow in our grounds and, in the late 1980s some of our ladies were housed there and, under supervision they were trained to look after themselves.

Now in the 1990s there are further changes. More care staff are employed. Eight ladies have gone into houses with resident care staff. Two have gone to family homes, eleven into group homes with non-resident staff and two to Carr Gomm House. Then we have three units of six in each Home being trained to go out into the community. Except during work time we may go anywhere without permission. We also have a work training centre established in the home. We handle our own money from social security £79.04 monthly for clothing, travel, entertainment, etc. . £16.00 weekly for food and, if we take on responsible jobs we get a little more for doing them. I now enjoy living in our beautiful furnished flat.

The staff in the old days were the nuns. They were trained to keep rules and were strict with us, but they were also kind to us when we were ill. I have a lot to be grateful for. Now we have many lay staff and care workers.

Mary Adams 1992, Fountains Centre Newsletter

3. Poems written by residents of Angel Convent

Talking about Sister
She's strict
She makes people get up in the morning whether they want to or not
She's strict about people doing their work
She doesn't like them lazing
She tells them to get on with it
She doesn't have to tell us

Sometimes she helps in the laundry when we're short
I've folded sheets with her
She knew what to do
She was alright to work with
She tells you she's going to stop your money sometimes, to frighten you
But on Saturday you still get your pounds!

She likes the sun
She likes to lie on the grass when it's sunny
But I sit in the shade 'cause I don't like the sun
She's usually happy
She's got a sense of humour
She likes watching television
She likes Songs of Praise and anything to do with Church
She likes Coronation Street, Crossroads and East Enders,
They're always in the pub in East Enders but she doesn't mind,
She's quite broad minded.

Bullies
They keep on at you
They shout at you
They aggravate you
Thy ask you for money
They kick you
They punch you
They hit you
They pinch you
They bite you
They pull your hair
They get you to do things you don't want to do for them
If they see you with any sweets or crisps or drinks
They keep on at you
And asking you
Until you give them some
They never buy their own

They don't have any friends because they keep on giving out.
Alice, Anne and Jane.

4. Pictures drawn by Residents of Mother and Angel Convents

a) Tess' picture of her family home before her family moved to Wales.

b) Roberta's view from her window at the convent

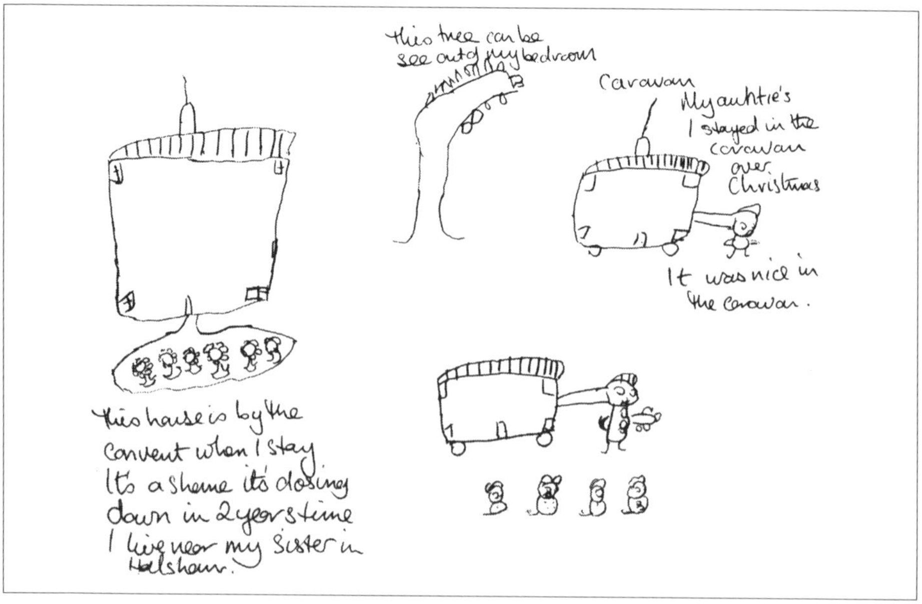

c) Jane's picture of one of the adult education classes at Angel convent

Bibliography

Adams M (1991) *The Atkinson Family Tree in words*, Unpublished hand-written work.

Adams M (1992) 'Mary' in *Fountains Centre Newsletter*, No 4 December 1992, Bexhill on Sea.

Adams M (1994a) 'Our Holiday in Malta' in *A book of Students' Work. Access to Information Technology with Word for Windows and Paintbrush,* Centre for Continuing Education: Brighton.

Adams M (1994b) *Those Lost Years – The Story of Mary Adams' Life,* Unpublished draft.

Adams M (1995) *Those Lost Years*, QueenSpark Market Books: Brighton.

Ahmad B (1990) *Black Perspectives in Social Work,* Venture Press: Birmingham.

Ahmad W and Atkin K (1996) *Race and Community Care,* OUP: Buckingham.

Alaszewski A (1986) *Institutional Care and the Mentally Handicapped: The Mental Handicap Hospital,* Croom Helm: London.

Alaszewski A and Nio Ong B (1991) 'From Consensus to Conflict: the impact of sociological ideas on policy for people with a mental handicap' in Baldwin S and Hattersley J (eds) (1991) *Mental Handicap Social Science Perspectives,* Routledge: London

Assopardi Monsignore M (1975) *A Breeze of Faith and Hope in Mental Handicap Human Relationships Sexuality* collected papers from the international symposium under the auspices of the International League of Societies for the Mentally Handicapped. Unpublished paper.

Atkin K (1996) 'An Opportunity for Change: Voluntary Sector Provision in a Mixed Economy of Care' in Ahmad W and Atkin K (1996) (eds) *Race and Community Care,* Open University Press: Buckingham.

Atkinson D (1993) 'I got put away: group-based reminiscence with people with learning difficulties' in Bornat J (ed) (1993) *Reminiscence Reviewed,* Open University Press: Milton Keynes.

Atkinson D (1997) *An Autobiographical Approach to Learning Disability Research,* Ashgate: Aldershot.

Atkinson D, Jackson M and Walmsley J (1997) *Forgotten Lives: Exploring the History of Learning Disability,* BILD: Kidderminster.

Atkinson D and Shakespeare P (1993) 'Introduction' in Shakespeare P, Atkinson D, Bornat J (1993) (eds) *Research Reflecting Practice,* Open University Press: Milton Keynes.

Atkinson D and Ward L (1987) 'Friends and Neighbours: Relationships and Opportunities in the Community for People with a Mental Handicap' in Malin N (1987) *Reassessing Community Care (with particular reference to provision for people with mental handicap and for people with mental illness),* Croom Helm: London.

Atkinson D and Williams F (1990) *Know me as I am. An Anthology of Prose, Poetry and Art by People with Learning Difficulties,* Hodder and Stoughton: Sevenoaks.

Ayer S and Alaszewski A (1984) *Community Care and the Mentally Handicapped. Services for Mothers and their Mentally Handicapped Children,* Croom Helm: London.

Barnett J (1954) *The American Christmas: A Study in National Culture,* Macmillan: New York.

Barron D (1989) 'Locked Away: Life in an Institution' in Brechin A and Walmsley J (1989) *Making Connections,* Hodder and Stoughton: London.

Barton L (ed) (1996) *Disability and Society. Emerging Issues and Insights,* Longman: Harlow

Bayley M (1997) 'Empowering and Relationships' in Ramcharan P, Roberts G, Grant G and Borland J (1997) *Empowerment in Everyday Life: Learning Disability,* Jessica Kingsley: London.

Begum N (1992) 'Disabled Women and the Feminist Agenda' in *Feminist Review,* No 40, pp. 70–85.

Benjamin J (1983) 'Master and Slave: The Fantasy of Erotic Domination' in Snitow S, Stansell C and Thompson S (eds.) (1983) *Powers of Desire. The Politics of Sexuality,* Monthly Review Press: New York

Bernstein M (1976) *Nuns,* Collins: London.

Bhabha H (1986) 'Of Mimicry and Man: An Ambivalence of Colonial Discourse' in Donald J and Hall S (eds.) (1986) *Politics and Ideology*, Open University Press: Milton Keynes.

Bhabha H (1994) *The Location of Culture,* Routledge: London.

Bogdan R and Taylor S (1982) *Inside Out,* University of Toronto Press: Toronto.

Booth T (1996) 'Sounds of Still Voices: Issues in the use of narrative methods with people with learning difficulties' in Barton L (ed) (1996) *Disability and Society. Emerging Issues and Insights*, Longman: Harlow.

Booth T, Simons K, Booth W (1990) *Outward Bound: Relocation and Community Care for People with Learning Difficulties,* Open University Press: Buckingham.

Booth T and Booth W (1994) *Parenting Under Pressure. Mothers and Fathers with Learning Difficulties*, Open University Press: Buckingham.

Bornat J (1977) 'Women's History and Oral History: An Outline Bibliography' in *Oral History,* Vol. 5 No 2, pp. 124–136 .

Bornat J (1992) 'The Communities of Community Publishing' in *Oral History,* Vol. 20, No 2, pp. 23–30.

Bornat J (1993) (ed) *Reminiscence Reviewed,* Open University Press: Milton Keynes.

Bornat J, Pereira C, Pilgrim D and Williams F (eds) (1993) *Community Care a Reader,* Macmillan: Basingstoke.

Bornat J and Walmsley J (1994) 'Oral History with Vulnerable People: Challenges to Concepts and Practice' Paper given at the International Conference on Oral History, New York, October 1994.

Borromeo Sr. M Charles CSC (ed) (1968) *The New Nuns,* Sheed and Ward: London.

Brearley P, Black J, Gutridge P, Roberts G and Tarron E (1982) *Leaving Residential Care,* Tavistock: London.

Brechin A and Walmsley J (1989) *Making Connections*, Hodder and Stoughton: London.

Brigden P and Todd M (eds) (1993) *Concepts in Community Care for People with a Learning Difficulty*, Macmillan: London.

Brothers J (1964) *Church and School. A Study of the Impact of Education on Religion*, Liverpool University Press: Liverpool.

Brown H (1994) 'An Ordinary Sexual Life?: A review of the normalisation principle as it applies to the sexual options of people with learning disabilities' *Disability and Society*, Vol. 9, No. 2, pp. 123–144.

Brown H and Craft A (1989) *Thinking the Unthinkable. Papers in Sexual Abuse and People with Learning Difficulties*, British Institute of Mental Handicap: Kidderminster.

Brown H and Smith H (eds) (1992) *Normalisation: A Reader for the Nineties*, Routledge: London.

Brown Y (1994) *Closure of Laundry Facilities Attached to Registered Care Home*, Unpublished paper.

Buchanan T (1996) 'Great Britain' in Buchanan T and Conway M (1996) *Political Catholicism in Europe 1918–1965*, Oxford University Press: Oxford.

Burman R (1982) 'The Jewish Woman as Breadwinner: The Changing Value of Women's Work in the Manchester Immigrant Community' in *Oral History*, Vol. 10, No 2, pp. 27–37.

Byrne L (1992) 'Lavinia Byrne' in Loudon M (1992) *Unveiled. Nuns Talking*, Chatto and Windus: London.

Cale M (1993) 'Girls and the Perception of Sexual Danger in the Victorian Reformatory System' in *The Historical Association*, Vol. 78, No 253, pp. 201–217.

Cambridge P, and Knapp M (eds) (1988) *Demonstrating Successful Care in the Community*, PSSRU University of Kent: Canterbury.

Cambridge P Hayes L and Knapp M (1994) *Care in the Community Five Years On*, Ashgate: Aldershot.

Campbell-Jones S (1979) *In Habit: An Anthropological Study of Working Nuns*, Faber: London.

Carabine J (1996) 'Heterosexuality and Social Policy' in Richardson D (ed) (1996) *Theorising Heterosexuality. Telling it Straight*, Open University Press: Buckingham.

Cattermole M, Jahoda A and Markova I (1988) 'Life in a Mental Handicap Hospital: the View from the Inside' in *Mental Handicap*, Vol. 16, no 4, pp. 136 – 139.

Chew D N. (1982) *Ada Neild Chew: Life and Writings of a Working Woman*, Virago: London.

Chodorow N (1978) *The Reproduction of Mothering. Psychoanalysis and the Sociology of Gender*, University of California Press: London.

Collins J (1992) *When the Eagles Fly: A Report into the Resettlement of People with Learning Difficulties from Long-Stay Institutions*, Values into Action: London.

Collins J (1996) The Unseen Costs of Secluded Communities in *Community Living*, Vol. 10, No. 1, pp. 6–7.

Collins J and Gimenez M (eds) (1990) *Work without Wages. Domestic Labor and Self Employment within Capitalism*, State University: New York.

Coman P (1977) *Catholics and the Welfare State*, Longman: New York.

Conneally S (1988) 'Developing the Sexuality of People with a Handicap' in McConkey R and McGinley P (1988) (eds) *Concepts and Controversies in Services for People with Mental Handicap,* Woodlands Centre: Galway.

Cooper M (1997) 'Mabel's Life Story' in Atkinson D, Jackson M and Walmsley J (eds) (1997) *Forgotten Lives: Exploring the History of Learning Disability,* BILD: Kidderminster.

Coward R (1984) *Female Desire. Women's Sexuality Today,* Paladin Books: London.

Cox P (1997) 'Girls Deficiency and Delinquency' in Wright D and Digby A (eds) (1997) *From Idiocy to Mental Deficiency. Historical Perspectives of People with Learning Disabilities,* Routledge: London.

Craft A (1987) *Mental Handicap and Sexuality. Issues and Perspectives*, Costello: Beckenham.

Creative Writing Group (1985) *Creative Writing Autumn Term,* Streatham and Tooting Adult Education Institute: London.

Cross G (1990) *A Social History of Leisure since 1600,* Venture Publishers: New York.

Dalley G (1988) *Ideologies of Caring: Rethinking Community and Collectivism,* Macmillan: London.

Dalley G (1989) 'Community Care: the Ideal and the Reality' in Brechin A and Walmsley J (eds) (1989) *Making Connections. Reflecting on the Lives and Experiences of People with Learning Difficulties,* Hodder and Stoughton: Sevenoaks.

D'Arcy F (1914) The Northern Whig, 12 February, 1914 in Jones G (1986) *Social Hygiene in Twentieth Century Britain,* Croom Helm: London.

Davidoff L and Hall C (1992) *Family Fortunes: Men and Women of the English Middle Class 1780–1850*, Hutchinson: London.

Davis D (1989) 'Goffman's Concept of the Total Institution Criticisms and Revisions' in *Human Studies,* Vol. 12, Nos. 1–2, pp. 28–40.

Delmar R (1986) 'What is Feminism?' in Mitchell J and Oakley A (eds) (1986) *What is Feminism,* Blackwell: London.

Deacon J (1977) *Tongue Tied,* National Society for Mentally Handicapped Children: London.

DHSS (1971) *Better Services for the Mentally Handicapped,* Cmnd 4683 HMSO.

Digby A (1997) 'Contexts and Perspectives' in Wright D and Digby A (eds) (1997) *From Idiocy to Mental Deficiency: Historical Perspectives of People with Learning Disabilities,* Routledge: London.

Douglas M (1970) 'Purity and Danger' in Bocock R and Thompson K (1985) (eds) *Religion and Ideology*, Manchester University Press: Manchester.

Douglas M (1973) *Natural Symbols: Explorations in Cosmology*, Barrie and Jenkins: London.

Douglas M and Nicod M (1974) 'Taking the Biscuit: The Structure of British Meals' in *New Society*, December, pp. 11– 15.

Douglas T (1983) *Groups Understanding People Living Together,* Tavistock: London.

Dowson S (1997) 'Empowerment within Services: A Comfortable Delusion' in Ramcharan P, Roberts G, Grant G and Borland J (eds) (1997) *Empowerment in Everyday Life. Learning Disability,* Jessica Kingsley: London.

Edgerton (1967) *The Cloak of Competence. Stigma in the Lives of the Mentally Retarded,* University of California Press: Berkeley.

Emerson C, Cullen C, Hatton C and Cross B (1996) *Residential Provision for People with Learning Difficulties: Summary Report,* Hester Adrian Research Centre: Manchester.

Ferns P (1992) 'Promoting Race Equality through Normalisation' in Brown H and Smith H (eds) (1992) *Normalisation: A Reader for the Nineties,* Routledge: London.

Finch J and Groves D (1983) (eds) *A Labour of Love: Women, Work and Caring,* Routledge and Kegan Paul: London.

Finnegan R (1992) *Oral Traditions and the Verbal Arts: A Guide to Research Practices,* Routledge: London.

Foucault M (1977) *Discipline and Punish. The Birth of the Prison,* Allen Lane: London.

Foucault M (1978) *The History of Sexuality: An Introduction,* Penguin: Middlesex.

Foucault M (1979) *The History of Sexuality Vol. 1,* Penguin: Middlesex.

Foucault M (1984) 'What is an Author?' in Rabinow P (1984) (ed) *The Foucault Reader: An Introduction to Foucault's Thought,* Penguin: Harmondsworth.

Francis Taylor Foundation (1993) 'Residential Services for People with Learning Disabilities' Unpublished publicity leaflet.

Gilchrist R (1994) *The Archaeology of Religious Women,* Routledge: London.

Gilpin Wells C (1988) *A Woman of Her time and Ours: Mary Magdalen Taylor SMG,* Laney-Smith: Charlotte.

Gladstone D (1997) 'The Changing Dynamic of Institutional Care: The Western Counties Idiot Asylum 1864–1914' in Wright D and Digby A (eds) (1997) *From Idiocy to Mental Deficiency: Historical Perspectives of People with Learning Disabilities,* Routledge: London.

Gluck S B and Patai D (1991) *Women's Words: The Feminist Practice of Oral History,* Routledge: New York.

Goffman E (1961) *Asylums: Essays on the Social Situation of Mental Patients and Other Inmates,* Doubleday: New York.

Grant G, Ramcharan P and McGrath M (1993) *Living in the Community: Views of three people with a learning disability,* CSPRD: Bangor.

Grossman H and Chester N (1990) *The Experience and Meaning of Work in Women's Lives,* Lawrence Erlbaum Associates: New Jersey.

Groves R (1996) 'Intentional Communities: Interesting Social Experiments or Ghettos?' in *Community Living,* Vol. 10, No 1, pp. 12–13.

Hall C (1979) 'The Early Formation of the Victorian Domestic Ideology' in Burman S (1979) (ed) *Fit Work for Women,* Croom Helm: London.

Hatton C and Emerson E (1996) *Residential Provision for People with Learning Disabilities: A Research Review,* Hester Adrian Research Centre: Manchester.

Heimann M (1995) *Catholic Devotion in Victorian England,* Claredon Press: Oxford.

Hockney J and James A (1993) *Growing Up and Growing Old: Ageing and Dependency in the Life Course*, Sage: London.

Holloway G (1995) *A Common Cause? Class Dynamics in the Industrial Women's Movement 1888–1918*, Unpublished thesis: University of Sussex.

Hornsby-Smith M P (1987) *Roman Catholics in England. Studies in Social Structure Since the Second World War,* Cambridge University Press: Cambridge.

Hudson B (1990) Social Policy and the New Right – the Strange Case of the Community Care White Paper, *Local Government Studies,* 1990, pp. 15–34.

Humphries S (1998) *Sex in a Cold Climate,* Channel Four.

Humphries S and Gordon P (1992) *Out of Sight: The Experience of Disability,* Channel Four/ Northcote Press: Plymouth.

Hunt N (1982) *The World of Nigel Hunt: The Diary of a Mongoloid Youth,* Asset Recycling: Norwich.

Jackson M (1997) 'Images of the Past: Using Photographs' in Atkinson D, Jackson M and Walmsley J (eds) (1997) *Forgotten Lives: Exploring the History of Learning Disability,* BILD: Kidderminster.

Jacobus M, Fox Keller E and Shuttleworth S (eds.) (1990) *Body Politics. Women and the Discourse of Science,* Routledge: New York.

Jay Committee (1979) *Report of the Committee of Inquiry into Mental Handicap Nursing and Care,* Vol. 1 Cmdn. 7468–I HMSO: London.

Jerrome D (1992) *Good Company. An Anthropological Study of Old People in Groups,* Edinburgh University Press: Edinburgh.

Jones G (1986) *Social Hygiene in Twentieth Century Britain,* Croom Helm: London.

Jones K (1975) *Opening the Doors. A Study of New Policies for the Mentally Handicapped,* Routledge and Kegan Paul: London.

Jones L (1995) 'Introduction' in Adams M (1995) *Those Lost Years*, QueenSpark Books: Brighton.

Kavanagh S and Opit L (1996) *The Prevalence Balance of Care Cost and Cost Effectiveness of Care for People with Learning Disabilities in. Great Britain,* University of Kent at Canterbury, Personal Social Services Research Unit: Canterbury

Kelly B (1988) Gift and Call in McConkey R and McGinley P *Concepts and Controversies in Services for People with Mental Handicap,* St Michael's House: Dublin.

Kings Fund (1988) *Ties and Connections: An Ordinary Community Life for People with Learning Difficulties*, Kings Fund Centre: London.

Knox R (1982) *Autobiography of a Saint Theresa of Lisieux. The Story of a Soul,* Collins: Glasgow.

Lawrence S, Walker A and Wilcocks D (1987) *She's Leaving Home*, PNL Press: London.

Leicester M (1989) *Multicultural Education. From Theory to Practice,* Berkshire: Nelson

Lewenhak S (1988) *The Re-evaluation of Women's Work,* Croom Helm: New York.

Lewis H (1971) *Shame and Guilt in Neurosis,* International Universities Press: New York.

Lewis R (1997) *Living in Hospital and in the Community,* Pavilion Publishers: Brighton.

Lister T and Ellis L (1992) *Survey of Supported Employment Services in England Wales and Scotland*, National Development Team: Manchester.

Loudon M (1992) *Unveiled Nuns Talking,* Chatto and Windus: London.

Lyotard JF (1992) *The Post Modern Explained to Children Correspondence 1982–1985*, Turnaround: London.

MacDonald I (1990) 'Similarities and Differences between Client Groups: Values and Myths' in Sharkey S and Barna S (eds) (1990) *Community Care. People Leaving Long-stay Hospitals,* Routledge: London.

Mace J (1994) 'Reminiscence Retailing and Change' in *Oral History*, 1994, pp. 46–55.

Mahood L (1988) 'Prostitution and Social Control in Glasgow 1869 -1890' in *Women's Studies International Forum,* Vol. 13, No 149–161, pp. 55–67.

Malin N (1987) *Reassessing Community Care (with particular reference to provision for people with mental handicap and for people with mental illness),* Croom Helm: London.

Malin N (1995) *Services for People with Learning Disabilities,* Routledge: London.

Manning P (1992) *Erving Goffman,* Policy Press: Oxford.

Margolis M (1984) *Mothers and Such: Views of American Women and Why they Changed,* University of California Press: Berkeley.

Marks L (1990) *Dear old Mother Levy's The Jewish Maternity Home and Sick Room Help Society 1895–1939*, Oxford University Press: Oxford.

Mathew D (1955) *Catholicism in England,* Chapel River Press: Andover.

Mayo M (1994) *Communities and Caring: The Mixed Economy of Welfare*, Macmillan: London.

McCarthy M and Thompson D (1994) *Sex and Staff Training. A Training Manual for Staff Working with People with Learning Difficulties,* Pavilion Publishing: Brighton.

Mead G H (1934) 'Mind Self and Society' in Thompson K and Tunstall J (1979) *Sociological Perspectives*, Penguin: London.

Mercer C (1981) 'Pleasure' in Middleton R and Mercer C (1981) *Form and Meaning,* Open University Press: Milton Keynes.

Miller D (ed) (1993) *Unwrapping Christmas,* Clarendon Press: Oxford.

Mitchell J (1971) *Women's Estate*, Penguin: Harmondsworth.

Morris J (1993a) *Community Care or Independent Living,* Joseph Rowntree Trust: York.

Morris J (1993b) 'Us and Them? Feminist Research and Community Care' in Bornat J, Pereira C, Pilgrim D and Williams F (eds) (1993) *Community Care: A Reader,* Macmillan: Basingstoke.

Morris P (1969) *Put Away: A Sociological Study of Institutions for the Mentally Retarded,* Routledge and Kegan Paul: London.

Murray B (1988) 'Training for Adults with Mental Handicap in Community Workshops' in McConkey R and McGinley P (eds) (1988) *Concepts and Controversies*, Woodlands Centre: Dublin.

Murray C (1990) *The Emerging British Underclass: Choice in Welfare Series :2,* Institute of Economic Affairs Heath and Welfare Unit: London.

Noonan Walsh P (1988) 'Handicapped and Female: Two Disabilities?' in McConkey R and McGinley P (eds) (1988) *Concepts and Controversies,* Woodlands Centre: Dublin.

Norman E (1985) *Roman Catholics in England from the Elizabethan Settlement to the Second Vatican Council,* Oxford University Press: Oxford.

Okely J (1992) 'Anthropology and Autobiography Participatory Experience and Embodied Knowledge' in Okely J and Callaway H (1992) *Anthropology and Autobiography*, Routledge: London.

Oliver M (1990) *The Politics of Disablement,* Macmillan: Basingstoke.

Oliver M (1993) 'Re-defining Disability' in Swain J, Finkelstein V, French S and Oliver M (1993) *Disabling Barriers Enabling Environments,* Sage: London.

Opie A (1992) 'Qualitative Research Appropriation of the 'Other' and Empowerment' in *Feminist Review,* No 40, Spring 1992, pp. 52–70.

Paul, Bishop of Rome 'Forword' in Abbot Walter R SJ General (ed) (1966) *The documents of Vatican II All sixteen official texts promulgated by the ecumenical council 1963/65*, Translated from the Latin Geoffrey Chapman: Dublin.

Peace S, Kellaher L and Willcocks D (1997) *Re-evaluating Residential Care,* Open University Press: Buckingham.

Phillips A (1994) 'Women on the Shop Floor. The Colchester Rag Trade 1918 -1950' in *Oral History,* pp. 55 -66.

Platt J (1981) *Whatever Happened to the Case Study? Or From Znaniecki to Lazansfeld in One Generation.* Unpublished paper.

Platt J (1988) 'What can case studies do?' in *Studies in Qualitative Method* , Vol. 1, pp. 1–23.

Plummer K (1977) *Documents of Life,* Routledge and Keegan Paul: London.

Plummer K (1995) *Telling Sexual Stories: Power, Change and Social Worlds,* Routledge: London.

Potts M and Fido R (1991) *A Fit Person to Be Removed. Personal Accounts of Life in a Mental Deficiency Institution,* Northcote Press: Plymouth.

Potts M and Fido R (1997) 'Using Oral Histories' in Atkinson D, Jackson M and Walmsley J (eds) (1997) *Forgotten Lives: Exploring the History of Learning Disability,* BILD: Kidderminster.

Ramcharan P, Roberts G, Grant G and Borland J (1997a) *Empowerment in Everyday Life: Learning Disability*, Jessica Kingsley: London.

Ramcharan P, Roberts G, Grant G and Borland J (1997b) 'Citizenship Empowerment and Everyday Life: Ideal and Illusion in the New Millennium' in Ramcharan P, Roberts G, Grant G and Borland J (1997) *Empowerment in Everyday Life: Learning Disability,* Jessica Kingsley: London.

Reading P (1994) *Community Care and the Voluntary Sector,* Biddles: Guildford.

Richardson A and Ritchie J (1989) *Developing Friendships Enabling. People with Learning Difficulties to Make And Maintain Friends,* Policy Studies Institute: London.

Riggins S (1990) *Beyond Goffman: Studies on Communication Institution and Social Interaction,* Mouton de Gruyter: Berlin.

Rioux M, Bach M and Crawford C (1997) 'Citizenship and People with Disabilities in Canada: Towards the Elusive Ideal' in Ramcharan P, Roberts G, Grant G and Borland J (eds) (1997) *Empowerment in Everyday Life: Learning Disability*, Jessica Kingsley: London.

Roberts E (1988) *Women's Work 1840–1940*, Macmillan: Basingstoke.

Robinson T (1989) 'Normalisation: The Whole Answer?' in Brechin A and Walmsley J (eds) (1989) *Making Connections. Reflecting on the Lives and Experiences of People with Learning Difficulties,* Hodder and Stoughton: Sevenoaks.

Rosenfeld R A (1985) *Farm Women,* University of North Carolina Press: Chapel Hill.

Russell J (1995) 'Leisure and Recreation Services' in Malin N (1995) *Services for People with Learning Disabilities,* Routledge: London.

Ryan J and Thomas F (1980) *The Politics of Mental Handicap,* Penguin: Hanmondsworth.

Saunders A (1995) 'Introduction' in Adams M (1995) *Those Lost Years*, QueenSpark Books: Brighton.

Sayers J (1986) *Sexual Contradictions: Psychoanalysis and Feminism*, Tavistock: London.

Scheff T (1994) *Microsociology Discourse Emotion and Social Structure*, University of Chicago Press: Chicago.

Scheff T (1996) *Parts and Wholes: Integrating the Human Sciences*, Cambridge University Press: Cambridge.

Segal L (1994) *Straight Sex: The Politics of Pleasure*, Virago: London.

Segal S (ed) (1990) *The Place for Special Villages and Residential Communities,* AB Academic Publishers: Bicester.

Shakespeare T (1996) 'Power and Prejudice: Issues of Gender Sexuality and Disability' in Barton L(ed) (1996) *Disability and Society: Emerging Issues and Insights,* Longman: Harlow.

Shakespeare T, Gellespie-Sells K and Davies D (1996) *The Sexual Politics of Disability. Untold Desires,* Cassell: London.

Simons K (1992) *Sticking Up for Yourself: Self Advocacy and People with Learning Difficulties,* Joseph Rowntree Foundation: York.

Simons K (1995) 'Empowerment and Advocacy' in Malin N (1995) *Services for People with Learning Disabilities,* Routledge: London.

Singer P (ed) (1986) *Applied Ethics,* Oxford University Press:Oxford

Singer P (1999) in Toolis K (1999) The World's Most Dangerous Man in *The Guardian* 6, November, 1999

Sister Loyala Parsons and Sister Thomas Dunleavy (1968) 'Renewing Religious Power Structures' in Sister M Charles Borromeo CSC (ed) *The New Nuns,* Sheed and Ward: London.

Sister Mary Aloysius Schaldenbrand (1968) 'Asylums: Total Societies and the Religious Life' in Sister M Charles Borromeo CSC (ed) *The New Nuns*, Sheed and Ward: London.

Sister M St. Pius 'Forword' in Gilpin Wells R (1988) *A Woman of Her Time and Ours: Mary Magdalen Taylor SMG,* Laney-Smith: Charlotte.

Smart C (1996) 'Collusion Collaboration and Confession' in Richardson D (ed) (1996) *Theorising Heterosexuality. Telling it Straight,* Open University Press: Buckingham.

SMG (1992) *Social Care Advisory Board – Learning Disabilities.* Unpublished document.

Smith H and Brown H (1989) Whose community, whose care? in Brechin A and Walmsley J (eds) (1989) *Making Connections. Reflecting on the Lives and Experiences of People with Learning Difficulties,* Hodder and Stoughton: Sevenoaks.

Smith K and Stuart M (1995) 'Our Right to Know: Women with Learning Difficulties and Sexuality Courses' in Stuart M and Thomson A (1995) *Engaging with Difference The Other in Adult Education,* NIACE: Leicester.

Snitow S, Stansell C and Thompson S (eds.) (1983) *Powers of Desire: The Politics of Sexuality,* Monthly Review Press: New York.

Sperlinger A (1992) 'Changing Services' in Brown H and Benson S (eds) *A Practical Guide to Working with People with Learning Disabilities,* Hawker Publications Ltd: London.

Stanley L (1991) *The Autobiographical 'I'* , Manchester University Press: Manchester.

Stedman Jones G (1981) *The Threat of Outcast London* in Fitzgerald M, McLennan G and Pawson J (1981) *Crime and Society*, Routledge & Kegan Paul: London.

Steele D (1993) 'Stop Wasting Money on Futile Training' in *Community Living,* Vol. 9 (3), pp. 18

Steele D (1996) 'Supported Employment, the Prospects' in *Community Living* Vol. 10, No l, pp. 22–23.

Stevens A (1997) 'Recording the History of an Institution: The Royal Eastern Counties Institution at Colchester' in Atkinson D, Jackson M and Walmsley J (eds) (1997) *Forgotten Lives: Exploring the History of Learning Disability,* BILD: Kidderminster.

Stuart M (1993) 'Speaking Personally: The Self in Educational Research' in Miller N and Jones D (1993) *Research Reflecting Practice,* SCRUTREA: Manchester

Stuart M (1997) *Looking Back, Looking Forward: Reminiscence with People with Learning Difficulties*, Pavilion Publishers: Brighton

Sutcliffe J (1990) *Education For Choice and Empowerment: Adults with Learning Difficulties,* NIACE: Leicester

Swain J (1989) 'Learned Helplessness, Theory and People With Learning Difficulties: The Psychological Price Of Powerlessness' in Brechin A and Walmsley J (eds) (1989) *Making Connections. Reflecting on the Lives and Experiences of People with Learning Difficulties,* Hodder and Stoughton: Sevenoaks.

Szivos S (1990) 'Attitudes to Work and their Relationship to Self-Esteem and Aspirations Among Young Adults with a Mild Mental Handicap' in *British Journal of Mental Subnormality,* Vol. 36, pp. 55–70.

The Remembering Project (1988) *We Speak for Ourselves,* Streatham and Tooting AEI: London.

Thompson D (1993) 'Against the Dividing of Women: Lesbian Feminism and Heterosexuality' in Wilkinson S and Kitzinger C (eds) (1993) *Heterosexuality: A Feminism and Psychology Reader*, Sage: London.

Thomson M (1992) *'The Trouble with the Mental Deficiency in England and Wales 1913–1946'* Unpublished PhD Thesis: University of Oxford.

Thomson M (1997) 'Family Community and the State: The Micro-Politics of Mental Deficiency' in Wright D and Digby A (eds) (1997) *From Idiocy to Mental Deficiency. Historical Perspectives of People with Learning Disabilities,* Routledge: London.

Thrift N (1989) 'Images of Social Change' in Hamnett C, McDowell L and Sarre P (eds.) (1989) *The Changing Social Structure,* Milton Keynes: Open University Press.

Urry J (1989) 'Cultural Change and Contemporary Holiday Making' in McDowell L, Sarre P and Hamnett C (eds) (1989) *Divided Nation,* Open University Press: Milton Keynes.

Vanier J (1982) (ed) *The Challenge of L'Arche,* Darton Longman and Todd: London.

Walker A, Walker C and Ryan T (1996) 'Older People with Learning Difficulties. Leaving Institutional Care – A Case of Double Jeopardy' in *Ageing and Society*, Vol. 16, pp. 125–150

Walkowitz J (1982) 'Male Vice and Feminist Virtue: Feminism and the Politics of Prostitution in Nineteenth Century Britain' in *History Workshop Journal* No 13, pp. 62–77.

Wall K (1998) *Friendship Skills and Opportunities amongst People with Learning Disabilities*, Social Work Monagraphs: UEA Norwich.

Walmsley J (1993a) 'Citizenship and Learning Difficulties' in Swain J, Finkelstein V, French S and Oliver M (1993) *Disabling Barriers. Enabling Environments*, Sage: London.

Walmsley J (1993b) 'Explaining' in Shakespeare P, Atkinson D and French S (1993) *Reflecting on Research Practice: Issues in Health and Social Welfare*, Open University Press: Buckingham.

Walmsley J (1995) *'Gender Caring and Learning Difficulties'* , Unpublished DPhil thesis: Open University.

Walmsley J (1997) 'Telling the History of Learning Disability from Local Sources' in Atkinson D, Jackson M and Walmsley J (eds) (1997) *Forgotten Lives: Exploring the History of Learning Disability*, BILD: Kidderminster.

Walmsley J and Downer J (1997) 'Shouting the Loudest' in Ramchran R, Roberts R, Grant G and Borland J (eds) (1997) *Empowerment in Everyday Life: Learning Disability*, Jessica Kingsley: London.

Weeks J (1981) *Sex Politics and Society. The Regulation of Sexuality Since 1800*, Longman: London.

Weeks J (1986) *Sexuality*, Ellis Horwood: Chichester.

West J (ed) (1982) *Work Women and the Labour Market*, Routledge and Kegan Paul: London.

Wilkinson J (1989) 'Being There: Evaluating Life Quality from Feelings and Daily Experience' in Brechin A and Walmsley J (eds) (1989) *Making Connections: Reflecting on the Lives and Experiences of People with Learning Difficulties*, Hodder and Stoughton: Sevenoaks.

Williams F (1989a) *Social Policy: A Critical Introduction. Issues of Race Gender and Class*, Policy Press: Cambridge.

Williams F (1989b) 'Mental Handicap and Oppression' in Brechin A and Walmsley J (eds) (1989) *Making Connections: Reflecting on the Lives and Experiences of People with Learning Difficulties*, Hodder and Stoughton: Sevenoaks.

Williams F (1992) 'Women with learning difficulties are women too' in Day L and Langam M (eds) *Women Oppression and Social Work*, Unwin Hyman: London.

Williams F (1993a) 'Women and Community' in Bornat J, Pereira C, Pilgrim D and Williams F(eds)(1993) *Community Care: A Reader*, Macmillan: Basingstoke.

Williams F (1995) 'Postmodernism Feminism and the Question of Difference' in Parton N (ed) (1995) *Social Work Social Theory and Social Change*, Routledge: London.

Williams F (1996) 'Race Welfare and Community Care – A Historical Perspective' in Ahmad W and Atkin K (1996) *Race and Community Care*, Open University Press: Buckingham.

Williams P (1991) 'Village Communities' in *Community Living*, Vol. 5 (1), pp. 10–11.

Williams P (1995) 'Residential and Day Services' in Malin N (ed) (1995) *Services for People with Learning Disabilities*, Routledge London

Wilson E (1977) *Women and the Welfare State*, Tavistock: London.

Wolfensberger W (1972) *The Principle of Normalisation in Human Services,* National Instititute on Mental Retardation: Toronto.

Wolfensberger W and Tullman S (1982) 'A brief outline of the principle of Normalisation' in Brechin A and Walmsley J (1989) *Making Connections: Reflecting on the Lives and Experiences of People with Learning Difficulties,* Hodder and Stoughton: London.

Wolfensberger W and Thomas S (1983) *'Program Analysis of Service Systems: Implementation of Normalisation Goals (Passing)'*, National Institute on Mental Retardation: Toronto.

Wright D (1997) 'Childlike in His Innocence: Lay Attitudes to Idiots and Imbeciles in Victorian England' in Wright D and Digby A (eds) (1997) *From Idiocy to Mental Deficiency: Historical Perspectives of People With Learning Disabilities,* Routledge: London.

Yeo E (1992) 'Social Motherhood and the Sexual Communion of Labour in British Social Science 1850 – 1950' in *Women's History Review,* Vol. 1, No 1, pp. 63–87.

Yeo E (1996) *The Contest for the Social Sciences: Relations and Representations of Gender and Class*, Rivers Oran Press: London.